To Annette

best wi

SCRAMBLING FOR ENTHUSIASTIC BEGINNERS

HOW I SURVIVED THE 1960S WITH A SMILE

FRANK MELLING

A Collie Press Book

First published in Great Britain in 2021 by:
The Collie Press
Manley Lane, Manley, Cheshire WA6 0PB.
Reprinted February 2022

Cover Artwork by Mike Baumber

Text and Design © Frank Melling
Layout by Geoff Fisher geoff.fisher@yahoo.co.uk

ISBN 978-0-9527987-9-8

A CIP catalogue record for this book is available in the British Library
Printed and bound by CPI Group (UK) Ltd, Croydon, CR0 4YY

Other Books by Frank Melling

A Penguin in a Sparrow's Nest

The Flying Penguin

Hostie

A Very Greek Romance

A Sixpence in the Settee

Ride of My Life

Classic Superbikes

February 2022 Update

I am writing this micro newsletter just after
Christmas 2021 – and with some degree of pride!

Very few self-published books even cover their base production
costs and at best sell only a few copies. "Scrambling" has been very
different. Thanks to the wonderful support of readers – and you
have been incredible – the book was ranked #1 on Amazon in
its category and we're now in the happy position of having to re-print.

Thanks to everyone for your support without
which Carol and I couldn't make our books.

Making Scrambling for Enthusiastic Beginners

Writing a book is both an extremely solitary activity whilst being very much a team effort - and that statement is not merely a politically correct or polite form of words. Any writer who thinks that they can produce a book entirely independently really is fooling themselves – and badly so too.

The idea for the book was mine and came about simply and directly because so many readers enjoyed the first part of my autobiography, *A Penguin in a Sparrow's Nest*.

Every writer likes to be praised because we have very fragile egos which need all the support that we can get! However, the comments I most enjoyed were from people just like me – ordinary men and women who have made their own way in life just as I have ricocheted from one near disaster to another.

In this respect, *Scrambling* is hugely different from the vast majority of those autobiographical works which are recollections of this world championship or that great success. For me, it's been a case of just avoiding falling down a big hole or avoiding the pallet of bricks which someone has knocked off the roof. Rather than being tales of a champion, they are the true story of a working class kid, with no advantages, trying to navigate his way through the minefield of growing up in the 1960s.

I was chatting to quite a well-known ex-rider last year about the book he had written and his experience is worth relating in the context of *Scrambling*. His book had come about because a fan had meticulously collated all the rider's race results over the years – and had documentary evidence to support them. This meant that it was a straightforward job to write them down in a book.

By contrast, no-one has ever kept a record of what I have done in my life – not even me – and my early days are particularly short of dates and times. So, *Scrambling* is put together from memories of incidents from a long time ago. Please be assured that they did all happen, and as I describe them, but the precise dates may well be wrong - as is the chronology. For sure, don't rely on the stories for pub quiz answers!

Working with my wife Carol, we have tried to cross reference dates and places but any errors and omissions are entirely mine.

This brings me to the team element of making the book. I could write pages and pages about how highly I value Carol's efforts but I will stop at saying that she is the best editor I have ever worked with bar none. She is meticulous, professional, determined and empathetic and has taken the text to the best level that we can achieve.

I was very apprehensive about writing a book like *Scrambling* which, in the final analysis, is the story of an incredibly ordinary person, so I sent early versions of the text to a group of test readers who I trust – friends who had the intellect and self-confidence to tell me if they thought I was wasting my time and should take up embroidery or jigsaw puzzles! They spent many hours reading the text and making invaluable suggestions so thanks to Peter Wilson, Farida Wilson, Andy Henworth, David Clarke, Jane Clarke and Oliver Presswood. Their feedback reassured me that the project was worth completing.

The book covers have been designed by Mike Baumber and this is the fifth we have produced together – and he's still working with me, which I guess shows something about how well we get on.

Geoff Fisher continues to typeset all our books to old-fashioned, craft skill levels which make it look so good. CPI have printed *Scrambling*, as they do all our books, for the simple reason that they are the best!

Finally, we have been extremely lucky to enjoy the financial support of Mike Owens, of Owens Moto Classics. Mike is one of the most enthusiastic people in the classic bike world and his help has enabled us to produce a book with the highest production values: thanks Mike.

Thanks again for reading *Scrambling* and I hope that you enjoy my journey through the 1960s.

Mike Owens of Owens Moto Classics

"Deciding to sponsor "Scrambling" was an easy decision. I have been reading Frank Melling's articles as long as I can remember - and I'm still enjoying them today.

"I like the fact that Frank tells things as he sees them with a direct honesty which is brilliant. He's also the best writer in the motorcycling world with a fantastic ability to tell stories in a way which keeps you wanting to read more.

"When I read the proof copy of "Scrambling" I couldn't wait to be involved. There are stories which made me laugh out loud and a few which nearly brought to tears to my eyes. But, most of all, it was a master story teller in action and the worst part was when I reached the final page.

"I think that this is one of the best motorcycling books ever written and I am proud that Owens Moto Classics is its sponsor."

Contents

Chapter One

It Seemed Like a Good
Idea at the Time

Carol, my wife, best friend, editor and business partner, says that I have the mind of an enthusiastic four year old. Pick something up; play with it; drop it on the floor; emotionally easily stressed; excitable; hyperactive; physically brave; better after a mid-afternoon nap; incredibly easily bored; super enthusiastic; inquisitive and – most of all - not that closely attached to reality.

If I'm in the right mood to accept the truth – and that's not always – her assessment is accurate.

All these traits came into full, living colour action as I sat on the edge of my bed in the chilly bedroom of a not very desirable Warrington council house, in 1965.

I was seventeen years old and, in just twenty months, had established a chaotic employment record. I had no job prospects, was penniless – almost literally – and had no hope for the future. If I was lucky - very lucky - I would get a council house like my parents and maybe a steady job as a labourer or, in my wildest dreams, even a trade. I would marry a nice girl who worked at Woolworths or the Army and Navy store, and we would have a week in Blackpool with our two kids every year.

I had no contacts, no help, no idea of what I should or should not do and I even looked precisely what I was: a poorly dressed member of the lower working classes with a rough, northern accent to match.

Anyone with half a grain of brain would see that my life's path was clearly mapped out and so what came next was so odd as to be almost certifiably strange. "No, Doctor. He's not violent or abusive but he's not with us either…"

My most prized possession was a little Adler portable typewriter. It was cream coloured with a brown, faux leather carrying case. I loved that typewriter so much that I actually used to talk to it last thing at night before I went to sleep – or often not to sleep, as thoughts tore endlessly round my mind.

"Yes, Doctor. I've heard him having a conversation with a typewriter. Is this normal?"

I never got on with my dad, and to be fair he didn't like me much either. However, there are always exceptions and he had noticed my manic zeal in writing to motorcycle club magazines, newsletters and even advertising notice boards, in my surreal, scrawling and rather Gothic, horror movie handwriting.

I even subjected real, paid for publications to my ideas and, no doubt, provided the offices with plenty of kindling for their coal fires.

In an act of near genius, my dad had found the Adler somewhere and simply gave it to me. It wasn't for Christmas, a birthday or any other celebration, it just arrived one day and I fell head over heels in love.

With the Adler, I had now weaponised my writing. Pecking away, ever so slowly with two fingers, I could now hit the poor editors with longer, more detailed comments - and often with proper capital letters.

The slight problem for everyone was that I really could write. The ideas might not have been well developed or even properly informed - but the words most certainly were.

I had been a voracious reader since early childhood and, because my parents had neither interest in nor knowledge of literature, I read whatever I wished - from science fiction to philosophy and everything in between. For example, I gobbled up *Commando* comic, *Oliver Twist* and *Viper* – an early book on drug addiction - as a twelve year old. I only remember that particular sequence because my mum found them all together under my bed at the same time. This was a bit different from finding the *Health and Efficiency* magazine which was the go-to soft porn publication for boys at that time.

I swam in the ocean of literature from the moment I could read. This meant that I really did know how to tell a story – and in good, Standard English too.

So, in the light of a 60w bulb, and with the faint heat of a paraffin fire on its lowest setting, I decided to write my first book. It was to be called *"Scrambling for Enthusiastic Beginners"* and, after just eight months of racing experience and zero success, I would tell readers how to excel in off-road sport.

You see what I mean about not being wholly attached to reality?

Surprisingly, I never did finish the book – although I did start it – and so I thought that I would do the job now - because *Scrambling for Enthusiastic Beginners* is also a good strap line for my life. Always scrambling about from one near disaster to the next, as the beginner in life's race that I am – and always managing, often only just, to survive for the next adventure.

The other reason for telling the story is that the lives of ordinary people don't often get recorded in print. If you are rich or famous, or extremely infamous, then you're fine: you will be everywhere and history will note your every moment – good or bad.

There is now also a seemingly endless stream of sports autobiographies which tend to be a list of the person's successes and championship wins which, although of interest to statisticians, rarely reveal anything about the actual lives they have led.

Where I spent my childhood and my first years after leaving school was a no-go area for anyone who had access to the media except, perhaps, some sociologist researching how the underclasses survived. So, this book is for everyone who wasn't top of the class, captain of the school rugby team or a hit with the girls.

Alternatively, if you were – this is how life was lived on the other side of fence!

As the saying goes, I didn't absolutely have to be mad to survive – but it did help that I was...

Chapter Two

In the Beginning There Was Smog

There are two dangers in recording memoirs like this one – and they are twin sisters.

The first is to go down the road of the immortal Monty Python sketch where Yorkshire men are reliving their youth, each trying to out-do the other in terms of their humble origins. "It were tough in them days when we had to drink from a puddle in t'road…" and so on.

I got breakfast and an evening meal every day and I had a bed of my own to sleep in. The front room was usually warm with the coal fire, and we had a toilet and bathroom inside the house.

Although my dad did knock my mum about, he never laid a finger on me. That job was left to my mum!

Really, there were many more people vastly worse off than me – and I do mean a lot.

The obverse side of the coin is that I would ask younger readers to accept my life as I have described it and not to see things through a 21st century filter. Every single day was a lot more physically dangerous, and not nearly so comfortable, as it is now - but against this was immense personal freedom.

It was a world free of e-mails, texts and social media, and there would have been riots in the streets at the very thought of CCTV surveillance. As for the idea of being told what to do by this advisory group or that charity, we would not even have laughed because the idea would have been too ludicrous to consider.

We never thought of ourselves as "disadvantaged", or any of the other trigger words which are now so important. Rather, we were just ordinary, like everyone else we knew, and what was special about that?

There was more social mobility than there is now too. Kids like me, with the wrong family background, the wrong address and a lack of formal education could be given chances by older people who saw some spark in them – and we were.

The problem was the smog, literal and metaphorical, which lay over my life in the first few months after I left school.

Smog was a thick, venomous version of fog, caused when the smoke from coal fires got mixed up with conventional, benign fog. Smog stops you seeing even the most obvious things and it chokes, crushing all desire to do anything but survive.

Smog blanketed Warrington, literally and metaphorically, with soul destroying regularity. It prevented kids from my background perceiving so many things which would be invaluable to them – including where they were at the time and the road ahead.

Both my parents had left school aged fourteen. My mother was a talented seamstress and so she had been fed directly into one of Warrington's many shirt factories, to satisfy their never sated appetite for nimble fingered girls. She left school on Thursday, had Friday as her "gap year", and started a forty-four hour, five and a half day week on Monday morning. She was lucky. My Auntie Nellie wasn't as good with her fingers so ended up on the production line at Rylands Wire, filling scrap bins – hard work for a fourteen year old.

My mum used to have a picture of her when she was a bit older but still at Rylands. There was Auntie Nellie, a tall girl with a huge smile, in a skirt covered by a leather apron, with her hair tied back in the style of northern, working class women. She was standing next to a big scrap bin with no gloves, protective goggles or anything: just a big grin to get her through the 44 hour week. She died very young, in childbirth – another element of life in the early 1960s which is now largely forgotten.

*****

At the risk of reiterating this ad nauseum, I want to stress how well off I was compared with a lot of kids in my community. I never went hungry and my clothes were okay too, especially my pullovers which my mum knitted beautifully. However, clothes had to be meticulously preserved. The consequences for not doing so were severe.

The rule was, inviolably, that I had to get changed out of my school clothes before I did anything, and I do mean anything, else at all. Not getting changed was like being slightly pregnant or a bit dead: it wasn't a negotiable act.

The reason was simple. I had one blazer; one pair of grey school trousers; one pair of grey school socks and two shirts. Damaging any of this ensemble could have painful consequences.

The problem, for me at least, was that I was becoming quite a competent cannon maker. Saltpetre (the traditional name for potassium nitrate), charcoal and sulphur were all available over the counter at Boots the Chemist. Now since these are the ingredients for gunpowder, and I can't think what else they are used for together, clearly the chemist had a relaxed view about twelve year olds making explosives.

Lots of lads did it – I was just rather better than my peers.

The big challenge was the cannon barrels. I lacked both the expertise and equipment to produce high quality barrels and so I used bits of brass tube of varying qualities. Fortunately, I couldn't cast cannon balls because these put an enormous extra load on the barrels when they were fired. In lieu of balls, I used the heaviest lead shot from my fishing tackle box.

Regardless of the set-backs, and I suppose that has been the cry of development engineers over millennia, I was making ever better progress.

The latest batch of black powder had burned well when I tested a small amount on the pavement, so I was confident of a good performance on my test range which was, fittingly, on the old small arms range at the, by then abandoned, Padgate RAF camp.

I tamped the powder into the barrel nice and hard, added a bit of paper and then the lead shot. All this was normal cannon loading procedure and very familiar to me.

I had made a slow match by soaking a bit of coarse string in a strong saltpetre solution overnight and then letting it dry out on the kitchen window ledge. After all, you never know when you'll need a slow match!

On site, I lit this with a conventional match. The end of the slow match glows red when it is lit and has been the standard tool for firing cannons since the invention of the gun.

Every designer has to know their weaknesses and mine was that I always struggled a bit with touch holes. These are the holes on top of the cannon which link the outside of the gun to the charge inside. A bit of gunpowder is put into the touch hole. Apply the red end of the slow match and whuff! - a little cloud of white smoke, followed by a satisfying bang as the cannon fires.

The snag is that touch holes are tricky to design and mine were never top class. I put the slow match to the touch hole and the black powder fizzed around a bit, as it tends to do, but the cannon didn't fire.

I blew on the slow match, to make it glow more strongly, and poked it round again but still no luck. Now at this point, any experienced gunner will tell all concerned to stand very well back and wait – and for a long time. But I was still learning my trade so I carried on poking around with the slow match - and then the cannon did fire.

Fortunately, it fell off its cradle and on to its side. Less fortunately, the breech split and a small piece of brass flew off towards my face. Fortunately #2, I fell over with the shock and, fortunately #3, the piece of brass embedded itself in my left foot just above my ankle. It was bless my soul hot too!

I admit that I did jump around a bit but, when I looked, the brass hadn't sunk very deeply into my foot so I could dig it out easily enough with the penknife I always carried.

Fortunately #4, the wound had been nicely cauterised so it was quite neat. I've still got a little hole and a scar on my foot today - which is a really authentic bit of body art. I was mortified that my new cannon had been destroyed but I was sure that the next one would be better.

The destroyed cannon wasn't my only problem. When I got home, I did get changed out of my school clothes but my mum found the left sock with the hole burnt in it. She went bonkers and really laid into me – I mean properly. I just rolled up into a ball in a corner of the kitchen until she was finished.

It's worth noting that I didn't get a good hiding for making the gunpowder, the cannon or almost getting blinded. The key issue was burning a hole in a pair of school socks with wear left in them: that was the major crime.

As things happened, she darned them expertly and none of the kids at school said anything. Lots of the poorer kids had darned clothes and a pair of socks was a long way down the embarrassment list.

*****

Getting a smack from Mum didn't particularly bother me. I was really well treated because I never once had a belt used on me. But there was a lot of institutional violence too and this did upset me - but emotionally rather than physically. I want to tell you a couple of stories because I hope that they will explain why motorcycles were so important to me. In my mind, bikes were almost mythical creatures and lived in a land where the sun shone endlessly – they were freedom, excitement and all the things which were missing from my daily life where survival was the key factor.

My parents had moved me right across Warrington just before my 11+ exam – a mixture of callous disregard for my future and immense parental incompetence. It was such a silly thing to do that you really couldn't make it up – and I'm not.

There were three options in Warrington resulting from the 11+ exam. The first was the secondary modern schools. Next, there were the girls' and boys' technical schools and finally – again separately for both genders – the two grammar schools.

Each level of school had a very clear aim – and I do mean clear. The boys' secondary modern schools churned out the workers who would power Warrington's hundreds of factories. The standard of trade skills imparted by these schools was jaw-droppingly high. The usual piece of work that the lads used to turn out before they left school was a copper and brass vase, beautifully shaped in a rather art deco style, with immaculately soldered joints.

If you could get anyone to make a vase like this for you now, it would cost a fortune and yet there were hundreds of them displayed in house windows throughout Warrington – put there by parents proud of their fifteen year old's achievements.

Girls produced immaculate dresses, aprons, skirts and goodness knows what else. They were the future seamstresses for the shirt making factories. At a level a bit further down were the girls who would work in the retail shops. Unlike today, shop assistants were invariably female.

Both genders could be found on production lines like the huge soap works at Crosfields, where Surf soap powder was made. My mum's friend worked there and she lived just outside the factory. Whenever we went to see her, I used to get coughing fits and stinging eyes but the received wisdom was that the fumes and steam gave you a good appetite! I guess that was the same story propagated by British Officers when the gas attacks took place in the First World War!

The role of technical schools was to produce Warrington's industrial elite. The lads learned engineering, a bit more engineering and then a lot more engineering.

The girls mastered clerical skills and became the zillions of highly skilled secretaries, engineering drawing tracers and shop managers.

The grammar schools were odd places really. There were working class kids there, because admission was by selection via the 11+, but the bulk of the intake was from south of the Manchester Ship Canal. These children knew about universities, the professions and how to make the most of the opportunities grammar school gave them.

To those people who hearken after a golden age of grammar schools the only thing that I can say is that, for me at least, grammar school was an immense waste of talent and a thoroughly horrible experience.

Around the top 11% of children, by the measure of the 11+ at least, went to the two grammar schools – one for boys and the other for girls. This was around 130 boys and about the same number of girls. So, immediately, 89% of kids had "failed".

The successful eleven year olds were then put into four classes. At Boteler Grammar School these were 1, 1P, 1A and 1B.

1 and 1P (One Parallel) were considered to be the kids worth educating and the bottom two streams were just makeweights – really!

So, out of the 130 boys who represented the brightest 11% of that year's intake, 65 were considered sub-standard: what an obscene waste!

Another problem for the working class kids was staying on at school to do "A" Levels. Common sense told anyone with a grain of brain that kids left school at sixteen and earned money. What sort of fruit cake kept their kids in school when they could be at work?

I know a lad a little bit older than me who has a PhD and has never been full time to university. He left school, aged sixteen, to work as a lab assistant at Crosfields and had such enormous ability that he achieved the highest academic standards – and still kept earning money!

*****

Inevitably, I managed to not fit in any box – not a single one.

There were numerous issues and they caused no end of problems for even those teachers who liked me. A strange one was that I was both very shy and nervous, whilst on occasions also being precociously confident and assertive.

I can give you a good example of this dichotomy. Warrington Library had a strict policy that children could not be given tickets for the adult section of the library until they were eleven years old. To be fair, this was sensible and practical for two reasons. First, most kids needed some help and guidance with choosing books and, alongside this, the large collection in the adult area of the library would have been overwhelming.

Then there was the additional issue of children not looking after books and so reducing the material available to the rest of the town.

I didn't see things in this light – not at all. By the time I was ten years old, I was bored out of my mind with children's books and wanted more – much, much, much more. Normally, I would have been reticent with adults but the unfairness of the situation pulled the pin from the moral grenade which has been both my saviour, and my sworn enemy, over the years.

I launched into a full-on tirade, stating that the Children's Librarian had no right – and that's another major trigger word in my lexicon – to deprive me of my choice of books. So there we have a scruffy little boy, in short trousers and with a music hall, joke Northern accent arguing philosophy and human rights with a professional adult. It was a literary version of bare knuckle fighting and it attracted a good audience of both kids and adults.

Eventually, some Boss Librarian was attracted to the fracas. She stopped me dead in my tracks and then ordered everyone to calm down and be silent. Even after all these years, I can remember her grey pleated skirt, stiff white blouse and hair tied back in a bun.

She asked me to explain what I felt was the issue, hushed the Children's Librarian, and listened to me in silence. Then, without any encouragement or agreement that I had been correct, she took me down the stairs to one of the pair of desks in the adult library. There, she gave me two adult library tickets, warned me to look after any books I borrowed and told me to choose something. There was no leading, hints or suggestions. Rather, "Okay Sunshine – you've mithered to be an adult reader – now get on with it."

And this suited me down to the ground because, to use that most hackneyed metaphor, I was like a kid in a candy store.

By contrast, my mum was absolutely mortified – out of her head with shame at the behaviour of her wayward son. There he was, a decent kid who had been taught good manners, arguing with adults - and posh ones too! I'm surprised I wasn't immediately put into service as a goatherd or chimney sweep! But I wasn't.

Because of books, my general knowledge exploded exponentially but so very untidily. For me, two might follow one and three might be the next number after two – but not necessarily. One could be followed by hedgehog, or perhaps blue, 633 Squadron or anything else which made sense to me. For a child of my social background, my general knowledge was outstanding.

I also wrote well, with a vivid imagination, but was terribly hampered by handwriting so bad that it was often dismissed by adults who could not, or would not, see beyond the untidy and apparently careless scrawl.

Once the grown-ups got past my reading, writing and general knowledge the good news came to an end.

My maths was weak and my handwriting would have defied a GCHQ code breaker. We also had a "Reasoning" exam which required shapes to be fitted into boxes and so on – and I really didn't reason well at all – and still don't!

So, what to do with this confusing eleven year old? Well, I wasn't going to fit in at a secondary modern school, and there were big problems with sending me to grammar school when clearly I couldn't "reason" and had handwriting which had been produced by a hyperactive spider with ink on its feet!

The answer, although it wasn't really a solution, was to pack me off to Beamont Technical School to learn engineering.

The school was in a Victorian building with some "temporary" classrooms which had been there for ages. Coming from a light, airy primary school, built straight after the war, these surroundings immediately terrified me.

I was a very young, very dreamy and very impractical child – and these were not good traits for anyone beginning a secondary education in industrial Warrington.

I need to stress that Beamont wasn't a bad or unusual school. I was chatting to a lady last year who had been to a girls' grammar school in the West Midlands at the same time that I was at Beamont. She said that her class teacher used to discipline the girls with one of the leather straps which raised and lowered train windows in the 1960s. I'll not go into the lurid details, except to say that the teacher would be banged up for a long time today.

Now we go on about the snowflake generation, and how some of the things which happen really are Big Woossie soft, but there had to be a change from how things were in the '60s. Let me give you two, completely accurate and exaggeration free examples.

Everyone did wood work and most of my class were incredibly good at it. The single exception was me. In the summer term, the whole class made a stool from oak. The stools had mortise and tenon joints, and a seat made from woven raffia. They were finished with wood oil and would cost £250 in any artisan designer shop today. Remember too, that they were made by eleven and twelve year olds.

However, the first stage in the manufacturing process was to plane a piece of oak square. I couldn't do this. My eyes and hands had no connection so every Monday afternoon I was made to plane and plane and plane until I could complete the task. And every week I failed. I must have used several large trees and made not one micron of progress but still Mr L insisted that I would continue until the wood was square. What a total waste of everyone's time when I could have written a really nice poem for him about trees or even about making stools.

Mr L also had rigid rules in the workshop. No-one was allowed to touch the circular saw – not for any reason. That was the rule.

The saw had a wooden cover on it and was unplugged at the wall when not in use because, very sensibly, a circular saw is a dangerous thing if misused and the kids needed protecting from it.

Mr L was demonstrating how to sharpen one of the small chisels which were used for making the joints on the stool legs. The lad next to me leaned across to get a better view and, in doing so, he accidentally put an elbow on the circular saw bench – and remember that the saw is unplugged and has its cover on.

Mr L leaned across and hit him with a stool leg – along with a warning not to touch the circular saw.

The lad fell on the floor but didn't cry or complain. He had been told not to touch the saw, did, and paid the price. That was that – and we all made certain that we gave the saw, and its wider environs, a very wide berth. My mouth used to go dry just looking at the thing from the other side of the workshop!

Being able to produce an engineering drawing was roughly the Beamont equivalent of breathing. Warrington had thousands of draughtsmen in its factories' drawing offices and the thirst was unquenchable. So from week one at secondary school we were taught how to draw. Interestingly, I can still produce a very passable drawing today – although I have the engineering expertise of a short sighted hamster with a hangover.

We sat in four rows for Tech Drawing. In front of each of us was a drawing board just like you might have seen in ancient black and white films. We each had our own set of basic drawing instruments which was purchased from the school. I kept mine all the way up until my cataclysmic divorce decades later.

The paper on the drawing board was secured by little spring clips and the first job was to line this up against the t-square at the bottom. Mr N demonstrated this on a great big board at the front of the room and then we did it – in silence.

In the coming weeks, we learned how to draw the job box on the bottom right hand side of the drawing and then began to produce plans with the various elevations – at eleven years old.

And we worked in complete silence…

For the avoidance of doubt, I need to clarify this word in case you mistake "silence" for "quiet" or "focussed." Silent meant no speaking unless you raised your hand to ask a question, which I never did, and Mr N gave you permission to speak.

I was sat in the third row back, on my high stool, and concentrating like crazy on the task in hand. I hated my place because there were two muppets sitting to my left who were always whispering to each other. I prayed, quite literally to God, that they would shut up so that I would not be caught up in their sins through a case of mistaken identity.

Mr N was at the back of the room and the idiots – no, far worse than just incredibly stupid – whispered. Mr N arrived and, without speaking, knocked one miscreant right off his stool and left him on the floor. I never even dared look down and, like everyone else, continued to work in silence.

And you wonder why I can still do a drawing?

*****

I was also developing a reputation for being a misfit – and quite badly so.

If I couldn't plane a piece of oak square, I did have other talents. Morning assembly followed a rigid pattern every day, a key part of which was a Bible reading on stage by a pupil.

The service operated on a rota basis. The Head was always present, along with the senior staff, but each day a different teacher was supposed to organise the rest of the gig. It soon became known amongst the less enthusiastic teachers that Melling, you know, that odd kid who wanders around as if he's lost, could actually sort out a Bible reading by himself and then deliver it on stage without any practice. Well done Melling – get on with it, there's a good lad, and don't bother me unless you have to...

So, at eleven years old, I became a semi professional organiser and reader in public.

The standard of my writing was also outstanding – when it could be deciphered – and I was beginning to register as being more than a bit different from my peers.

Things came to a head when the class was kept in for detention for talking during registration, or some other minor infringement of the rules: I can't remember the precise misdemeanour.

You will see that I have used initials for teachers because I don't want some relative to recognise them and not be best pleased with what they read. I do want to tell the absolute truth in these stories but upsetting someone unnecessarily is pointless and undignified. However, I want to name Mr Alfred Hart explicitly because, for the first time, he saw something in me that had passed every other teacher by.

Mr Hart was my form teacher and, just after our last lesson of the day, the class dutifully trooped back to our form room for the detention. We sat silently in our desks whilst he handed out sheets of paper and told us to spend the next half an hour explaining why "Silence is Golden." The class, seething with resentment, dutifully scribbled any nonsense to fill in the next thirty minutes – but I didn't.

In my immature way, I wrote an essay on the power of speech, gave it in, went home and got stuck into *The Motorcycle* and the world where I wanted to be.

The following morning, after assembly, Mr Hart pulled me out of class saying that he wanted a word with me.

We went through the hall and along to the Headmaster's Office and I was told to sit outside until I was called. I was neither brave nor confident and came very close to projectile vomiting on the floor, as I wracked my brain to remember anything I had done which was so bad that it warranted a visit to the Head: I couldn't think of a single thing.

After what seemed like days, Mr Hart called me in and there, on the Head's desk, was my essay. I felt sick and dizzy because I was certain that I was going to get a real walloping for insurrection or treason, or perhaps for just being a gobby smarty pants.

Mr Hart picked up the essay from the desk and smiled. He said: "This is a very thoughtful piece of writing. You were the only one who took any care. Why did you?"

So I explained my reasons to the two teachers, who listened in silence.

Then the Head gave me a few words of praise and off I went to my first lesson.

I didn't dare tell anyone about the incident, not even my parents, in case I had misunderstood what had happened and I was in trouble but just didn't know it.

*****

The one secret which I hoarded, and which kept me from feeling a complete and utter failure, was motorcycles.

After my 11+, my mum decided to take me on holiday – and to the Isle of Man. I didn't know what the Isle of Man was and did not have the vaguest concept of the TT races but off we went. I think that my mum decided on the Isle of Man because of the warm memories she had of holidaying there before the war.

Her whole family travelled to the Isle of Man for their annual holiday and the three daughters went to the dances which were held in the Villa Marina every day. I have just a few pictures of my mum from that time and she was catch your breath beautiful with thick, copper coloured hair and a vivacious smile.

My dad was handsome too, with a cocky, bring-it-on smile which must have captured the hearts of a lot of young women.

Things were going right for them in every way. My dad was making top money as an electrician and he was such a valued customer at Jack Frodsham Motorcycles that he was allocated one of the very first Triumph Speed Twins – which were like gold dust at the time.

The following year, 1939, he had a Triumph Tiger 100. I have a picture of my mum with the Speedtwin, dressed in a lovely, long leather coat, a flying helmet, and with a smile to die for.

My mum rarely spoke of what happened during the war, and my father never. She once told me that dad had left as the man she knew and loved, and came back a completely different person. He had found drink, infidelity and the influence of other men with similar tastes. Innumerable other marriages suffered the same fate so my family wasn't anything special or unusual.

Because of her fondness for the Isle of Man, and I guess as a rites-of-passage treat for me, we set off for Douglas. I remember very little of the trip over there. Looking back, I think that this was because kids were done unto rather than did. Whatever the decision, good children – and I was well behaved – did what they were told; ate when they were given food; went to whatever bed they were put into and followed the orders of whatever adult was in charge of them that day.

Your opinion was neither sought nor given and, truly, children were expected to speak only when spoken to.

In my case, the situation was somewhat worse than even this. I am trying to be objective with these memories – impossible task though this is - because the 1950s' world is being portrayed through my eyes. Even so, I am sure that I had already begun to realise that I was brighter than my parents. I need to clarify this statement. Both Mum and Dad knew more than me but, when I did have the knowledge, I could use it better and in a more organised fashion. The more I could, and did, do this the greater became the gap between my parents and me.

I have no memories of the cheap boarding house where we stayed. It felt just like our house so it must have been pretty grim, but we did have a cooked breakfast every morning and I remember the smell of burning toast and hot fat, which was in sharp contrast to the Cornflakes and Frosties we had at home.

My mum took me for a walk along Douglas Promenade but the tide was in, so I couldn't go on to the rocky beach and skim stones. In every way, the holiday was militantly ordinary.

We got up early on Monday morning and caught a bus to Creg Ny Baa. This is a 90 degree, right-hand corner at the end of the ferocious downhill straight from Sarah's Cottage. The bus was packed with laughing race goers and I began to catch the atmosphere. It was also incredibly smoky. The premier seats on the bus were right at the back, where a group of noisy, younger fans were laughing and shouting. I looked round to try to see them but they were obscured by a dense layer of cigarette smoke. If you didn't smoke, whether you were male or female, you were in a minority.

My mum found us a place on the high bank, after the corner, and I listened – albeit uncomprehendingly – to the adults discussing the forthcoming 350cc, "Junior" race. The sun was shining and there was a palpable excitement in the air – like the tightening of the atmosphere before a thunderstorm.

The traffic on the roads stopped and now I could taste the tension. A man near us slipped down the bank and ended up in a heap on the road. The women, and there were many, laughed. A big, jolly lady – with a cascading waterfall of thick, curly black hair said: "You'll have to leave him there now. You're not allowed to pick up any rubbish that you drop."

Her friend giggled. "The soft sod. I've been trying to get rid of him for years. I wish I could leave the silly bugger there." Then she reached down and helped him up.

After sixty years, I can still recall the conversation and the faces around us. The smells of cheap perfume and always, always, always the acrid stench of strong cigarettes remain etched into my memory forever.

But what was to come next is far more than just a memory – it was to become me.

From far behind us, over my left shoulder, came a wailing, sonorous howl – not tortured or distressed but a war cry of some unnatural being, the like of which I had never seen nor could even imagine.

The noise came from a 350cc, four cylinder MV Agusta ridden by the greatest rider of his era, John Surtees. He came down through the gears and the wail rose and fell like the mating call of some mythical beast. I was transfixed and leaned forward. Then, with a clarity still burnt into my mind today, the MV screamed past us with Surtees buried in the fuel tank.

The noise tore into my very soul. This was something magnificent. It sliced through the bonds which tied me to the sepia world of my council house with its paraffin fire, the bus trips into town sitting alongside the ancient women who smelled of age and oldness, and the fights and arguments which were the corrosive liquor of my daily existence.

The sun shone, the red and silver MV gleamed and the noise was a war cry of freedom and joy. That night, I lay in bed and the wail of the MV sang me to sleep.

Later in the week, we met my dad off the boat. He had come to watch the Senior TT – the premier event of the week – but he was soon in the pub so I didn't see him very much.

*****

Over the years, I have developed a range of reactions about what my dad did or, more accurately, didn't do.

At the time, seeing my dad ignore me and head for the pub was not upsetting. Probably, I was rather happy because there were no cataclysmic rows which meant that Mum and I were on a winning streak. Also, lots of kids were ignored by their parents so his behaviour seemed completely normal to me.

I think the saddest thing was that directly after the war, when my dad was making a lot of money with the taxi business he started, he achieved some modest success at grass track racing. He knew all about motorcycles and racing, and now he had a bright, hyper-enthusiastic, eleven year old son – and in those days having a male child was still important – who had just fallen in love with racing. Yet, the best he could do with this golden ticket was to ignore me and go drinking.

When I began to make my own way in the world, I bitterly – and I use that word advisedly – resented the neglect and the drink which caused it...

Now, at my age, I have nothing but pity for my dad. What a tragic thing alcoholism made him do – to trade all the fun and pride I have could have given him, for drunkenness.

*****

Another important event in my life occurred at about the same time: I was given the key to the door through which I would walk into the rest of my life, because I rode my first motorcycle. In fact, that's stretching things a bit because calling a 32cc Cyclemaster a motorcycle is like saying that the dinghy I sail on Coniston Water is the same as a round the world racing yacht – because they've both got sails!

The Cyclemaster's story begins with DKW and pre-war Germany. The Zschopau based company was the world leader in two-stroke technology and developed the Schnurle loop scavenging system which is the basis of all two-strokes, even today. From this high-tech environment came a vast range of two-strokes, from the utilitarian RT125 to exotic, supercharged GP bikes. In this mass of leading edge designs was an incredibly neat, disc-valved 25cc power unit designed to be fitted directly in place of the rear wheel of a conventional pedal cycle.

DKW never actually manufactured the new power plant and, after the war, the original drawings found their way to Holland via Bernhard Neumann, an ex-DKW designer. Neumann reworked the original DKW design with the help of Rinus Bruynzeel and Nico Groenerdijke and, in 1949, the neat power plant went into production in Holland, retaining its original 25.7cc form.

The new engine was outstandingly the best of the "cyclemotor" power plants - tiny engines, designed to provide power for bicycles - and its potential was soon recognised in Britain. In 1950 an uprated, 32cc version of the original design was in full production and almost 250,000 British built Cyclemasters were manufactured over the next eleven years. This makes the Cyclemaster outstandingly the most successful British built motorcycle of all time, in terms of numbers produced.

The reason for the Cyclemaster's success is simple: it is an extremely clever, effective piece of engineering which far exceeded its design brief. To begin with, the power plant was universal and easy to install in any bicycle. The whole unit, including the fuel tank, simply slotted in place of the bicycle's rear wheel, leaving only two cables - one for the throttle and the other to lift the clutch - to be routed to the handlebars. By contrast, other cyclemotors required mounting brackets and friction drives on to the front or rear wheels of the bicycle.

Being disc-valved, the tiny engine was incredibly torquey and a genuine 20mph cruising speed was possible. Starting was easy too. Because the Cyclemaster had a clutch, the bicycle could be pedalled up to a speed where the engine would fire, the clutch dropped and then, with a little light pedal assistance, the Cyclemaster would power away.

The tiny engine produced 0.6bhp at only 3,700rpm and, despite having no gears, this was enough power to deal with hills - if the rider provided a little help with the pedals.

Even driven hard, 200mpg was comfortably achievable. Being fitted with a coaster rear brake, operated by reversing the bicycle's pedals, the Cyclemaster also stopped better than other cycle motor equipped bicycles, which often contaminated the rubber block rim brakes with two-stroke mix.

Finally, the Cyclemaster was affordable. Costing around £30, at a time when an average wage was £5.00 a week, the power plant was Purchase Tax free and could be bought on the newly introduced Hire Purchase schemes imported from America. For the first time in history, a reliable, practical, personal transport system was available to the masses.

The social impact was immense. No longer were workers locked into living in the terraced houses adjacent to their places of work - or reliant on trams, trains and buses. Now, they could commute from the newly built suburban housing estates on the outskirts of towns.

Mothers rode Cyclemasters too. My mum collected me from my first infant school in Warrington town centre and carried me home, along with a shopping bag balanced on my knee, in a little seat bolted to the rear mudguard. No helmet, no seat belt, but hold on to the shopping bag love: that's what made the British Empire great!

At weekends, the Cyclemaster carried fishing rods and baskets to new areas of canals and rivers which had previously only been accessible by coach or train. My dad often did this with his fishing basket strapped to the same seat which housed me Monday to Friday, and his rods running parallel with the mainframe on the bike.

Truly, this modest little vehicle changed the lives of millions of Britons.

Even when we had a car, the Cyclemaster was still used as a second vehicle in the house and this is how it came to be my golden ticket into the world of motorcycling.

Because my dad was inebriated most of the time, he had a rather laissez-faire attitude towards me using the Cyclemaster – so I did!

Very near to our council house were the remains of RAF Padgate. This base was where many thousands of RAF recruits had their first taste of military life. When I was a child it had been abandoned by the military but the road systems were still largely intact.

I took the Cyclemaster round to Padgate Camp and then pushed and pushed and pushed, trying to make the little bike start. It didn't - until a kindly adult walking his dog turned the fuel on for me. A lack of mechanical awareness has remained with me to this day!

With fuel now feeding the engine, I ran alongside the full sized bicycle and then dropped the clutch. The motor fired and, somehow, I clambered on to the saddle and perched high in the air with no chance of ever getting my feet to the ground if anything went wrong.

But why should there, or could there, ever be a problem? I opened the throttle lever and the Cyclemaster surged forward on what felt like a magic carpet wave of fire and power.

As I am writing these words, I can still remember the dark brown wooden huts flashing by on the right hand side of the road, while I was transformed into some new creature - no longer boy, but now a mechanical hybrid of motorcycle and man.

In my mind, from now on, there would be no more walking to the shops. No more queuing for buses outside the market. No more pedalling up the ramp to the Cantilever Bridge at Grappenhall, with aching legs and panting lungs. Simply, the God-like power of pulling the lever towards me and feeling the power of the engine take me to new worlds. When I got a bike licence…

There was no drug more addictive – nothing in the world I wanted to do more. I was hooked: a hard core junkie! It was a life sentence. From now on, bikes and books were to be inextricably wound into every day of my life.

*****

My year at Beamont concluded with an incident which had a huge impact on my thinking for the rest of my life. At the end of the final term, I was called into the Head's Office and told that I had won the first year prizes for the best work in English and History.

My first reaction was one of confusion because I still walked round with a vast lack of self-confidence. Regardless, I was delighted. I had worked hard, was better than my peers and my efforts had been recognised. So far, so good.

The Head then told me that I couldn't have both prizes because it wasn't fair to the other boys. In summary, the argument was that I was so much better than everyone else that I somehow enjoyed an unfair advantage.

I didn't say anything but I was mortified. No-one came along when I was rubbish at rugby and said that I should get a place in the school team on the grounds that all the other lads were bigger, stronger and more competent than me. When I was planing wood on a Monday afternoon, I hadn't noticed the Head intervening then and showing some sympathy for my incompetence.

Yet, when I was good at something it wasn't fair to the other pupils: that didn't seem like natural justice!

I told my mum, but she just shrugged her shoulders and said if that was the rule then tough.

The prize-giving was held in the Parr Hall, in the centre of Warrington, and was quite a formal affair. Neither of my parents came so I sat on my own, collected the prize for History, returned to my seat and clapped politely when some other lad collected my prize for English.

I didn't make a fuss or complain, because kids from my background didn't: that was life - so get on with it!

But, in the silence of my bedroom, the injustice burnt into me and led me to a love of motorcycle racing. Racing bikes is one of the purest forms of human activity. It doesn't matter whether you are rich or poor, confident or shy, have a profession or work with your hands: no, none of this carries one molecule of value. With bike racing, life is condensed into one singularity point. When the flag drops, the bull***t stops and if you ride faster, have more skill and are braver than everyone else, you win - and if you aren't then you don't. That is fair.

Chapter Three

Glory, Glory Hallelujah . . .

Glory, glory Hallelujah
Teacher hit me with a ruler
Mother hit me with a walking stick and made me black and blue

(1950s playground skipping song)

In the summer term I was called into the Head's Office again and told that I was transferring to Boteler Grammar School. This was not unusual because each year one or two kids, who were considered to be "late developers" were shuffled out of Beamont and across town to Boteler Grammar.

Those who couldn't hack it at Beamont moved the other way. Of mild interest, the muppet who Mr N had knocked off his stool in Tech Drawing was one of half a dozen kids who got relegated. Served him right too, for almost causing me to get caught up in the collateral damage following his talking!

The system was inhumane - even for kids with supportive families. For me it was an utter disaster. Two of us went to Boteler Grammar – a lad from a middle class family who had been ill during the 11+ and me, the school misfit.

We made no preliminary visit nor did we have any information about what to expect. The only good thing was that I had outgrown my first school blazer, so my mum could replace it with a new Boteler Grammar one. The rest of my school uniform moved across easily, along with new grey socks for the start of the term to replace my cannon damaged pair.

I had never even visited my new school – not once – and so the first job of the new term was to actually find out where it was. I set off early on my bicycle and eventually located Boteler Grammar on the far side of town from where I lived.

I was not at all proud of my apparent promotion. On the contrary, I was deeply unhappy. I had moved house three times in three years and had been to three different schools. Without fail, each time I thought that I had arrived somewhere - everything changed. Things were made more difficult because I was entirely on my own. I had no siblings and my parents were absentee landlords in every practical sense, so I groped and stumbled through the darkness and chaos of my life. Truly, scrambling for beginners.

I duly arrived at the bike sheds on the right hand side of the school – and got punched because the section I had chosen was controlled by a group of Mafiosi from the Upper School. Of course, I was supposed to know this.

There was no mentor, or even casual advice, when I went to class. I was just supposed to divine what to do and where to go. Mr S, my form teacher, made it clear that in his opinion I should never have been allowed into an academic institution.

From there, things only went downhill...

I am happy to admit that it wasn't either Beamont or Boteler Grammar which was at fault, but me. Throughout my life, the snag has been finding something which fits my abilities. If the employer/institution/situation can find something I can do, then it's happy days all round. However, trying to fit me into the wrong shaped slot for my very, very odd set of talents leads to certain failure – and it did at grammar school.

In the second year at grammar school, the emphasis was on rote learning of every subject and, even today, I struggle with this skill set to an embarrassing degree.

Let me explain just how bad I am at remembering facts out of context. Currently, I take part in dementia research because I have seen the results of this illness at first hand and it is a truly sad thing to witness. In one piece of research we were given tasks to do which are proven, reliable indicators of early onset dementia. Some of these involved remembering number or letter sequences, and other sections asked participants to recall the names of people we had met in the past or places where we had put things. Not being able to find basic household implements in your own home is often a good indicator of dementia.

I completed one extensive exercise and a nice lady contacted me to suggest that I should see my GP soonest because my symptoms were clearly indicating that either I already had, or was well on the way to having, dementia.

I wrote a, fairly, polite note to her explaining that if this was the case then I have had dementia all my life because I have never been able to successfully do any of the things on the questionnaire. Interestingly, I never received a reply.

Had they known that I was an early onset dementia sufferer, perhaps my teachers would have been a bit kinder and less inclined to say that I was lazy or indolent – neither of which were true.

Instead, I was kept in detention, whacked with a wide range of objects including – and this was a first – lengths of Bunsen burner tubing knotted together in a sort of modern cat o' nine tails. That was creative on the part of my chemistry teacher.

*****

I am going to make some further comments about corporal punishments and it is important to see these in context. In the 1960s there was a lot of gratuitous violence in society and there is no point in looking at this through a 21st century prism. To do this distorts both the truth of situation and the reality of daily life and I really do not want this to happen.

2,000 years ago, when a cohort had failed its Legion, Roman legionaries were forced to beat one in ten of their comrades to death in the act of decimation. In the 1960s, we would have considered this to be a barbaric act. Yet, the Romans thought decimation to be a fair, reasonable and effective way of maintaining discipline and cohesion within the army.

Flogging, up to 1000 lashes, was common in the British Army and Navy in the 19th century and was accepted as being a sound and sensible way of maintaining discipline

So it was with corporal punishment when I was growing up. The mantra was – quite literally – "Spare the rod and spoil the child."

In fact, it was a joke. A popular TV comedy sitcom at the time was "Whacko" – originally called "Six of the Best" (six strokes of the cane on a pupil's bottom) – and it ran all the way up 1972. I used to think that it was hilarious, with Jimmy Edwards, the Headmaster of Chiselbury Public School, cheating the kids out of their pocket money and caning them left, right and centre. It was a very popular show and was enjoyed by both children and adults.

However, I was much fonder of "Hancock's Half Hour" with the truly gifted Tony Hancock in the eponymous role. Hancock was always being conned out of money, when he wasn't cheating other people, and got knocked about all the time. This was simply what happened and it is wrong to say that we should have all been appalled at the subject and content of the shows – wrong and completely inaccurate. Everyone thought that they were great.

What I objected to, and it did upset me deeply, was not the actual corporal punishment but its gratuitous use – a simply mindless hurting of kids for no reason. I was perfectly sanguine about getting punished for breaking whatever rules and regulations that were in place – and there were many of all grades. If you smoked behind the bike sheds, and got caught, you were going to get caned and that was that: serves you right.

I could, sort of, understand getting knocked off your stool in Tech Drawing for talking. We were ordered not to speak, and the instruction was unequivocal, so if you spoke the outcome was predictable: harsh but not unfair.

Where it became mindless were instances such as when I was caned for reaching into my satchel during a class examination. I had leaned down to get my bottle of ink because my fountain pen had run out. Okay, we were supposed neither to open our desks nor go into our satchels to avoid cheating but my teacher saw exactly what was happening and I still got hit. There were endless other cases like this which just seemed petty, silly and counter-productive.

So, the stories I am going to relate are not complaints about how badly, or unfairly, we were treated by 2021 standards but rather the unreasonableness of corporal punishment even when it is considered from a 1960s' view point.

*****

An additional problem to that of getting whacked was that I was small, nervous, timid, very late into puberty and immature. How's that for a hand of cards?

Already, many of the lads were developing "bum fluff" – the precursor to proper facial hair. They also knew about girls and sex, and the unmentionable things like bras, knickers and sanitary towels all of which were still closely guarded secrets in the 1960s.

They looked at girls in a very different way from me. The fit, athletic ones got to play on the best pitches, right next to the girls' grammar school. In between scoring tries, kicking goals and all sorts of other acts of physical prowess, they were able to study the fit, athletic girls in their short, green PE skirts and yellow knickers.

Afterwards, when we were getting changed, they gave lurid descriptions of the girls' attractions.

I was in bottom set for PE and so my physical education lessons took place in a patch of mud behind the sports pavilion. I stumbled around in the slime, along with a lad who wore incredibly thick glasses and another who stuttered so badly that we could never work out what he wanted so he just stood around, jumping up and down, desperately gesticulating with his arms.

The rest of the group were merely disastrously incompetent - like me. I remember one of my cohort having three attempts at kicking the rugby ball to restart a game - and failing. Not failing to kick it well, but totally and completely defeated by the task of making his foot connect with the static ball!

Overall, we were a truly memorable group of losers.

As we limped and shuffled back to the changing room, like Napoleon's Grande Armée after the retreat from Moscow, I sometimes wondered whether there was our doppelgänger of physically hopeless girls on the other side of the campus, also trudging back to get changed whilst wondering what decent boys looked like.

*****

Boteler had a very different atmosphere from Beamont and it was yet another problem for me. At Beamont, I had been rather liked, and accepted, for being an odd ball but Boteler looked to mould pupils in a very restrictive way.

I have tried to be fair in these recollections and, as far as I can judge anything objectively this distant from the time, I was an outstandingly good writer.

There was a school magazine and I wrote a piece for it. This was home ground for me. My story was based around resources running out on earth and our species seeking supplies from nearby planets: not bad for a twelve year old who was reading a huge amount of science fiction from Ray Bradbury's *Martian Chronicles* to the *Day of the Triffids* and *The Midwich Cuckoos* written by John Wyndham.

I dutifully presented it and waited. Mr D had a quick glance, ripped it up before my eyes and threw the story in the bin, telling me not to be so stupid in fantasising about ridiculous things. Then he ordered me to write a report about the school cricket team – which I didn't.

I never told my parents or anyone else what had happened, but seeing my work destroyed in front of my eyes really hurt me so much that I actually stopped writing anything for a long time – even for my own amusement.

*****

What kept me sane were motorcycles. It was a big effort for my parents to find the money, but for my 12th birthday I was given a Dansette record player. In the red, vinyl covered box there was a turntable and at the front a small, built in speaker controlled by knurled, plastic knobs. It was a symbol that I was growing up and ready to become part of the rock 'n' roll generation.

My mum bought me the Beatles' *I Wanna Hold Your Hand* and my avant-garde older cousin gave me a quite badly scratched, long play vinyl record from the film *GI Blues*, and I sang along with Elvis and *Wooden Heart* as I did my homework.

But my parents failed in their noble attempt to both civilise and convert me into a mainstream teenager, for I had a secret sin.

No, not illegal drugs - which hadn't been invented in Warrington yet.

Nor was it looking at partially undressed ladies in magazines which were only sold to grown-ups from secret supplies under the counter.

No, my addiction had come from the second-hand shop which was located just next to the railway bridge, opposite the Horse and Jockey pub. In there, for the princely sum of two shillings and six pence (12½ p) – a whole week's pocket money – I purchased a well-worn copy of the Stanley Schofield recordings from the 1957 TT.

And so I would go into my bedroom, close the door tight, put on the Dansette under my bed sheets and, in the claustrophobic darkness, listen to the wailing, siren call of Bob McIntyre winning the 1957 Golden Jubilee TT on his four cylinder Gilera.

The crackle of the British singles was the heart and body of Grand Prix racing in motorcycling's Golden Era but the warbling wail of the four cylinder Gilera touched my soul. My 1960s monochrome world was rent asunder by the technicolour ululation of the Gilera's war song which scarred my young brain forever.

*****

Getting hit by teachers was such a common occurrence that I never gave it a second thought. It didn't matter how much you tried to stay on the straight – and very narrow – path of righteousness, you were bound to do something wrong.

I'll give you an example. When your jotter was full, you presented it to a teacher, showed that there was no wasted room and got a new one. Whilst I was waiting in line for my new jotter, I filled in a tiny space on the back page with a little drawing of a Gilera Four engine – canted slightly forward and looking like a very racy, motorcycling Holbein miniature.

The teacher, I forget who it was, raged at me for defacing school property - and so it was bend over and a whack with the board ruler. It was this petty, unnecessary violence which I really didn't think was either fair or acceptable.

I was also permanently scarred by something else I saw at school. In fact, it is still pellucidly clear today. Rules were everywhere at Boteler Grammar and they were rigid. I'm not quite sure why kids who were well behaved and under control were constantly punished - but we were. The sanctions were so much a part of life that I never took much notice of them. However, there was one example which strayed very clearly into the area of perversion.

Mr G was our PE teacher and he was utter rubbish – uninspiring and a thug. His rule was that we had to have a spare pair of underpants to wear in PE. After PE, we showered and then got changed back into our normal pants.

One of the kids came from a very poor family and he only had one pair of pants. He might have had two at some point, but anything could have happened in a family with a herd of kids all sharing the same bedroom and often one bed too.

Mr G went berserk with him, screaming and raging in apoplectic fury. Clearly, the lad was going to get whacked with the large gym shoe kept just for this purpose. So what? Except for the merest hint of schadenfreude I didn't have much interest. He didn't have his spare pants so he was going to get what was coming.

If that was fair by the dreadfully low standards of the school, then what came next most certainly wasn't – and it still upsets me today.

The class was divided into four teams of around eight lads in each. Three teams were sent to sit on the wall bars – probably so that we could get a good view of what was going to happen next.

The remaining group got the wooden vaulting box out, removed the bottom section and placed the remainder in the centre of the gym. The miscreant was made to stretch out across the box and each member of the team was told to hit him with a gym shoe – and hard. If the blow wasn't considered to be sufficiently hard, then the boy who had failed would get whacked – along with a second stroke for the lad stretched across the box, given by Mr G.

One lad actually did only make a nominal effort and I was torn between admiration for his courage and incredulity at his madness. Even to this day, I wonder whether I would have done the same thing.

The beating took most of the lesson and then we all trooped back to the changing room, showered – because that was the rule - and sat in silence. The lad who took the punishment didn't cry overtly but tears ran down his face – not surprising when he showed us the welts on his bottom.

Meanwhile, Mr G smirked and warned us that the same thing would happen to us if we made the same mistake.

So, did I eventually rise to the top and make a success of grammar school? The answer would have been almost a certain no. The school had no use for what I had to offer - and for me, each day was merely a matter of survival.

My saviour came in the most bizarre form. My dad worked for the Air Ministry Works Department and he was offered a well-paid job in Libya. Had I been the star of Boteler Grammar, it still wouldn't have mattered because the family was off to Tripoli. Four houses and four schools in four years!

In Tripoli, I attended an army school which was so laid back that it could have been a hippy commune. No-one was hit, or shouted at, but equally there was no pressure to work or succeed. It suited me down to the ground and I collected a nice haul of good "O" Levels.

Chapter Four

What's Libya?

I had almost nothing to pack up - so I didn't. I had no idea of where Libya was or even what it was. I had never seen even a picture of the country until a few days before we left England, but then I have a vague recollection of looking in a library book and being excited at the image of a Bedouin with a rifle, sitting on a camel. Maybe that was what all Libyans did.

There was no goodbye party but Lyn Jones, a friend of mine from grammar school, bought me a book as a parting gift and that was nice.

I got on the train at Bank Quay Station in Warrington and sat in the seat where I was put. I ate what I was given and read a book. My only choice was when to visit the toilet.

We got off the train at somewhere. I think that it was probably Luton. I walked, stood, sat, ate and shuffled along in the queues just like any other piece of luggage. I guess that if I'd had a headache my mum would have given me two aspirin but, other than that, I was of no interest to anyone.

At the risk of reiterating the same point ad nauseum, I wasn't badly treated compared with many other kids I knew. I never went hungry and had sound clothes and shoes but as for my feelings, they were utterly irrelevant to my parents, other adults or the world at large.

So I remember nothing of the journey – except for a few minutes. Those moments were burned into my brain and, as I am writing these words, I can still feel the tension in my hands.

I have a picture of me as a baby, being held by my dad on the steps of a Dakota airliner just after the war - but I have no memory of the flight. Other than the Dakota, I had never been on an aircraft and so the flight to Libya was a new experience for me. I want to mention not so much the journey itself but how little say kids had in anything. At twelve years old, I had about as much influence on my life as one of the green, faux crocodile skin cardboard suitcases which contained all our life.

British Forces' families and troops were transported round the world by the RAF and also a charter company called Eagle Airlines. On this flight, we flew with Eagle. At the time, I didn't know the aircraft type but, later on, I found that it was an American Douglas DC6 – a post war, propeller driven aircraft.

I must have asked to be given a window seat and it was wonderful – absolutely breath-taking. I sat just behind the two engines and, in the darkness, I could see the exhausts from the Wright Cyclone engines glowing a dull red.

We took a long, long time to get airborne and I sat on the edge of my seat, not with fear but with excitement, as the exhausts became ever brighter and we bumped down the runway. Then there was a surge and we were airborne, the heavily laden plane struggling to break free of its gravitational chains.

Was this some mystical metaphor for the next stage of my life? No, not really; in fact, not at all. There was nothing to see, so I got out my book and read. Books and books and books - my friends, my support, my doors to other worlds.

A long time later, the plane landed at RAF Idris, some distance from Tripoli city, and we had arrived. I shuffled off the plane along with all the other luggage and began a new chapter in my life.

*****

We were given a small villa on the outskirts of Tripoli, in an area called Colina Verde. It was a very well established area and extremely cosmopolitan. Our next door neighbour was an American family and, later, I did some babysitting for a member of the Libyan judiciary who lived a few hundred yards away. There was a good sprinkling of Italian families who had been in Libya since the 1930s, and plenty of British too.

Not far away was the British Forces' hospital, surrounded with woods of fragrant juniper pines to play in.

Two other aromas remain with me and they both came from the little convenience store where the Libyan owner had befriended me. There was shay – stewed tea drunk from little cups – and peanuts roasted on a large metal dish heated over a charcoal fire. I was liked there for being friendly, kind and helpful and so started to form the first pre-dawn hints of a happiness which would have been so important to me as both an outsider in life and a physically slow developer.

There was also not so much a scent but a taste – everywhere the background flavour of the fine, khaki dust which permeated every molecule of my existence.

I loved Colina Verde and was just beginning to find my feet and form friendships – so we moved again! Six houses, in six different areas, in five years: it didn't make for a stable upbringing.

I never knew why my parents moved us. This time, I was so upset that I actually did object but kids had little say in what happened in those days, so we loaded up and went to Georgian Popoli and another small villa. There were two orange trees in the garden, and the whole house was surrounded by a tall, whitewashed wall. It was okay but lacked the warmth, intimacy and inclusivity of Colina Verde. At Georgian Popoli I always felt that we were foreigners in someone else's country, instead of being part of the happy community which Colina Verde was.

*****

The laissez-faire attitude of the British Army Children's School in Tripoli allowed me to stumble along in a fog of misunderstanding and misfittery, and yet still get a good set of "O" Levels. Later, these were to be invaluable to me.

I was still hugely behind my peers in terms of maturity but, slowly, I was beginning to think of girls – albeit just not very adequately. It's important to understand how little respectable boys like me - and, except for being somewhat manically inclined, I was a nice lad – knew about girls. Lots of other teenagers in my generation did know a vast amount – but not the cloud dweller Frank Melling.

Daily talk amongst the lads in my class was about girls: it was constant. Everyone seemed to know much more than me – vastly more – so mainly I listened. Unfortunately, when I did try to participate, everything went wrong. Imagine trying to join in a conversation with Professor Brian Cox and a group of astrophysicists chatting about the Higgs Boson elementary particle: that was me trying to sound knowledgeable about girls.

There was a truly lovely girl in our class who did babysitting in the Colina Verde area and, sometimes, she smiled shyly at me. She was small, had jet black hair and a laughing face. She was also gentle and had shown me much kindness - a difficult thing to do at the time in a co-educational class. Eventually, I saw her leaning on the green metal gate outside the house where she was babysitting and I asked her to be my girlfriend. I knew how to pronounce the words, and I could spell them accurately, but had not even the vaguest hint of what they meant in reality.

She smiled and said that she would be my girlfriend. I should have kissed her on the cheek or held her hand – or made some first, tentative gesture towards a nascent manhood: but I didn't. I felt several galaxies beyond inadequate and incompetent, and so did nothing – nothing at all.

The following day at school I was torn apart. Inside, I felt so much for her. I desperately wanted to say something appropriate – something kind, affectionate even, but I didn't have the words. More than anything else, it was a fear of being rejected, of being laughed at by her or the other lads so, when she was talking to someone else or was distracted, I used to look at her surreptitiously – longing to be with her – just the two of us sat on the wall above the playing field and talking: nothing more.

As I have mentioned she showed kindness to me, and on unexpected occasions. If I had stayed in Colina Verde I am sure that we would have become proto-girlfriend and boyfriend.

And, in the one in ten million chance that you ever read this JW – you of the dark hair, tied back, and smiling face – I'm sorry that I didn't play my part because you deserved whatever affection I could have given you at the time and I have always regretted my inadequacies in this first, tiny, hesitant, stumbling step towards being in love.

*****

In Tripoli, I gradually did begin to find myself and, in retrospect, discovered the traits which would later allow me to fall in love with motorcycle racing. I wasn't brave in the conventional sense of wanting to get into fights with other lads. I was small, somewhat timid because I was a misfit, and had an abhorrence of violence. I had sat with my mum, nursing her injuries, too many times not to be deeply upset at the thought of hurting someone.

However, I was super ice-cool under pressure and in the face of physical danger.

During the summer holidays, the girls used to come over from the various boarding schools to visit their parents who were stationed in Tripoli. Lads did too, but they weren't of any interest!

I was showing off to three girls, as lads have done since the invention of the two sexes, by diving down to an arch which was about 20 feet (7m) below the surface, whilst the ladies looked down at me through their face masks, hopefully admiringly.

I snorkelled almost every day and could manage a lot deeper dive than this without any effort. I used to regularly fin down 30 feet (10m) or more without any effort.

My efforts to impress were going as well as usual – which meant very badly! The answer was to up the stakes and so, hopefully, get some recognition. At one side of the arch was a short tunnel, no more than six or eight feet long (2m). I often swam through this and came up past the two huge rocks which were on either side. This was spectacular when the brilliant Mediterranean sun was sending shafts of light down the flanks.

The trick was to grab each side of the tunnel entrance and pull really hard. This catapulted you through and out the other side in just a few seconds.

I made my "look at me" sales pitch, explained that I was going to dive out of sight and when I reappeared they should be suitably impressed. I surface dived beautifully and never even left a ripple on the surface. By the time I had equalised the pressure in my ears, I was at the tunnel entrance. One good pull and I was – stuck!

There had been a storm a few days before and sand had been pushed into the tunnel. As a result, I was jammed on the bank in the centre. I have been happy to admit my inadequacies in these stories but this was the other side of my character. I knew that I had a problem but I was totally calm – not a hint of panic.

I carefully swept the sand away, released my snorkel which had been getting jammed on the tunnel roof, wriggled out and kicked for the surface.

I had been underwater for around two minutes but the girls only made passing mention of this and then swam back to the beach - where a group of eager suitors from the 14/20th Kings Hussars was waiting with open arms – metaphorically and literally.

Despite the inevitable failure with the girls, I had learned a valuable lesson – one which proved to be a reliable indicator of a life-long trait. I don't panic, ever, under pressure or danger and this mind-set has got me out of endless scrapes – some merely very dangerous and others fully life threatening.

Being able to handle physical danger calmly is also one of the key attributes for a motorcycle racer, as I would later find out.

*****

I also discovered another sliver of information about myself during one snowy PE lesson. You might find this hard to believe but we did actually have snow, at sea level, for a few days during each winter. We couldn't use the gym because this had been booked by the girls, and no-one, including our PE teacher, wanted to slosh around in the sleet and sandy mud of the quagmire that was our football pitch.

To entertain us, Mr K got out a ruler and tested our reactions. He held the ruler between our fingers and, when he released it, the point at which we caught it measured the speed of our reactions. I beat everyone, time and again, because I had, and still do have, lightning quick reactions. In the normal manner, I didn't get any credit for winning but I did know how fast I could move. Tick box #2 for bike racing.

*****

The final thing that I learned was that I could organise things – and in a rather odd way. I was not the most charismatic pupil at the school nor did I manifest traits which showed the traditional young leader in action.

Despite the absence of any of the normal indicators, I was an absolute and completely natural organiser and leader. I liked writing things down and could break tasks up effortlessly into their sub-elements. I knew that if "A" was done then "B" would result – and it did.

The problem was that the rest of the package was missing. I came from a working class background and lacked social finesse so my ideas were often badly expressed, and this led to me not being given the credit I would have received had I been more polished.

I could give you examples but I abhor "poor me" whinging and whining. Every time I was knocked back I cried a little, on my own and in silence, but learned a bit more. I also promised myself that if I ever did have a position of power I would try to be kind to those around me.

They wouldn't get their metaphorical stories ripped up in front of their eyes, and nor would there be punishments in order to humiliate or cause pain. I would have things done how I wanted them to be done, and without question, but I would also try to be kind.

I couldn't have expressed these ideas as lucidly then, with my clumsy, shy, teenage voice, as I have done now – but that is what I felt.

*****

I have commented on the costs of maintaining a British presence in Libya already – and they were really horrendous. Being an imperial power might have been good business for GB Plc in the 19th century but it certainly wasn't by the 1960s.

The British bases were scattered over a very wide area of Greater Tripoli, as were the living areas for British personnel. These were all linked by a free bus service. Some of the vehicles were actual, real buses but most were Bedford army trucks which you climbed into via foot holds in the tail gate and a rope. It wasn't at all unusual to see mums hauling themselves up with the rope - which speaks volumes for the standard level of fitness which was prevalent.

On Saturdays, I would go into Tripoli to visit the city centre Naafi shop – just down the way from King Idris' gold leafed palace.

There were actually two Naafi shops. The main one sold food and other items from Britain, but round the corner was a second shop, where teenagers could find all the latest records from home. This was the height of rock 'n' roll so clearly it was popular with my peer group: but not with me.

There was a small area in the main Naafi which had British newspapers and a scattering of magazines. Like some human truffle hunter, I would dig around in the disorganised pile and snaffle everything with a bike in it. I was, by any standard, a full-on addict.

It wasn't a shortage of money which stopped me buying records. On the contrary, I had a very lucrative babysitting business. I arrived promptly for my customers and was reliable and trustworthy. I didn't steal their alcohol or bring my girlfriend with me – not that I had one to bring!

On the contrary, I was utterly reliable and also good under pressure. I remember babysitting for a Jamaican diplomat on one occasion and one of his two daughters had a bad nose bleed. I staunched the bleeding, changed her bed clothes, ensured that she got washed and put on a clean nightie, and had her tucked up and asleep before her parents came home.

Mum and Dad were very pleased, and gave me a £5 tip – a lot of money when a skilled tradesman in Britain was earning £20 a week.

I could also pick and choose my customers so I had a clientele of senior army officers, diplomats and oil company executives.

With the babysitting money, I bought a 50cc Tomos motorcycle. This was a three speed, licence built copy of a Puch but was made in Yugoslavia. It was a sweet little thing which I rode and rode, simply for feeling the joy of controlling the power. This might sound a rather odd thing to say, because the Tomos probably only made 3 or 4 hp, but when I had a throttle in my hand the world changed.

I was more than a competent cyclist but push bikes held no attraction for me. They were just a way of getting from one place to another.

Motorcycles belonged to a different world – and one I very much wanted to be in. The throttle not only gave me power but freedom too. And something very strange happened – really, very odd. You may remember my lack of co-ordination with the wood plane at Beamont and my outstanding lack of success at games? Well, bikes were different. My body did work harmoniously when I was riding a bike and everything came naturally to me. I was connected to the engine and the chassis in a very intimate, anthropomorphic way and it was good – really good.

I have read how Spitfire pilots felt in their aircraft, and bikes were like this for me. In his iconic book, *First Light,* this is how Battle of Britain ace Geoffrey Wellum describes his first flight in a Spitfire:

"You didn't get in, you strapped it to you. A Spitfire could almost think what you wanted to do and it did it. And you didn't think anything about it."

I got a hint of the same feeling with the Tomos. I never had to look for the controls. They just grew into me – as if I had always had a throttle in my right hand and a clutch lever beneath my left.

Much later, I became quite competent at riding a motorcycle and race bikes in particular are very similar to how Geoffrey Wellum describes a Spitfire. I still race a Seeley Suzuki, a bike I've had now for around thirty years, and I never think about how to ride this machine. I sit on it and the bike almost rides itself, it is so much an extension of me – and perhaps I am of it. It is an utterly wonderful experience and I feel very blessed, and yes I do want to use that emotive word, every time I ride a motorcycle.

I also discovered something else which was equally strange. I became an inveterate borrower of bikes and I soon developed the knack of riding all of them. In short, with motorcycles I felt that I was in my natural home – and I loved it.

*****

The Services tried to be compassionate, especially with families where the kids were either reaching, or concluding, primary school or coming up to GCEs. It was something of an administrative nuisance which is why the cost of a boarding school was subsidised and many families took advantage of this allowance.

The stay was called a tour and, after three and a bit years, my dad's tour was over so it was yet another move – this time back to Warrington.

We left RAF Idris on a brilliant October morning. The sky was almost cobalt blue in colour and the air was so clean that it scoured my lungs. I had a last look round at the flight of Canberra bombers on the hard standing, at the light brown, sun bleached sand outside the perimeter fence and took a deep breath of the sweet, aromatic juniper pine scents which blew across the apron.

It would be more melodramatic to say that I trudged mournfully up to the steps of the Hastings transport plane which was taking us back home but I didn't. Home? Was Warrington or Tripoli my home? I didn't know. So I did as I was told and settled down in a canvas seat, next to a generator which was going back to England for repair. My mum and dad were located somewhere else in the aircraft and I didn't much care where they were.

I was glad that I was sitting next to a generator because this was all the company I wanted. Again, if this were fiction, I would say that I wondered about my future – but I didn't. I hoped that we were going to have some decent sandwiches and that I could find something to make a pillow so that I could sleep in between reading but, as for hopes or dreams or aspirations – no, not really. I was far more used to being done unto, rather than doing - and nothing that I could see was going to change this.

*****

We landed at RAF Lyneham in a gale, with the rain pouring down. In place of the searing, technicolour brilliance of Tripoli, I looked up at the turbulent grey and black hues of an angry storm. I was home – possibly.

There were rigorous customs' checks at Lyneham, but I was ignored. I could have been smuggling half a dozen Rolex watches in my bag – the standard end of tour bonus for those with a relaxed view of tax regulations – but no-one paid me any attention. If I was remarkable for anything it was for being remarkably unremarkable.

We stayed the night in transit rooms at Lyneham, and the following morning had a really substantial breakfast. Then we caught a train and headed north. I stared silently out of the window at the greys and greens and wet browns of the English countryside. I saw the terraced houses packed cheek to jowl with their tiny gardens, each gasping for breath. There were pale people with caps pulled down tight on their heads, and head-scarfed women bravely butting the rain as they rushed through the streets, their infants clinging like drowning sailors to the lifeline of their extended hands. I saw the queuing cars and motorcycles waiting, pushing to what and for what? This was my England and my country now.

*****

We left the train at Bank Quay Station in Warrington, right next to the Surf factory. The sweet, cloying steam swept across the platform, obscuring the far side of the track and choking me. Maybe this was a metaphor for my new life – with my past out of sight forever and no way forward.

Then I heard the soft thump, thump, thump of a British single cylinder bike, plodding its way dully up the hill towards Bank Park. It wasn't much of a call to arms – but it was vastly better than nothing.

Chapter Five

Welcome Home

My world was one defined by the aspirations of the working classes - drawn in cigarette stained, fern green and grey. It wasn't a question of being slow to join life's race, but much more of not even knowing a race existed.

I need to stress just how great my alienation was from the world around me. It was as if I had been left as an embryo, on a strange planet which was not mine and with human foster parents who had raised me. The gulf between what inspired them and what inspired me, what made us laugh or cry, excited or depressed was so immense that it was unbridgeable. In another book, I described it as like being a penguin chick living in a sparrow's nest.

At the same time, I was even more distant from Warrington's middle classes, who lived south of the Manchester Ship Canal. I occasionally, very occasionally, shopped in Stockton Heath which was, in my eyes, such an incredibly upmarket area that I thought the shop girls should all be wearing tiaras. The reality was that Stockton Heath was next to the canal and half a mile from Greenall's Brewery.

In Stockton Heath, there were cars parked outside the shops and people didn't greet each other with "Ey up" and insert "love" into every sentence. This species on my alien planet spoke a different form of English, and I never heard words like mithering and skryking from my own tribe's dialect.

I felt even more distant from the posh people than I did from the poor, and so I bumped around in the swamp like some tiny creature looking for a safe bit of driftwood that I could cling to and grow.

Had I started an apprenticeship then things would have been much better. Right from the start, I would have worked alongside a tradesman. I would have been treated as a servant, ribbed endlessly and undertaken the most menial jobs but, and it was an enormous but, I would have been on the first steps to that most glorious achievement in Warrington – a trade. After five years, I would have "served my time" and been a tradesman. And what a magnificent achievement this was. A welder, fitter or turner who had come through an apprenticeship at one of the Warrington factories was a true master of his craft – as good as anyone anywhere in the world.

There was immense pride in being a tradesman in Warrington and I looked up to this elite in awe. By contrast, I had fallen through the cracks in the system. Despite my family background, I was naturally academic – and properly bright too. I had a bag full of good "O" Levels but, clearly, I was never going to stay on to take "A" Levels.

As for university, I had only the very vaguest idea of what one was and even less knowledge about what it did or where it, or they, were. I want to press the analogy to illustrate just how little I knew or understood about further education. What do you know about the rings of Saturn? You will be aware that they are there. Perhaps you know that they are made of different sizes of rock? Or is it rock, dust and ice?

So it was with tertiary education or a profession. Once, in a fleeting moment of recognition that I had abilities within me that she could very vaguely see, but not recognise or understand, my mum said that if she had any money she would have paid for me to become a solicitor's clerk – the most prestigious job she could possibly imagine.

As for the thought of the teacher that I would later become, this was so far from utterly inconceivable that she would not have devoted a second of her time to even considering the question. You could have asked her about authors and journalists and she would have smiled – and rapidly changed the subject because only deities appeared in the *Warrington Guardian* unless, of course, you were the subject of one of that week's extensive list of court cases - and everyone on our street knew all about those.

So I left school at sixteen with my "O" Levels, which was a considerable achievement for someone who had largely flown solo throughout secondary school, and my mum gave me a copy of the *Warrington Guardian* and told me to find a job. Note that I was not told to find a satisfying job, or one with prospects or where I would use my talents. No, it was a case of get a job now, because the family needs the money.

There were also cultural issues which are now overlooked. The thought of a fit young man not working would have been abhorrent within my very conservative, working class community. Only people who were sick, or – heaven forbid – lazy, didn't work. Even the idea of accepting money for not working was shameful.

I went into town on the bus and rocked up at one of the big engineering merchants, and said that I had come about the job as an assistant storeman which was advertised in the *Guardian* - and ten minutes later I had been appointed.

I duly turned up for work on Monday morning and was met by the dour, and deeply suspicious, Chief Storeman. I was highly literate, articulate, smiling and bursting with energy. The Chief Storeman was an ex-Navy gunner who was partially deaf after a misfire in the turret of a cruiser.

He was extremely suspicious of young people, rock and roll, showers and especially reading and writing – skills which he felt were for officers and posh people - not "Other Ranks", the likes of whom applied for jobs in stores.

To avoid a conflict of interest, I was sent deep into the bowels of the stores to paint shelves. There were a lot of them, and so I spent many weeks in the crepuscular half-light, kept company only by the occasional 60 watt light bulb, many gallon tins of Jellipex paint and a single brush – whilst wondering if the sky was blue outside, or if the rain was caressing the rooftops, or perhaps the trees were rustling in the breeze.

As a treat, I used to allow myself to stir the last quarter of the one gallon tin of Jellipex paint so that it was no longer non-drip but was liquid. Liquefied jelly paint – a magnificent blow for freedom!

During tea break I sat in the crude canteen, in a corner away from everyone else. My workmates studied the *Sporting Pink* for likely horses, and ogled the pictures in *Health and Efficiency* magazine - whilst I read a copy of Chaucer's *Canterbury Tales*: we didn't have a lot in common.

This was lower working class life in 1960s Warrington, and it should have been mine too – except for one miraculous act of good fortune: I was in love.

Love is a much misused word in the instant, social media obsessed world we live in now - where love is achieving fleeting fame on a TV dating show, or 1000 likes for an Instagram post. The sort of love I had was the one which eats into your soul and gnaws at your very being, the ache is so great.

Love as I understood the word, and aged sixteen I really did think that I knew all about this state, meant that you would – happily – go without food or sleep to feel the touch of your loved one.

Cold, rain and all other discomforts were mere inconveniences if you could be there with, and alongside, your loved one.

I wanted to write about my love, in poems and prose, just to let the whole world know how badly I was smitten.

In short, I loved motorcycles more than life itself.

In a world of dullness, make do and eyes cast down, motorcycles swept away the tired, stained hues of Warrington and broke through the restraining doors. Pushed wide open, they revealed a brave new world of soul stirring noises, glorious colours, hedgerows disappearing in grey green blurs and, most of all, freedom.

Without bikes, I was a labourer painting shelves in semi-darkness. With a motorcycle, I sloughed off the chrysalis which bound me to mediocrity and I became something I neither knew nor understood - except that it was glorious.

Bikes were me – and I was bikes, with every molecule in my body.

*****

My first craving was for a full bike licence. I was in full survival mode in every other aspect of my life but a bike licence was different: the very thought of it kept me awake all night, every night.

Today, bikes are very much recreational vehicles. You might see the odd courier on a bike or, more likely, a pizza delivery being made with a 50cc scooter but, overwhelmingly, motorcycles are now toys. In the 1960s, things were very different with bikes being used as the primary method of transport for a lot of people. In fact, pure recreational bikes, in the sense that such a thing existed, were quite rare and the province of what were called "serious" riders.

There was a range of reasons for the popularity of bikes and they coalesced into a powerful argument for motorcycling. At the head of the queue was that you could ride a bike aged sixteen – and with no training. The machines you could ride were limited to a maximum capacity of 250cc but that was it. You found a bike, stuck a pair of "L" plates on it and away you went – and I did, everywhere and very frequently.

By contrast, it wasn't possible to start driving a car until you were seventeen - and then it was compulsory to have a qualified driver alongside you until you passed your driving test.

Another reason for their popularity was that motorcycles were cheap. Warrington was awash with second-hand bikes and £40 got you a decent 250 with a strong second-hand value. Even an exotic and very desirable machine like the Honda CB72 was under £300 brand new - and this was within the range of richer sixteen year olds, when their parents guaranteed the HP payments.

Finally, motorcycles were much more socially acceptable than they are today – perhaps because so many people rode them. They weren't the exclusive province of the working classes either. Teachers came to their schools on motorcycles, clerks to their banks and even district nurses visited their patients using two-wheels.

As I have mentioned, there was no training necessary to get a bike licence – as in none. Everyone I knew could ride a bike, in the same way that everyone could brush their teeth. Riding a motorcycle wasn't so much a skill but just a simple fact of life. Even so, if one had any aspirations to become a real motorcyclist you needed a full bike licence.

The bike test was notoriously basic but still a major hurdle to jump – a true rite of passage. I knew one lad who not only failed his bike test but, when he returned to the Test Centre in Warrington – somewhat ironically located almost opposite the cemetery – the police were waiting to sort him out for reckless driving. To be fair, cutting up a police panda car during your driving test and then making a non-complimentary gesture with two fingers was perhaps stretching even 1960s' tolerance.

I was more than very competent before I took my test but, even so, I had to get the pass paper in my hand. I was desperate for a full licence and there was a way to get one quickly. During my lunch break I went to a phone box in the market, and I rang round all the test centres near to us to see if they had any cancellations. Clearly, this was eons before computers and internet booking systems.

I found a cancellation, at the end of the week, in Bolton and my mum lovingly agreed to phone my employers and explain that I was ill. It was worth losing a day's pay for the early test appointment. All that I had to do was ride to the test centre and, clearly, pass.

The bike I had was a 250cc BSA C15 – a truly loathsome thing. It had come from an advertisement in the *Warrington Guardian*, which carried a lot of bike ads every week. There were more machines available in the weekly bike press – *Motorcycle News* in particular – but to get at these meant travelling and I was reaching a stage in life where even thinking about a bus was a total anathema.

I got the BSA because it was being sold in Orford, not very far from where we lived, and it only cost £25. This was the sum total of its virtues. Otherwise, it was an odious creature. So why did I buy it and not something like the beautiful little Honda S90 or a 125 Suzuki which I could have had for around the same price?

Once more, there is a danger of current commentators rewriting history and seeing it through the filter of 21st century mores. My very first memory of infant school was having my hand held by a slightly older girl and being told to swing my arms high, as we marched into class to the tune of *We're Soldiers of the Queen…*

Empire Day was still in full flow, with this aim:

"*To* remind children that they formed part of the British Empire, and that they might think with others in lands across the sea, what it meant to be sons and daughters of such a glorious Empire."

and that:

"The strength of the Empire depended upon them, and they must never forget it."

Also, in the 1960s the Second World War was still a very active memory – not ancient history. I met a man at the scrapyard where I later worked and he delighted in telling me, and everyone else, how much he had enjoyed killing the Japanese in the Burma campaign.

The mood was changing, and quite rapidly too, but for some young men like me – and remember I had been three and a bit years in Libya, which was then a British Imperial outpost – the idea of having a Japanese motorcycle was unthinkable.

Paradoxically, my patriotism was also the reason I detested the C15.

The C15's story started when BSA announced their all new, one stop motorcycle shopping experience: the C15. The idea was that this single machine would replace the 250cc C12 as a commuter motorcycle capable of taking the working masses from the new, post war housing estates to their factories. The same bike would then carry the head of the family, always a man of course - at least in the demographic which the C15 inhabited - to the football match or the canal for a day's fishing. In short, it was intended as a working, utility vehicle.

The recreational motorcycling slot, such as it existed at all, occupied by the dull, heavy, expensive to produce, and poorly performing, 350cc B31 would also be taken over by the C15. Now, the cute little woman of the house could cuddle adoringly up to her man as he took her for a ride in the countryside on a Sunday afternoon.

Better still, the C15 would be the core DNA for a whole range of motorcycles which would enable BSA to amortise the tooling costs of the new bike very effectively.

At this point, the historical context becomes important. BSA were located at Small Heath, in Birmingham, the epi-centre of manufacturing in the world. Anything and everything which could be made was made in Birmingham and its environs, from jewellery to jet engines.

1955, when the C15 project was started, was only ten years after the end of the war in the Pacific - in which Japan had suffered a humiliating, total defeat. If anyone at BSA had bothered to look at Japan, which they most certainly would not have done, they would have seen that the most successful manufacturer was Honda. And what were they offering in competition to the mighty BSA group? In 1953, Honda launched the Model E "Dream" – a three speed, 150cc oddity producing a far from earth-shattering 5.5hp.

In every way, even including reliability, the 15hp C15 massacred the little Japanese pretender.

If BSA trounced the non-existent Japanese opposition, they didn't do nearly so well against the other beaten foe in WWII – the Germans. BMW produced the slightly less powerful R25 but this little bike had shaft drive, a four speed gearbox and could be ridden flat out all day – albeit not very fast with only 12hp.

If you wanted speed and reliability, BMW's neighbour NSU would sell you the fabulous 18hp, overhead cam, 250cc Supermax complete with leading link suspension and an enclosed rear chain so that the not too reliable chains of the day lasted well and needed adjusting only rarely.

The NSU Supermax was state of the art for the early 1950s and had a huge influence on Soichiro Honda and his right hand man, Takeo Fujisawa. Not only was the Supermax technically advanced, it was designed for mass production. Instead of a conventional frame fabricated from steel tubing, the German bike made extensive use of steel pressings. A frame made from tubing required vastly less investment in tooling than a chassis made, like a car, from pressings but – until the arrival of automated manufacturing processes – tubed frames were slow and expensive to make.

NSU built sufficiently high numbers of the Supermax machines to be able to commit to press tools and, of course, the production costs plummeted.

But we were British. We had saved the world - and we were the chosen people.

Having won the war, the idea – even the merest hint of the concept – that we could learn anything from either the Germans or the Japanese, who had lost to us, was inconceivable.

Added to this mind set – and it was still prevalent all the way into the Swinging '60s – was the accurate belief that the world lay at BSA's feet: which it did.

Large swathes of the British Empire had only just been granted independence and lumps of prime, African real estate were still ruled from London. These colonies, and the former ones, were open doors for BSA sales. If BSA deigned to grant you a motorcycle, you should feel blessed.

Finally, and again it's due to the victory in the war, Britain was exhausted. When my mum was very elderly I remember pressing her, to try to discover what an ordinary, working class woman thought of the decline in Britain's manufacturing prowess. She was weary with 21st Century Britain, but what followed was a rather touching moment as she held my hands between hers. I wrote her words down at the time. This is what she said, and with tears in her eyes. "We were tired, love – tired out. We were tired of the fighting and going without. We were tired of seeing people killed.

"My cousin Arthur was a rear gunner in a Lancaster, and he was shot down and killed on the last day of the war. Everyone was the same. Lovely young men - killed when they should have been dancing with their wives and girlfriends.

"After the war, we wanted a break with proper clothes and no rationing, and so we were just worn out and that was the start of all the trouble, love. I really believe that was the start."

So, with BSA we had a heady combination of a complacent management, with a conservative and risk-averse frame of mind, encouraged by very strong sales. There were designers and engineers capable of producing world class motorcycles, but it was never going to happen without the support of a management which was willing to invest in the future.

When the British motorcycle industry collapsed, it became popular to say that we lacked the designers capable of producing a world beating lightweight motorcycle but this was simply untrue.

Valentine (Val) Page was at the head of the queue. He had drawn the overhead cam JAP engines which, in 1922, dominated racing. Moving to Triumph, he showed that he had a fine eye for mass production with his range of single cylinder engines. Page's problem was that he wasn't political and, in a sea where the egotistical Edward Turner swam as the predatory shark, Val was always going to be a long way down the food chain.

Alongside Page, not literally but within a short motorcycle ride, worked the world's finest motorcycle development engineer - in the form of the genius which was Doug Hele. Given management support these two could have produced a world leading, lightweight motorcycle. Instead, the C15 crawled inconsequentially into life.

At the heart of the C15 was a unit construction engine – a concept where the gearbox and engine are one unit. To anyone under 60 – or who isn't a classic bike fan – it probably seems bizarre that the gearbox could be separated from the engine and the two joined by a chain. But in the British motorcycle industry of 1950s, this was common practice.

Unit construction engines were not unknown. In the case of BSA, the idea was actually very well understood because they produced the BSA Bantam – a right-hand side gear change version of the pre-war German DKW RT 125 design, which BSA were given as part of the war reparations.

So BSA had the talent, the capital available and – potentially at least – the engineering ability. What it lacked was vision and drive.

The engine element of the C15 was a desperately unambitious push-rod motor with an iron cylinder barrel and a two-valve, aluminium cylinder head. Ignition was via a car-type points distributor which sat uncomfortably on top of the crankcases. The points gap, the key element in getting the ignition to provide a spark, was usually set using a handy cigarette paper – really, truthfully, honestly – or about 4 thousandths of an inch. I was at a distinct disadvantage in this respect since I was one of the very few non-smokers in my peer group.

Not that the antiquated ignition system was the only problem. The core issue was that the Lucas alternator was only 6v and so the lights were immensely underpowered. I rode through the pouring rain and sleet of an English winter – or at least part of it – and my abiding memory is of peering out through a tiny arc of tired, yellow light which barely indicated the pavements - and never the road ahead.

In fact, that's not actually wholly accurate. My C15 was one of the better ones because the lights did, usually, come on when asked. Frequently, the Lucas alternators failed altogether.

The crankcases were split vertically and inevitably leaked oil. In fact, a C15 without at least some sign of minor incontinence on the garage floor was considered to be "A right good 'un."

The big-end bearing was a simple plain bush and was, from birth, not up to the job. As penniless teenagers, my peer group often ended up with C15s because we could afford nothing better, and we simply destroyed the plain bearing big ends and cast iron crankshafts. The fix then was to fill the engine with a monograde SW50 oil and advertise the bike in the local paper. There was usually a greedy older person who thought that he was spanking an innocent youth in terms of the price, so we could invariably off-load a C15 with the treacle thick oil concealing the clonking from the bottom half of the engine – at least for a few miles!

A duplex chain linked the engine to a fragile four speed gearbox which had a thoroughly feeble clutch fitted. We reduced both the gearbox and clutch to scrap too.

Compared to the C12, something akin to deciding whether you prefer dysentery or typhoid, the C15 looked smart(ish) and modern(ish). It had 6", full width hubs which sort of worked but these were cast iron drums with single, leading shoe brakes. The Japanese were simply producing motorcycles from a different planet.

Instead of the pressed steel frame, which would have permitted the right production costs, the C15 chassis was made from tubing which was joined with brazed lugs. This system was simple and went right back into 19th century bicycle manufacture. A piece of steel tubing is slotted into a cast iron lug and then the two parts are "glued" together using brass. Done this way, production costs are low and the system is tolerant of errors.

Again, it's not that BSA lacked the knowledge of how to use pressings. They were located in the very centre of Birmingham and the factory was surrounded by companies making things from pressings – notably the Austin works at Longbridge and BSA's own sister companies Carbodies and Daimler. The problem was BSA's utterly chaotic business model.

For example, in the 1963/64 selling season BSA offered 42 different machines - but made only a total of 18,000 units. Some models had ludicrously low production. Only thirty-one C15S motocross machines were made – which was less than many British specials' builders of the day were producing.

In an attempt to make the most of every opportunity, BSA produced a bewildering number of flavours of each model. Again referring to the 1963/64 season, there were eleven variants of the C15 alone.

Theoretically, a C15 could manage 70mph but this was only on a good day with a following wind, slightly downhill and so on. Also, if the bike was ridden towards its claimed maximum velocity it would self-destruct in a surprisingly short distance.

My C15 was not a fine example of the type – not at all. In fact, it had been passed around from owner to owner until it arrived with me, and I did not shower it with love.

*****

Still, it wasn't raining on the day of the test as I set off north from Warrington towards Bolton. It was mainly an urban ride and so plodding along on the C15 wasn't too onerous – right up until the point where I braked fairly hard for some traffic lights in Wigan town centre. I pulled the front brake lever firmly – and, almost immediately, felt the lever come all the way back to the handlebars.

Bless my soul – and other similar expletives!

Cables used to break all the time on British bikes, but whoever had made a replacement for this C15's front anchor had done a singularly poor job and the nipple on the end of the cable had pulled out.

I have already mentioned that the bike test was not the world's most demanding challenge but the one thing that everyone said testers were hot on, was the use of the front brake in the critical emergency stop.

Using the rear brake, even the feeble ones on British bikes, could cause the rear wheel to lock and skid so all the emphasis had to be on the front anchor.

There was absolutely no way I was going to miss the test, so I got out the pliers from my tool kit – we never went anywhere without a tool roll – and carefully threaded the cable through the brake arm on the drum, tucking it well out of sight at the end so that, at a passing glance, it looked intact.

I duly arrived at the test centre, smiled at the examiner and called him "Sir". We young underlings knew our place in society… He stood on the pavement and sent me to lap the block. I dutifully held my arm rigidly at ninety degrees on the left hand corner that he could see, and arrived back riding like the paragon of virtue that I wasn't.

Then he reversed the route and this was trickier. Now, I had to rotate my arm in neat circles to show that I intended to turn right. Of course, the Japanese had indicators which worked but we were soldiers of the Queen.

Each time I came to a halt, I dutifully made short flapping motions with my left hand to indicate that I was slowing down. The C15 did have a brake light but it would have taken a fit, athletic, young owl to spot that it was actually glowing a subliminally dull red.

Now for the big one. I was to do another lap and this time, when the tester stepped off the pavement and held up his clipboard, I was to come to a stop as quickly as possible whilst still maintaining full control.

I arrived on the finishing straight with a suitable briskness – deliberate lethargy was not considered acceptable – and the tester stepped boldly into the road.

I made a huge, comic sweep of my right hand to prove, beyond all doubt, that I was indeed braking with the full force of the front brake – whilst applying the most delicate and subtle of pressures so that the cable stayed wrapped around the lever.

At the same time I hit the rear brake hard, just up to the point of locking, and brought the bike to a suitably impressive, brisk halt. A flicker of approval showed on the tester's face - and mine. If only he had known how lucky he had been.

There were a few perfunctory questions about the Highway Code – and that was that. I had a full licence and suddenly I was a new person. In the morning, I had been no more than a learner motorcyclist and three hours later I could ride any bike of any size, speed or type that my budget would allow.

I had a celebratory pie and then rode home with a smile which would not go away.

Chapter Six

Frank Must Try Harder

I have to keep repeating this but I wasn't at the bottom of the social tree. There were many sixteen year olds worse off than me – and a lot worse too. In fact, I didn't even know that things could have been much better because I had the sense of acceptance that comes from having limited horizons.

I think that not knowing what can be achieved is the single biggest hindrance to social mobility – and I wasn't even aware that there was a horizon, let alone that it was limited.

I was paid £10 a week in return for 44 hours of the most intellectually suffocating labour it was possible to imagine. If any task was beyond menial for even the least talented storemen then I was given it. Shelf painting was at the top of the list of jobs I hated but re-labelling the dull, grey, dented parts' boxes was a close second. I came into work in the morning, took a label from a little compartment at the front of the box and transferred it across the bench to another dull, grey, dented box. I never understood why I did this – I just did it, for hour after hour after hour.

Seven months earlier I had been delighting in translating Chaucer's *Nonne Preestes Tale* into modern English, swimming in a warm sea of wonderful words and magnificent imagery. Now, I moved a ⅝ BSF label from one grey box to another: the very act corroded my soul.

Of my £10 a week wages, I gave my mum £5 for my "keep." This was standard practice. This left £5 for everything else in my life. In fact, that's not quite true because my mum was often exceptionally generous and bought me essential clothes like working shirts, jeans, socks and underwear.

Sometimes, but not always, Mum made sandwiches for my lunch and these were always lovely, thick "doorstoppers" – a real filler for a growing lad, and I really was growing.

All the "extras" I funded. I had ridden to my bike test in Bolton wearing a duffle coat and without any gloves - seriously unsuitable for winter motorcycling so my first priority was a wax cotton jacket. Barbour still make similar jackets today and they are considered to be very fashionable and ultra-cool.

But I didn't want a fashion statement, just something to keep me dry and which didn't weigh a ton when it was wet! The problem was that Barbour jackets were a premium product and so very expensive. Another British company called Belstaff also made jackets, and one of their factories was in Caroline Street, in Stoke-on-Trent – not too far away from Warrington.

The rumour was that if you rocked up at the stores and made a sad face – and I was world class at looking glum – it was sometimes possible to get a "second" from underneath the counter.

Theoretically, these were jackets which were slightly sub-standard in some way. Maybe the grey -green colour wasn't consistent or the stitching not quite straight but these, it was said, could be bought for cash – minus the Belstaff label.

I negotiated with the Senior Storeman about leaving a couple of hours early on Friday afternoon, in return for working Saturday afternoon for no pay, and chuffed down the new M6 to Stoke-on-Trent on the C15.

Driving down the M6 now is like being in the cast of a horror film – a sort of *Mad Max* meets *Death Race* with *Fast and Furious* extras. However, it wasn't always like this.

My first memories of riding on the M6 are of the emptiness and silence. I can't really think of an accurate comparison now but something approximating the northern sections of the M6, near Penrith, at 2am in November: and yes, I was there before the dreaded Covid Lockdown.

The speeds were also incredibly slow. One would need a very powerful, suicidal bent now to plod down the M6 to Stoke at 45mph – even in the apparently permanent roadworks – but not then. A typical small family car like a Mini or Ford Anglia produced under 40hp and had a very optimistic top speed of 75mph so a C15, crawling along at the same speed was not out of place.

Belstaff's Caroline Street works was located in Stoke city centre and had the look and feel of a Victorian factory which, to be fair, it was. There was a trade counter and, sure enough, it was possible to buy a "seconds" jacket. It looked fine to me, and I already knew the rules regarding paying cash and not asking for a receipt, so I rode home ever so proudly in my brand new, wax cotton jacket which was wind and rain-proof. I couldn't stop smiling for the whole hour and a half journey home

*****

The next issue was to get a pair of gloves. I rode bare handed at the time and it was particularly uncomfortable when there was rain stinging my already frozen fingers. The answer lay in the centre of Warrington, at Market Gate, where there was a large Army and Navy store. This sold some new, military surplus equipment as well as civilian items. My Belstaff jacket had been the number one priority but during my lunch break, I had also seen some ex-army dispatch riders' gloves. These were big, clumsy looking things but I could almost feel my hands getting warm inside them so they became the next target on the acquisition list.

There was also another attraction: a pretty girl who served there. I watched her through the window when I was ogling - clearly the gloves! She had sort of mousy brown hair and was, objectively, a bit plain but from my social position she looked film star beautiful.

Once, she caught me looking at her through the window and half smiled before turning away to one of the shelves behind her.

I determined that when I bought my gloves I would also try to make myself known to her personally.

During these stories, I have tried to be as honest as possible and I'll continue to be so now because what happened next might seem odd in the 21st century. My hormones told me that I needed a girlfriend, and in teenage boys the chemicals really do send very clear messages!

Socially too, I felt that I ought to have a girlfriend. Lots of the lads I knew had girlfriends and they really got to know all about them – so much so that there was even a sprinkling of Warrington's equivalent of shotgun marriages.

The problem for me was that I had no social skills – as in zero. Additionally, I was very shy and my words tumbled out in an embarrassing torrent of confusion. Finally, I knew very little about girls. For example, I had never even seen a picture of a fully naked girl and so had no idea of what lay beneath the waist band of any young woman.

I had kissed girls, and clumsily touched them – poor things that they were to experience my beginner's attempts at intimacy – but how to take this level of experience to even the most basic level of girlfriendship was completely beyond me.

The gloves were ten shillings (50p) which was a fortune. I had only £5 a week surplus and this had to pay for petrol for the BSA – my absolute #1 priority – and then everything else.

My mum usually made me a sandwich for lunch but if circumstances intervened, and "things" did tend to occur in our family rather a lot, then I would jog round Warrington during my lunch break instead of eating anything. Clearly, this did no end of good for my fitness levels but the exercise was also a really good appetite suppressant so it was a win-win situation all round.

I went into the Army and Navy store at lunchtime and smiled at K – although I didn't know her name at the time. The conversation was fine at first. I was an experienced scrounger, with a skilful blagger's open smile, and so I was happy asking K to sort through the gloves and get me a good pair.

I can still remember the older lady smiling as K dug around in the box for me and found a mint condition pair, which were perfect except for smelling quite musty. I opened my wallet, ferreted around and found the red ten shilling note that I had reserved for this purchase.

K smiled, and the lady who had been watching us tactfully withdrew. I quite literally shut my eyes and, metaphorically, jumped – but not very far.

"I'm Frank. I've got a BSA." You will notice how quickly the conversation defaulted to bikes because having a full motorcycle licence was about the only vaguely meritorious card I had to play.

K smiled. "That's nice…"

I stopped.

What else to say? How about, "I really like Chaucer. Have you read *The Canterbury Tales?*"

That should get things off to a good start with a shop assistant who worked at the Army and Navy Stores.

Or perhaps: "I paint shelves all day in a half-light which gnaws at my mind and eats into my very soul?

How do you feel about selling gloves to teenage lads with no prospects or even the vaguest hope of escape?"

K helped me. "What time do you finish work? Mrs Barber is letting me off early tonight so that I can go to Woolies for my mum. I'll be out at quarter to five."

She hesitated, only very slightly better at this game than I was.

"I finish at half past four. I could meet you, if you wanted like…"

My voice trailed off into nothing, starved into oblivion by fear of having said the wrong thing and the resultant rejection.

"Okay then. I'll see you outside."

Then she turned her back to me and began tidying the shelves with excessive zeal.

Such was the courtship which you don't see recorded in words or pictures. Yes, there was a lot of frenetic partying, and all that went with it, taking place in the cities. There were fashion conscious kids of my age living the high life and probably, though I knew nothing of it, taking drugs too.

But for working class kids like me in a working class Northern town, the world was largely composed of grey and magnolia – in terms of sights, smells and sounds. We didn't so much look down as a life-choice but rather because we didn't know which way was up.

I finished at 4.30 and was out of the back door, underneath the stores, the moment I had clocked-off. We had a big clocking-on machine, with a brass handle burnished to a shine through decades of use. The highlight of my day, literally the moment I dreamed of from eight o'clock in the morning, was when I put my magnolia coloured card into the machine, pulled the lever – and escaped.

There was a satisfying clang from the bell and then I could put my card in the bottom of the rack. Note - the bottom, because even this part of my life was stratified and controlled by status - and there was no-one in the world lower down the scale than me. I was, in every way, at the end of everything.

Running round Warrington at lunchtimes did have its advantages and so I jogged to Market Gate in ten minutes – and without any effort. I'm smiling as I write this, at the thought of a modern teenager trotting through the streets, carrying his ex-Army gas mask bag, when a liaison is now just a couple of clicks away.

K was waiting outside and my heart soared – and then crashed through the floor. Yes she was there, which was indescribably wonderful, but then came the invoice for the experience: what should I do next?

You see all these super smooth chat-up lines on TV and Netflix, and there were some cracking one liners even in the olden days. Mine was a particularly impressive example of smooth talking flirting.

"Hiya."

K replied. "Hiya"

Me: "Hiya"

K: "I've got to go to Woolworths to get some Christmas paper for my mum."

Me: silence.

K: "Do you want to come?"

Me: silent nod.

James Bond was an amateur compared with me!

So we went and talked a bit, about nothing mainly because I both didn't have anything to say and wouldn't have known how to say it, had I thought of even a single molecule of vaguely interesting conversation.

I followed K around and finally managed to make some sort of contribution.

She picked up some Christmas paper and I said: "That's nice."

How about that for a smooth talking man about town?

K smiled at me and I thought that I was going to drop dead on the spot with pleasure and excitement.

Outside Woolworth's I plucked up every grain of courage I had and said to K, "Would you like to go to the pictures?"

She half smiled and said: "Yes, that'd be nice."

My first thought was that I hadn't asked just the right question. I should have said, "Would you like to go to the pictures with ME?" – not just would you like to go to the pictures…

I mean, she might have enjoyed the pictures a lot and liked going, but perhaps she only ever went with her friends or her mum and dad or someone.

"James Bond is on at the Odeon, if you like…"

K saw me struggling and helped out, good girl that she was. "Yes, that'd be nice. Do you want to go on Friday?"

I mainly nodded but also managed to croak an agreement.

"Right then, I'll see you outside at quarter past seven and then if there's a queue, we'll still get in for half past and see the trailers."

I nodded again but somehow managed, "Okay, I'll see you on Friday."

I had a real date with a real girl and she was going to the pictures with me! I jogged back through the cold and pre-smog mist to the BSA and, incredibly, it started first kick. This was going to be a brilliant week.

*****

Since it was Tuesday, there was all day Wednesday, the whole of Thursday and most of Friday before I could see K: I don't think that I slept for more than a couple of minutes during the whole time. Yes, there were the normal teenage boy fantasies but what was more on my mind was making a mess of the whole job.

The first problem was the cost of the actual cinema tickets. Clearly, I had to pay for us both and I wanted to do the job properly but I thought that I could reasonably get away with a pair of the mid-range seats, downstairs, which were two and six – 12½p – each! That was going to be five bob.

Then I was going to offer to take K for a drink and heaven alone knew what that was going to cost. I never drank alcohol but I knew that a pint cost around half a crown – 12½p – and goodness only knows how much a little bottle of Babycham cost – and the blokes at work said that this was what the posh girls drank on a date.

I was in another financial corner because the Odeon was two miles from Dallam. I wasn't keen on turning up to meet K with riding gear – even if she approved of my new gloves – and although I could have easily jogged into town, I didn't want to arrive all hot and sweaty. This was pre deodorant, and personal hygiene standards weren't what they are today but, even so, there were unacceptable limits - and meeting K after a two mile run was probably at that point.

The solution was to use the bus but this cost sixpence each way – another 2½p. Bloody hell! This was a whole additional shilling out of the increasingly battered budget.

We didn't have a shower at home but I had a bath and then sort of hosed myself down with the two rubber pipes which clipped on to the taps.

My mum thought that I was too young to be meeting girls but she eventually acquiesced and ironed my best jeans for me. I had a smart, fluorescent pink shirt, a crushed velvet flower tie and tweed sports jacket, which was as smart as I was going to get. Win or lose, K was getting a full power attack on this event.

I caught the bus outside the vicar's house which was, unfortunately for him, a convenient distance from the traffic island in the centre of Dallam. There were a few of us heading into town for all that Warrington could offer in terms of a wild Friday night's entertainment: the pictures, drinks in the innumerable pubs, a game of darts, perhaps a fight and then back home again.

I arrived early at the Odeon with mixed feelings. It was one of Warrington's better cinemas but I wasn't fond of it for a very personal reason. It was something my mum mentioned, albeit very rarely, when she was particularly upset. She had told me that the Odeon was where she had first seen my dad with another woman.

The war was such a bad thing - in so many ways and for so many people. Before my dad joined the Navy my parents had been deeply, passionately in love and making so much progress in their young lives but afterwards there was infidelity and alcoholism. I am sure that their story was repeated endlessly by other couples but, even now, that does not stop me feeling the poignancy of their position.

My dad was also a perfect example of the cloying, choking, rigid class structure in Britain at the time – and maybe even today. He joined the Navy as an Able Seaman but this state did not last very long at all. He was an outstanding electrician and the Royal Navy soon recognised his talents especially, it seems, with radar and the degaussing of ships – the technique used to reduce their electromagnetic signature and so make them less prone to being attacked by magnetic mines.

He got rapid promotion to Chief Petty Officer and then, in 1942, he was offered a commission. My father never once mentioned this but my mum did on several occasions. When I began to achieve success in my own life I was genuinely puzzled about why my dad didn't accept the commission. It turned out that the reason was that he was frightened – actually physically worried – about being with all the "posh" people who were Royal Navy officers. For many years, I was both angry at his lack of courage and dismissive of his fears – although, ironically, I felt the same trepidation myself in social situations. Now, I am more understanding. My dad was brought up in a tiny terraced house with an outside lavatory, comprised of a large bucket in a tiny building at the end of the yard. His world was focussed not on advancement but survival.

Like my mum, he left school when he was fourteen and he pushed the hand cart containing the electricians' tools and materials from job to job. He raised his eyes not to an Oxbridge degree but finishing his five year apprenticeship and having a trade. His eyes turned not to Ascot, the Boat Race and a test match at Lords but dancing in the Isle of Man, and owning the most desirable motorcycle in the world – the Triumph Tiger 100.

It was possible for men of his background to become officers in any of the armed forces but the odds were stacked hugely, immensely against them and so he felt – and with complete justification - that despite his intelligence and technical skills he would always be an outsider, and maybe this is why he found solace in drink.

Certainly, the transition from the working class to middle class in Britain was an immense leap and it took a vast amount of self-confidence and ability, and whilst my father had the latter, he lacked the former.

And his reticence is why I was steeling myself for the forthcoming trauma of meeting a nice shop assistant who worked at the Army and Navy store, instead of studying for "A" Levels and then the seamless transition to University.

I want to give this vignette of the challenges faced by working class kids in the 1960s, not to elicit sympathy but to explain the importance of motorcycles in my life then – and even today.

Motorcycles were democratic and individually demanding. If you were a duke or a dustbin man, a Tiger 100 didn't care: you could either ride or you couldn't, and no amount of privilege would change this – or will now. And if you couldn't ride, the bike would expose you and very likely inflict real punishment for your hubris in thinking that you could.

Motorcycles were also the magic door to another world, not of magnolia lit by 60 watt bulbs and merely making it to the end of each day. Bikes could, and would, open the portal into something vastly different – but all this was to be in the future. Now, my life was focussed entirely on meeting K and this required me to step out of the darkness and into the pool of light outside the cinema – and preferably without being sick on the pavement with fear.

I was desperate for K to see me so I stood under the light to make sure that I would be spotted easily. There was a gaggle of other lads waiting for their dates too and I couldn't help comparing myself to them.

I thought that they were all better looking me and certainly a lot more fashionably dressed. They also looked very old and sophisticated, smoking cigarettes and shouting to each other. I immediately thought that this was another case of being a penguin in yet one more group of sparrows.

K arrived on time and smiled - which made me feel a lot better. I counted the coins out at the pay booth with meticulous care: just one two shilling or a half a crown escaping now would have spelled utter disaster.

The seats were half way up the main body of the cinema. All around us other couples slurped on Kia Ora and munched popcorn but both these treats were way beyond my budget.

Before the main film were the Pearl and Dean advertisements. I can remember very little of them except that there were a lot of really high quality movies selling cigarettes. This was hardly surprising since a veil of cigarette smoke hung over the auditorium – even in the non-smoking section where we were sat. Non-smokers really were in a tiny minority.

Then there were the trailers but, again, I can remember nothing of these. After seeing all the properly grown up lads outside the Odeon, I couldn't imagine why K would want a second date with me.

At the conclusion of the ads and trailers there was a short break, and a lady stood at the front of the cinema selling ice-creams from a little tray which hung from a strap around her neck and was balanced on her ample chest.

Lots of the real lads bought ice-creams for their dates but I didn't. I was terrified, literally catatonic with fear, at the thought of asking K if she would like to come for a drink, then hearing her ask for a second Babycham - and my wallet being empty.

The lights dimmed and the familiar Bond music started with Sean Connery bashing people up left, right and centre and saving the world from *Dr No*.

After ten minutes I very, very, very tentatively reached out to touch K's hand – and she didn't move it away. So, game on. Now, what to do next?

I wasn't sure what one did with a girl's hand at this stage. Did you hold it like your mum's or maybe squeeze it in some form of a handshake or perhaps something else? My dog liked being stroked so maybe this is what you did.

Out of cowardice, or a total lack of any coherent plan of action, I sort of limply rested my hand on K's.

The film progressed in what was to become the familiar Bond pattern. People got beaten up and shot, whilst Bond seduced beautiful women and won shed loads of money playing roulette. You might think that many of the ideas would have been deeply attractive to a fit, healthy, heterosexual young man – but they weren't.

I didn't like fighting and was rubbish at it in any case, because hurting someone upset me. The thought of shooting anyone was even worse and as for some gorgeous lady wanting to jump into bed with me, or go anywhere else for that matter, I would have been utterly terrified. I was out of my mind with stress just sitting next to a girl who worked in the Army and Navy Stores, so having some temptress smile lustfully at me in some posh casino would have led to instant death.

The Coroner's report read: "Mr Melling died from a massive heart attack when an older lady, wearing a low cut dress, smiled at him."

That would have made the obituary section of the *Warrington Guardian* without any problem – and without having to pay for the space!

I waited for another very long time and eventually put my left hand on K's leg, just above her knee. She was wearing jeans so it wasn't very rude or anything. She looked at me and didn't object - and the merest hint of a smile passed her face. Yes!

The rules were clear regarding the next stage of the game and, if either of us had misunderstood them, the mass of writhing, murmuring – and considerably more – from the couples around us was a constant reminder of the route map.

I was supposed to begin passionate kissing and K had to respond enthusiastically. Then I should begin to touch her breasts and K should agree to this too. Next, we should go for a drink and then on to more complex and challenging tasks. It was almost like a Haynes' workshop manual for sexual relations.

Unfortunately for us both, whatever lived inside my head was unhappy with the plan. My hormones were right on message, and to a potentially embarrassing degree, but my mind wasn't. I wasn't sure if I liked K or not. Yes, she ticked all the right boxes in terms of being a potential girlfriend but I hadn't spoken more than fifty words to her socially. In terms of the numbers, we had spent more time discussing my gloves than finding out anything about each other. So, my hand remained where it was and we watched James Bond blast his way to glory.

Afterwards, we faced each other in the half-light outside the Odeon. During the film, the vessel containing my courage had slowly been filling up – albeit very slowly!

I said: "Do you have a phone?"

K nodded.

"Can I phone you then?"

She looked down, fidgeting and embarrassed. "No, me mum doesn't like lads phoning me or anything."

I was shattered but decided to stick at the job.

"Do you want to meet at dinner time then, and we could have pie or something?"

This time came the polite smile that I would soon come to recognise as a complete homily of rejection – without her ever having to say a single word.

"Yes, but I've got a lot on now…"

"See you then."

And she walked off, downhill towards Boots the Chemist, and out of sight.

I was hurt and confused but not surprised. By any standards, I was deeply undesirable boyfriend material and didn't even know what to do in the pictures – a truly impressive loser.

The only thing which stopped me becoming both intensely sad, and perhaps even angry or bitter, was that one of the fitters at work had made me an irresistibly attractive offer for the C15 and, with luck, twenty-four hours from now I was going to have £35 in my wallet.

With my brain developing almost by the second, and money in my pocket, I was going unicorn hunting – and the only way was up!

Chapter Seven

Unicorn Hunting

What I really wanted – no, actually needed merely to stay alive - was a Velocette Venom Clubmans with a Brooklands silencer which went braahhh, braahhh, braahhh at traffic lights, frightened nervous cats and made girls like K go weak at the knees and look at me lustfully. Well, slightly lustfully - but still with an encouraging smile.

I wanted my very own unicorn, powered not by wings but by a big British single that was impossible to start by anyone except a trainee MotoGod like me. That's what I wanted. But what I could afford had to fit into the sub-£35 price bracket because that was the outer edge of my budget.

The sales pitch to the fitter at work had been very subtle. If the C15 could actually get a talentless numpty like me through the test, just imagine what the thrusting, throbbing, loin tingling 15hp could do for him.

So, £35 found its way into my ever depleted wallet and I wrote my first ever receipt containing the immortal words: "Sold as seen, tried and approved" – a phrase I had seen scrawled on many bits of grubby, oil stained paper.

The problem was not so much a shortage of unicorns in the area but rather a desperate absence of second hand ones with a price tag of £35. So I settled for the next best thing, which was not very best at all: a 350cc AJS.

*****

There were a number of places to find a bike but all of them had problems. The three weekly motorcycling papers did have plenty of machines for sale but, except for an immense piece of good fortune, these were all likely to be too far away and there was no way on earth that I was going to eat into the £35 by spending any of it on train fares.

The answer lay in the Warrington Guardian, a rather serious, broadsheet publication first published in 1853. I wasn't much of a fan of it, except for the occasional glance at the court reports featuring one of our neighbours, but it did have a rather good second hand bikes' section.

There was a 350cc AJS Model 16 advertised there, at a rather posh address – by my standards at least – near the site of Saxon Warrington: very apposite in terms of the age and condition of the bike I intended to buy!

The bloke selling the bike had bought a car because, even in the late 1960s, the drift away from two wheels as practical transport was beginning to gain pace. The AJS had been his commuter bike but now, in its place, sat a Hillman Imp with a badly resprayed front wing.

Clearly, the AJS was going to go and, equally clearly, it was not a very desirable machine. The reasons for its lack of desirability were numerous. The bike looked deeply unattractive in every way – fat, black and oozing dullness from every pore. There was surface rust on the chrome, from being left out all day in various car parks, but I could see that it was basically all there and almost any way was up after the C15.

I listened politely to the seller explaining what a fine machine it was and the only reason for its departure was the arrival of the Imp. But it was interesting how he skirted round the ease of starting it because even dull, commuter, single cylinder machines like the AJS were not easy to fire up without the correct technique.

Having spent a lot of time riding ex-military machines like the Matchless G3L, and BSA M20, I could start these bikes, and easily too, but I was beginning to get suspicious that the vendor couldn't – so clearly I asked him to get the thing going.

He waffled and faffed about a bit and then said he had a bad knee – but that I could start it if I wished. There is an almost religious ritual to starting a British single and, if you don't follow the creed to the letter of the law, the thing will sit there all day, without making the slightest effort to burst into life.

The first step in the procedure is to "tickle" the Amal carburettor until fuel sloshes out of the breather. Next, ease the piston up to the top of the stroke with the kick starter. At this point, with the help of the valve lifter, just coax it the thickness of a gnat's eyelash over top dead centre – but only one eyelash.

Now, let the kick start pedal fully return. Take a long, thrusting – and trusting – kick, keeping the throttle fully closed. The piston will whizz down the barrel and as it comes up to top dead centre again, the charge will ignite. At this point, the acolyte must not, under any circumstances, open the throttle. No, this can only be done on the second stroke and then with the precision of a brain surgeon operating a laser scalpel. Just give the engine a Higgs Boson particle more fuel and it will burst into life as docile as a Blackpool Beach donkey.

If you get things even slightly wrong then one of two things will happen. It could be that the engine will misfire, kick back and try to break your leg. The other is utter silence, disturbed only by unhelpful wheezing and panting noises from the engine and a range of colourful curses from the startee.

Knowing precisely what to do, I set about not doing it. I began by not flooding the carburettor and avoiding having the piston in the correct position. I completed the procedure by giving the motor a huge handful of throttle.

Then I carried on desperately kicking it until my mouth became foam flecked with the effort and my eyes were bursting out of my head. Overall, it was a truly Oscar winning performance.

Since the bike was clearly a non-runner, it was not worth the £40 asking price. This would have been grossly unfair to an innocent sixteen year old who knew nothing about bikes. There was a modest degree of haggling and then we agreed on £27 and ten shillings (£27.50) which was brilliant. I had a new bike and £7.50 of capital – and I had ideas for this.

The problem now was how to ride the bike home when it was clearly a non-runner. The fix was easy. Everyone with a bike in those days had spares and so I politely asked – and I always was well-mannered – if the chap had a spare spark plug. He did and I fitted this in a few seconds.

There was already plenty of fuel in the engine from my previous attempts at not starting it, so it was merely a matter of getting the piston up to top dead centre, giving a long kick and away we went with the Ajay ticking over like a good 'un.

In fact, it was such a sweet motor that I was faintly embarrassed at the deal – but not very. I let the bike get thoroughly warm whilst the bloke filled in the log book and gave me the much loved "Sold as seen" receipt and I then rode off in my "seconds" Belstaff jacket and ex-Army gloves, whistling a happy tune.

*****

The pleasure of the deal on the AJS wasn't going to last because work wasn't going well – not at all. With the benefit of long sight, I can see the Chief Storeman's point of view. He had fought in the war and knew all about discipline and following orders. He had also faced death – and very closely too – when there had been misfire in the turret he was manning. From his point of view, my incompetence was a close relative of mutiny. This wasn't fair to me – but it did explain what was shortly going to happen.

The second issue was my ability at a whole range of tasks he found difficult, to the point of being impossible. If anything needed writing I could do the job instantly and well. This only confirmed his view that I was being deliberately difficult when it came to putting labels on parts' boxes. One job was simple and fitting for an assistant trainee storeman and the other, writing and spelling, could - and should - only be done by officers who spoke in posh voices.

If I could do the hard, officer things then I was simply being difficult by not putting the bloody labels on the boxes without trying to be a smart***e.

But back to the story...

I wanted to go to the International Motorcycle Show in London which meant that I couldn't work on Saturday morning. I did ask for permission but it had been a bad week, with numerous areas of petty disagreement between me and the Chief Storeman, so I was told that I had to clock-on.

There wasn't a lot of drama in what followed. I took Saturday off, without permission, went to London and enjoyed the show. On Monday morning I was called into the manager's office, sacked on the spot and given a week's wages. By half past nine, I was walking home. Then the trouble really started.

There were two problems and, ironically, they were of about equal importance. My mum was traumatised because I had been sacked. Me, a decent, well brought up lad – sacked! What would the neighbours say? And say they did, because the curtains were rustling at the sight of Flo Melling's lad home from work so early. In a few hours, I was the scandal of the street.

The second problem was that my mum needed the £5 a week I was chipping into the family pot.

As for me, I had a rather ambivalent attitude towards the whole exercise. I was concerned that my mum was upset but completely distant from the tirade I had faced in the Manager's Office. The dire warnings heaped on me regarding my attitude, work ethic, lack of responsibility and thought for others, didn't so much bounce off me as skim by me, as if I was sitting in a bubble.

This was strange because I was a sensitive young man, and very easily hurt on an emotional level, but when it came to being abused by adults somehow it had no effect. I simply sat quietly until he ran out of verbal ammunition, picked up my gas mask bag containing my copy of *The Motorcycle* - and left.

The real trouble was about to come. When I arrived home, my mum cried. I had seen her cry a lot over the years and her tears penetrated deep inside me to private, vulnerable places which should only be entered with extreme caution.

I had given her all my wages after being sacked and so had only a few pennies left in the world. Mum ordered me to go to the Unemployment Exchange and sign on – and do it immediately.

The Dole Office was about three miles from home but there was no thought of using my bike, and its precious remaining petrol, or a bus. It was a case of jogging and walking down to Bank Park - home to Warrington's famous, and quite stunning, Victorian Golden Gates - and sitting on the wall there whilst I picked up the courage to go through the door of the Dole Office.

By 11 o'clock, I was ready to cross Sankey Street - and another Rubicon in the process of growing up.

I watched with morbid interest, as the unemployed filed in through the door. They looked broken men – I never saw a woman – and they exuded sadness and world weariness. They were on the Dole – out of work and scroungers. This, in a town which exemplified the Protestant work ethic!

Eventually, I took a deep breath, crossed the street and opened the door. I felt that ten thousand eyes were looking at me. A fit, young man signing on for benefit – wanting money for not working: what could be more shameful?

In fact, I never actually went across the threshold but instead, I turned and fled back to Bank Park where I sat on the grass and cried and cried until there was not a single tear left.

My mum was neither condemnatory nor sympathetic. Yes, she understood how I felt and if I had chosen not to sign on then I had better find some work – any work – and fast too.

So began a maelstrom of employment, as I bounced from one job to another. Second-hand car salesman, bulldozer route planner (don't even ask), photographer's assistant, fitter's mate, farm labourer, administrator, trainee manager and scrap metal burner.

*****

Probably the physically toughest job I had was working with the potato pickers and this is another occasion when the 1960s sounds positively medieval. Women did the actual potato picking and it was back breaking work too, bent over in wet fields dragging spuds out of the ground.

I was young, fit and male and so I was given a different task more suited to my abilities. The potatoes went into 56lb bags (25kg) and these were laid out in long rows. The farm tractor pulled a trailer along the rows and my job was to lift the 56lb bag to shoulder height and then empty it into the trailer. As soon as one bag was in, I had to run in front of the tractor to get the next one ready.

I like telling stories so I should say that I loved the work and ended up fitter and stronger than I had ever been, glowing with health and manly vitality. Unfortunately, that wasn't the case. I was fit but after four days I was dead on my feet. I lay on my bed on Thursday evening and thought that the Grim Reaper was going to pay me a visit that very night.

During Friday lunch break, I saw the farmer and explained that I had managed to get a well-paid job and had to reluctantly leave him – which was not actually true. However, he had been so pleased with my efforts that he paid me for the whole five days and said that there was a permanent post available if I ever decided that farming was for me.

There was one interesting by product of being in the potato fields, and one which might be relevant today. Twice a day, Mrs Farmer arrived with huge, thick slices of white bread about an inch deep in home-made jam: there must have been 1000 calories a slice. In my case, she also gave me a proper lunch of Lancashire Hotpot, dripping with grease and lovely, fatty meat. If my mum's teas were added to this, I suppose my intake would have been around 4,000 calories a day and yet the weight sloughed off me.

There is no doubt that obesity is a problem today but what chance do young people have when they're stuck in a Call Centre all day, burning about 3 calories an hour?

*****

On several occasions, things went quite badly wrong. Let me give you an example. It turned out that I had something of a natural talent with an oxy-acetylene burning torch. These are the things you sometimes see on bank robbery films. A blue flame comes out of the end of the torch and, ten seconds later, the bank vault door falls conveniently open. In real life, it's not quite that easy – or fast.

I got a job burning a zinc plating bath into sections for a local scrapman. I had to work inside the bath, with no protective gear except a pair of gloves and some green goggles. The fumes were so bad that they quite literally almost killed me, and I was dragged out of the bath almost unconscious. Health and Safety legislation is currently manically oppressive but what I had to do then, for £3 a day, was ridiculously dangerous.

Being a dab hand with a burning torch, and it really is a useful skill, also got me into another very tight spot. This time, it was lusting after a lovely young lady who lived near us. S was archetypally English-rose gorgeous with a lovely, softly freckled face, ash blonde hair, such a winning smile and a bottom which used to make me physically ill just thinking about it.

I used to try to bump into her – not quite literally, although it would have been a very pleasant experience if I had – so that I could accidentally walk alongside her on the way home or give her a lift in my car. The problem was that she had a reputation of being on the top shelf of girlfriendshiposity and was renowned for her expensive tastes. One lad I knew had managed to wangle a date with her and she'd eaten chicken in a basket and had drunk two Babychams – and in one night! I fancied her so badly that I was prepared to make even this sort of immense financial commitment for an evening on our own together.

The *Warrington Guardian* came to the rescue again. I saw an ad for a labourer to work on a demolition job at a factory on the banks of the Sankey St Helens Canal. It was a good location for me because I could ride along the towpath from home more or less in a straight line and, with my off-road ability, at high speed too.

The base pay was £15 a week but, and this was real Babycham territory, when I told the foreman that I could burn beams, there was an instant offer of £5 a week bonus – all cash in hand. £20 was a good earner and verging on a meal in a Chinese restaurant - and with a Babycham!

The gang was mainly Irish and they were good company. Despite being dirty work, and my eyes hurting a lot from the fumes of burning decades of industrial filth off the beams I was cutting, I was enjoying being popular and looking forward to what £20 would bring at the end of the week.

The beams were huge things called RSJs – Rolled Steel Joists, but never known by their full name. The walls had been knocked down and my job was to sit astride an RSJ and burn the length in front of me largely through. I was really frightened of heights and thought that this was a seriously dangerous exercise. The fact that I was doing it at all is proof positive of the attractions of S' bottom.

With the beam almost cut, a thick wire was looped round it, the crane driver then gave it a quick tug and away it went: another nice length of good quality steel for the scrapman. What could be better?

After a couple of days, the Charge Hand asked me if I would mind working further along the beams. I was desperately not keen on doing this but he reminded me of the bonus, and S' bottom all wrapped up in her tight pink jeans flashed in front of my eyes, so I agreed. I wonder now what's the sum total of the damage caused by teenage hormones through the millennia...

I would like to claim some special, paranormal superpower intervening in what came next but maybe it was just down to me developing an ever stronger instinct for survival. I looked round and one of the Irish lads was burning the beam I was sat on: I went berserk!

The boys were actually a bit puzzled as to why I was making a fuss. As the lad with the torch pointed out, it wasn't as if he was going to do anything silly like burning the whole beam through. No, all that he was doing was giving me a flying start on the next section.

I was out of my mind. I was already terrified about being sixty feet up in the air sat on a knackered steel beam, and the thought that some nutter was reducing what already seemed like a very slim chance of not getting killed, was just too much.

I edged back along the beam and told the Charge Hand that was me finished. S' bottom or not, this was me out of the game.

The Irish lads were puzzled, not to say politely disappointed that I had proved not to be a team player. They were more than fair in paying me for the rest of the week – but no bonus.

Fate also conspired against me because I didn't see S again for some time – but she did come back into my life later, and in a major way.

*****

I think that one of the reasons I could deal with repeated failures and so many rejections was that, quite suddenly, someone had switched on the light in my head – and in a very profound way.

Since that very first TT when I was ten years old, I had been pretty well obsessed with racing. In Tripoli, I had assiduously studied every race report and I knew the names of all the top riders. Intellectually, I did understand about racing. However, I had no emotional feel for it until the 1965 TT.

Even visiting the Isle of Man was a complete sensory overload in every way. I travelled to the Island on the midnight boat, sleeping on the deck of the King Orry with my gas mask bag full of tools as a pillow.

When I arrived, it was if I was a new born baby who had just arrived in a world full of grown-ups. I smelled the sweet, salty, dawn dappled sea mist as I sat on the wall at the end of Douglas Promenade and drank deep draughts of the barely silenced Gold Stars and Bonnevilles as they snarled their way on to the TT circuit for a pre-breakfast lap.

I ate the Brylcreemed "Champ" hairstyles and gorged myself on the rows of TT badges displayed proudly on real leather jackets.

Everything was part of an opulent, extravagant banquet of colour and sounds and smells which pushed the mediocre magnolia of my Warrington life deep out of sight.

I wanted to see and smell and hear and taste everything - because that everything opened up vast doors on to another world – but this time, one of potential.

The feelings managed to subsume the actual experience in both a good and a bad way. Instead of spending time in the TT paddock, and soaking up the atmosphere which I would have loved, I was too shy to even go in there – too nervous of saying or doing the wrong thing and appearing to be inadequate, for I still carried a huge boulder of inferiority on my shoulders.

The good thing which came out of this mind set was that I could survive in dismal lodgings, where the number of rounds of toast which could be eaten with breakfast was rigidly controlled and there was a line on the bath, indicating that under no circumstances could more than 2" (50mm) of water be used.

I was also able to absorb, by osmosis rather than thought or intention, the sounds and sights which were to become my future.

The wail of the four cylinder works Hondas, with their silver fairings, and the screaming white and red Yamahas tearing at the air with two-stroke anger, were etched into my mind - and still are for that matter. These Japanese bikes were the future but I was also witnessing the end of an era. The booming, snarling AJS, Matchless and Norton singles were outdated and no longer race winners but still beating their chests anthropomorphically in defiance of progress.

This was my TT. All of this, everything in every way, was moulding and shaping me as if some celestial child had been given a handful of dull, grey plasticine and was now experimenting to see what, if anything, could be made of it.

Then, on the Friday of the TT week, came the experience which was to change me forever. I got up as a clumsy, shy, gauche and socially inept teenager who had achieved nothing and had zero prospects, and rode back to Douglas in the evening physically the same person, but spiritually someone very different – maybe even the first hint of a man.

On Friday was the Senior TT for 500cc machines – the pinnacle of the motorcycling calendar and the one event which every racer in the world wanted to win.

The weather was appalling - with cold, driving rain lashing the circuit. The favourite to win was Mike Hailwood, the greatest motorcycle racer of his generation – maybe even the best of all time. But Hailwood was not the normal sporting superstar. Mike the Bike was slightly shy, not very articulate and hopeless technically. He was disorganised, forgetful and amateurish in his approach – everything that ordinary club racers were.

His millionaire father did bank roll his racing, and to a lavish degree, but racing is a naked place. There is no "us" and "we" and bike racers are not team players. At the highest level they do need the support of a team and this is why you now hear the pronoun "we" so often. "We had a good day and we won" - or "things were not going well and we had problems". It is right and proper, both personally and professionally, that the efforts of engineers and sponsors are publicly seen to be appreciated. It would be both foolish and discourteous not to do so. Equally, it has to be acknowledged that "we" won't get hurt if "we" misjudge a corner or get a pass wrong. It is the rider's body on the line and it is only he who will wake up in hospital – or worse.

This is why Hailwood in the 1965 Senior TT was so magnificent, and his efforts so noble. First, he crashed on the uphill climb at Sarah's Cottage, almost in front of his team mate Giacomo Agostini who had fallen off just before him. Then he restarted his MV against the traffic on the course – an act which showed such ruthless disregard for the regulations that it was reckless.

But this act was also noble because Hailwood, the archetypal good sportsman who later won the George Medal for his bravery in rescuing Clay Regazzoni from a burning F1 car, not only wanted to win but needed to do so in order that some inner demon could be pacified.

I watched the race from the Gooseneck, one of the slowest corners on the TT course. The rain lashed across the moors and the road was flooded. The best riders of the day tiptoed tentatively through the torrent but Hailwood pitched the MV on to its side as if the conditions were perfect. But they weren't. The screen on the MV was smashed and Hailwood was bleeding from the injuries he had sustained but still he had the courage to race.

Later in the race, at Hailwood's insistence, the MV mechanics removed one damaged carburettor slide from the four cylinder engine - so now, in horrendous conditions, the motor would not fully shut off: still he won.

In the midst of the grey battalions of driving rain we, the ordinary folk, stood up and cheered - for we were in the presence of a better, greater person than us and yet one who was still a member of our tribe.

On the way back to Liverpool, I sat on the floor at the back of the King Orry's Lounge Bar sipping a bottle of ginger beer and listened to my elders and betters reliving Hailwood's win which they said, with a rare unanimity, was the greatest TT victory ever.

I would not disagree with their judgement but for me it was much, much more. Out on the track, no-one looked at who your dad was or where you lived. No-one knew if you were shy or confident – if you didn't know how to hold a girl's hand properly or kiss her. There was no-one measuring your social status or lack of it.

The flag dropped and the race was on. Rich or poor, council house or mansion, one of the boys or an outsider: no, nothing counted or was of any importance. If you rode better, were braver, more determined then you won and if weren't, you didn't – and no amount of excuses or mitigating circumstances meant a single thing.

In the fog of cigarette smoke, the cacophony of alcohol fuelled shouting, the laughter and the boasting, I came to a conclusion. I would be a bike racer and I would be judged not on my background but by what happened when I went underneath the chequered flag.

They were noble aspirations but the path I had chosen wasn't going to be an easy one.

Chapter Eight

Growing Up is, Quite, Hard to Do

One of the longest periods of employment that I had was as a fitter's mate at the Air Ministry Works Department in the old Burtonwood airbase. I want to try to give you a flavour of my life here because it was replicated widely throughout British industry – albeit in different shades depending on the actual business.

When I worked at Burtonwood, and I use the word "work" in only the very loosest sense, there was no flying taking place although many of the immense runways were still there. In fact, there was an awful lot of tarmac in the area with the main runway, at 1.7 miles, being the longest in Europe.

Across the way from the main base were the maintenance hangers. This was where the American planes, which had come across the Atlantic in kit form, were assembled. Battle damaged machines were repaired here too. The hangers were enormous – absolutely gigantic – and stretched away for what seemed like miles.

My job was as a gofor - as in "gofor for this and gofor for that." Once more, it was an immense mismatch of ability to task. This time, I was grossly under employed and so became even more restless.

The problem was that the whole operation was corrupt beyond imagination. I wasn't holier-than-thou about this, like some militant environmentalist or religious fundamentalist, but I wasn't comfortable with what was happening.

Let me give you some examples. The main work of the facility was in repairing and maintaining the huge, Ruston Paxman engines which powered the generators providing emergency power at RAF bases throughout the world. These engines were immense – absolutely enormous – so big that they had a walkway running along each side of the crankcases.

To supply the engines there was a big stores full of spare parts – millions of pounds worth. There was also a second stores, jam packed with high quality tools and specialist equipment. The Tool Store was very often target for the day and so was actually quite secure, requiring anyone going in to sign for the keys and then account for what had been removed.

The fix for the security was to get a pair of extremely long ladders which could reach up into the roof space – and that was a long way up – remove one of the aluminium panels and then lower the ladder down the other side into the tools.

The thefts were done quite thoughtfully with things being taken from the back of the shelves and then everything carefully rearranged so that, to a casual glance, the stock looked untouched. This wasn't the problem it seemed because the corruption was so widespread that it permeated every level of the base, and I don't think that anyone was particularly bothered.

But I had been taught that stealing was wrong. Not just getting caught which now seems to be the accepted norm, but that the act of taking something which did not belong to me was morally unacceptable. I have to thank my mum for this strong moral code. As an eight year old, I had found a Timpo lead soldier in the stockroom at my primary school. It had been confiscated by the teacher and then fallen in between two shelves and forgotten about - so I took it home.

Mum was quite tender with me and explained that since the soldier wasn't mine what I had done was to steal someone else's property - and this was wrong. I was made to take it back to my teacher the following day and it sat on her desk for ages, unwanted and unloved by anyone - except me. Regardless, my mum was right and I should not have taken the soldier.

One of the fitters I was working for said that he needed me to help with a job moving ladders. Fitters' Mates, the actual job title for Gofors like me, never questioned anything so I took one end of the very large extending aluminium ladders and off we went.

I never even saw what was coming next when we reached the hanger where the stores were located. Then he explained. He would go up the ladder and I would follow. My job was to help him pull the ladder up into the roof space and then lower it down into the tool store.

Why did I do something which was wrong, and that I knew was stealing? The truth is that I wasn't brave enough to stand up to him. I was very young and lacked confidence. I was also terribly shy and a loser and this wasn't a good hand of cards to play against a tough, adult man.

However, what happened next was considerably worse – and it influenced the rest of my life. The theft went according to plan and I was offered anything I wanted from the stores. Favoured items were the Britool socket sets which made good money in pubs. I would have walked across broken glass to own a Britool socket set which would have been a wonderful asset for working on my bikes.

The fitter thrust one of these at me and I really, desperately wanted it. However, even with all my inadequacy I wouldn't take it. He could see that things weren't going to plan and so put a Thor hide mallet in my hand. I didn't know what to do. As soon as it had touched me, he said: "Now you've been thieving as much as me so if the police ever find out, you'll get done with me and you'll do time with me."

I was terrified and hid the hammer inside my shirt, next to my chest, for fear of being found out and the consequences.

I still have the hammer and I look at it regularly because I owe a great debt to the tool. I am a deeply flawed and imperfect person but I was determined that if I was ever in a position to have power I would not use it cruelly and, in particular, I would not deliberately set out to hurt people who were vulnerable.

As I cycled home that night, with the hammer rubbing up and down against my chest, I could never imagine being able to exercise influence over anyone or anything but the nascent flame had been ignited, and my militant abhorrence of bullying remains with me today.

*****

Looking back, I think that the reason theft was tolerated, if this is the right word, on such an epidemic scale, is that the corruption ran right through the whole organisation. At the mild end, managers got their cars serviced by fitters in work's time, with work's material, but there was also a more calculated dishonesty.

The last hanger in the line was used for the sale of scrap metal gathered from bases all over Britain. Inside, the area was roped off into sections - each one with a number chalked on the floor. Scrap was put into each section - and this could be anything which had been declared unwanted or unusable. For example, there were always cracked locomotive wheels and prototype jigs made from steel channelling and RSJ beams.

On this occasion, one of the bays was filled with rubbish that wasn't going to make any decent money at all. The primary attraction was some battered, grey clothing lockers but these were so tired that they couldn't be used for their intended purpose so they would have to be "weighed in" for scrap.

One of the junior engineers took me on one side and said that he needed a job doing, and that I should report only to him. No-one else – just him or I would be in serious bother. Immediately, I knew that there was some sort of trouble coming but again, in my position, I didn't know what to do.

The job was easy. I was to take the electric pallet truck down to the scrap hanger and open the locker with the key he had given to me. When it was open, I was to put the heavy cardboard box he had given to me into the locker and then return the key to him – saying nothing to anyone.

Under no circumstances, and for no reason, was I to open the box.

Clearly, given such dire warnings not to open the box it was inevitable that I would! Inside were dozens of used copper buzz bars. These were long strips of copper about the size of a super-sized Twix chocolate bar and were used to connect a generator to the system it was powering.

In the next couple of weeks I made more trips, with more boxes of buzz bars and on the last one, I opened the box to see that it was full of glistening, brand new buzz bars, still in their protective wax coating, all of which had been withdrawn from the main stores.

Now, here is the scene. Come the day of the scrap sale, all the scrap men bid for the areas. This makes the whole process transparent and honest.

Clearly, one patch is full largely of rubbish and a few battered lockers – except that one is effectively a solid column of copper, six feet high.

Maybe someone was just going to get a very, very pleasant surprise when he got back to his yard…

*****

It wasn't only theft which was epidemic but "foreigners" – private jobs done in work's time. This story is slightly out of chronological order but it will, I hope, give you a flavour of what was happening at the time.

I had a really rough 350 Velocette with a particularly dodgy dynamo. This was driven by a pulley and v-belt. I decided to check if it was working at all, or merely intermittently, so I brought the unit into Burtonwood in my gasmask bag.

The concept was simple. We had enormous polishing machines, driven by huge electric motors. I intended putting the pulley against the polishing mop, spinning the dynamo and then checking to see if it was producing any current.

To check the voltage, I needed an AVO meter. This was a tool for metering and checking all sorts of things like voltage, amperage and earth continuity. Now, the same meter comes in a tiny box about the size of a cigarette packet but in the olden days an AVO was a big, chocolate box sized rascal weighing a porky couple of pounds.

In fact, the situation was even worse than this because the Air Ministry used a special heavy duty version of the Avo and this really was a big lad, complete with a thick leather carrying strap.

I stood at the wire grill of the stores and presented a request for an AVO signed by one of the electricians: except that it wasn't. In fact, it wasn't signed by anyone except me in the form of an illegible squiggle.

The storeman returned a few minutes later with the AVO and I signed for it. Now, my fate really was in my own hands.

The storeman was a miserable sod and issued a sneering warning that was surprisingly prescient. "You look after this AVO. I've only had it in three days and I want it back in the same condition you've taken it."

High above Burtonwood, in some other part of the Multiverse, a whole gaggle of deities were going to have a laugh.

I had persuaded one of the apprentices to help me with the exercise. He agreed but only with the utmost reluctance. "If anything happens to that AVO, they'll cut your balls off. For f***'s sake, be careful."

The young gods, watching from on high, passed the celestial Nacho chips round and got ready for the show.

I just smiled. I was going to come to a definite conclusion about the errant Velocette dynamo.

It needs stressing that the buffing machines at Burtonwood were nothing like the sort of thing you see in a home workshop. The ones at Burtonwood were huge, very heavy duty monsters designed to be used 24 hours a day during the war, powered by motors which would probably manage to run a small bus now. These boys could compete for the title of "World's Biggest Buffing Machine" and be certain of a win.

Coming out of the AVO were two thick leads – again, nothing like the bits of wire you see on a home electronic multi meter. Because the heavy-duty AVOs were designed for handling huge currents, the red and black leads were as thick as a washing line and covered with rubber insulation.

Even after such a long time, I can still remember starting the buffer. The machines did not leap into immediate action like a domestic tool. Rather, they sort of built up speed gradually, in the style of a jet engine coming into the power band and then sat there, throbbing purposefully on their cast iron bases.

The lad who was helping me held the dynamo pulley against the coarse rag of the wheel whilst I readied the AVO. To be fair to me, I now had the difficult job of poking the ends of the positive and negative leads into the dynamo whilst balancing the AVO on my thigh so that I could see the reading, if any.

The task was quite short lived. I juggled the meter but did not take precise care with the position of the leads. In less than a flash – much less actually – one of the leads got caught around the mop head of the buffing wheel – very closely followed by the second one.

The scene was truly memorable – maybe one of the most memorable of my whole life!

AVOs were fine examples of British engineering – made to a standard, not a price. There was no way that the leads were giving way without a battle, so the AVO did half a dozen ever faster laps, with the leads fighting to the last bullet to hold on to the meter. Then they failed…

The wheel was doing maybe 5,000rpm and so when the meter parted company with the leads it was really motoring. Taking off like a black, Bakelite missile it soared up into the hanger roof hitting one of the steel joists at a very considerable speed.

It didn't so much break, as explode with a real crack. You have to remember that most of the workforce had fought in the war and so they knew just what a grenade or incoming mortar shell sounded like. All over the place, fitters and electricians hit the floor and waited for the Germans to launch the second round.

Meanwhile, in quite a surreal manner, bits of AVO floated down around me.

*****

Later that day I was summoned to see the Station Engineer – the senior manager on site. The Air Ministry policy was that when some tool or machine was broken, what could be salvaged was retained for future use because, pre-electronics, it was possible to recycle lots of parts.

In the centre of his desk, the Station Engineer had a large folder containing pink blotting paper which was used to absorb the excess ink from when he signed a letter with his fountain pen. The blotting paper sat in a green, Moroccan leather holder which is still clear in my mind even today. In the centre of the pink paper was a small spring, about the size of those you see inside a ball point pen.

I had been marched in, military fashion, by the foreman and now stood before the Station Engineer awaiting either a death sentence, maybe a public flogging or perhaps disembowelling before the assembled workforce.

He looked up and pushed the spring around on his blotting paper with his forefinger. "Do you know what this is?"

My mouth was dry. "No Sir. I'm sorry Sir, but I don't – Sir."

"This is what we have recovered for salvage, from the brand-bloody-new-bloody-AVO you've destroyed."

"Am really sorry Sir. I really am Sir."

He put his head in hands and then looked up. "Just get out - and you're banned from the stores until I say different!"

In a world of chaos and dishonesty, what was one more incident and another waste of money? The truth was that this was his normal world and although what I had done was a minor irritation, it was only one of very many snafus.

*****

I guess that his real problem was that there was always something going wrong – sometimes like an archetypal Benny Hill farce and on other occasions, pure Monty Python surrealism. Here's a good one.

The diesel engines lived inside huge boxes made out of aircraft grade, alloy sheet. These were lovely pieces of British craftsmanship and clearly there were always bits of spare alloy left over from every job. These would go for scrap. Who could possibly object to a few bits of scrap being used for foreigners?

But the reality proved to be very different. The lads saw this is as a golden opportunity and, every night, cars were staggering home loaded with sheets of alloy. Even I got some little pieces which were considered to be too small to be worth stealing by the tradesmen.

Some years later, I drove through the nearby town of Newton-le-Willows and felt quite proud to see three immaculate pigeon lofts, all built to superb standards with our aircraft spec alloy. They're probably still there – examples of the very best of British craftsmanship.

In this case, things became so bad that they did reach a climax. So much sheet was being used, along with the alloy, angle iron and pop rivets which went with it, that some bloke from London or somewhere came up to find out why Burtonwood was using more alloy than the rest of the aircraft industry put together: the gypsies' warning was duly issued to all concerned.

However, probably the best of all the fun and games that happened during my sojourn at Burtonwood could have got someone into properly serious trouble with a manslaughter charge.

The diesel engines sat on steel frames so that they could be installed on sites all over the world. Because of the size of these engines, the bolts holding them to the frames were really substantial. Lots of things at Burtonwood were super-sized and none more so than the overhead crane which picked up the engines and moved them from one area to another.

There was some Saturday morning overtime being done and, on this particular occasion, the crane driver decided to get some time and a half pay. However, to make the morning more fun, he took his girlfriend into the cab. I went up there once and it was a brilliant view over the whole shop. You'd pay a lot of money for the experience at a theme park now.

He trundled the crane to and fro, eliciting ever more excited comments from his girlfriend who was in awe of his manly prowess. In fact, she was so ecstatic that she suggested he drop his trousers – as you would...

I heard the story second hand on Monday morning and, at the time, I really and truthfully did not understand what had actually happened. The word was that she knelt down in the rather cramped cab and her boyfriend was most appreciative – albeit somewhat distracted.

One of the fitters below was just removing the final retaining bolt which held the engine to the bed, when the crane driver began lifting it – probably because he had his mind on other things...

The bolt was ripped out of the bed and ricocheted round the hanger like shrapnel from an anti-personnel mine, before falling to the floor exhausted - and thankfully without having hit anyone.

Of course, this was considered to be utterly hilarious but even by the microscopically low health and safety standards of the time, getting walloped by an inch thick bolt doing a couple of hundred miles an hour would have not been that funny.

Chapter Nine

The Centre of the Motorcycling Universe?

In terms of being in the right place at the right time, Warrington really was the lucky lottery ticket for a sixteen year old in love with motorcycles.

There were two mainstream dealers in the town, both of whom sold British and Japanese bikes, as well as Sankey Bridge Motorcycles and Freddy's Breakers.

The biggest, by a long way was Jack Frodsham Motorcycles, who had a large shop on Winwick Street, quite near to Central Station. The firm also had a workshop and paint shop along one of the adjoining roads. Finally, there was another storage area on the other side of Winwick Street.

I first went into Froddies whilst I was still at school and then it was run, and I think owned, by an elderly, patrician gentleman called Bernard, or Barney, Rudd.

Mr Rudd, as I knew him, was already very old when I first saw him. He was immaculately presented in a dark blue suit, tie and gold cufflinks and looked more like one of my teachers than someone who worked in a bike shop. I was fascinated to hear the adults say that he lived, permanently, at the Victoria Hotel in nearby Stockton Heath, but not too surprised because he epitomised my stylised fantasy of a very important person.

When I later came into contact with Jack Frodsham Motorcycles as a potential customer, Mr Rudd had moved on and the firm was run by Mr Etherington who had been an RAF fighter pilot in the war. My sense, even as a very young man, was that Mr Etherington's heart was not in the bike business and perhaps the war was to blame for this.

He enjoyed talking to me about subjects other than motorcycles because I was polite and interested – both traits being natural for me. Mr Etherington had flown Hurricane fighter bombers in the Burma campaign and he told me that he had lost his best friend, in a senseless accident as he was returning to Chittagong.

The mission had been both long and very hazardous, with all the aircraft suffering from the extensive anti-aircraft ground fire. Mr Etherington thought that it was exhaustion from the intensity of battle but his friend flew out to sea, sure that a low cloud was an island where he could land. Mr Etherington followed him and desperately tried to attract his attention right up to the moment he crashed into the sea. Although Mr Etherington had continued flying, after this he had no interest in aircraft or fighting and left the RAF as soon as he could: another victim of the war.

Jack Frodsham sold a wide range of new and second-bikes including Triumph, Honda, Yamaha and Lambretta scooters. I seem to remember that they had a franchise for AMC products too – Matchless and Norton being the only two of any value by this time.

The company also sold the Reliant Regal three wheelers and these are worth mentioning in some detail. Reliants were little three wheeled cars made in Tamworth, Staffordshire. They have become iconic after starring with Del Boy in *Only Fools and Horses* and for Jeremy Clarkson's destruction of a whole herd of Reliants in *Top Gear*.

Reliants were a true good news/bad news story. Through a very odd quirk in road traffic legislation, they were classed as a motorcycle and sidecar, and so could be driven on a motorcycle licence without the need to take an additional car test. This led to the rather odd situation where bikers who couldn't master the complexity of driving a car could rock up at Jack Frodshams and immediately tootle off in a Reliant.

This was often a challenging experience because a Reliant, weighing almost nothing and with just a single front wheel, needed to be driven with a considerable degree of thought and a healthy sprinkling of circumspection. Okay, Clarkson did ham it up - and he later admitted that the cars he used had been modified to make them roll but, regardless, Reliants could be challenging if driven hard or carelessly.

To conform with legislation, all Reliants had to weigh less than 450kg so they were decidedly basic inside. To keep the weight to a minimum they had a fibreglass body mounted on a minimalist, steel box chassis.

Even with my social status I looked down on Reliants, which everyone thought were for losers. Certainly, I don't think that I would have done any better with K if I had turned up at the Odeon in a Reliant Regal!

The bizarre thing though, was that they were quite fast. Reliant made their own, all alloy, 750cc four cylinder engine which produced 40hp – ample enough for 70mph plus. At this speed, and especially if there was a bit of a cross wind, you really did need zero imagination and a strong belief that Karma had declared that nothing could ever go wrong in your life!

The obverse side of the coin was that the little trikes were ludicrously, amazingly light on fuel and, even when a gallon of petrol (4.5 litres) was just over five bob (25p), being able to drive over 80 miles on every gallon of fuel was a big plus.

New Reliants were popular at Jack Frodsham's because motorcycles were invariably put in part exchange against them, so it was a win/win situation all round. The problem came with tired Reliants which had been taken in these part exchange deals.

In the 1970s there had been a fire in the paint shop at Frodshams, and I remember meeting the then Sales Manager in Warrington Market. He looked really rough, still with blood shot eyes days after the inferno - but was beaming like someone who had just won the lottery. One of the interesting drawbacks of the Reliant is that they burn with great enthusiasm in an accident because the resin which bonds the glass fibres together is super inflammable. Once the flames take hold, there is no putting them out!

When the fire had begun in the paint shop there had been a mad panic to push every single second-hand Reliant the firm had in stock, into the inferno. This was a relatively easy job because they burnt out almost instantly, making space for the next one. When the lads objected, on the wholly reasonable grounds that the fumes were trying to kill them and lumps of burning roof were dropping on their heads, they were re-motivated by the promise of an all expenses night in the pub – truly, the Dunkirk spirit writ large in a Warrington paint shop!

The insurance assessor eventually came to visit and he was more than a little sceptical about how many Reliants were being painted at the same time, in such a tiny workshop – but he still paid out.

And there was an even happier ending to this most happy of happy tales. The sales manager did a deal with the local scrapman for the steel chassis, so he got a personal drink out of the inferno too.

Jack Frodsham's was on the cusp between the old-fashioned, enthusiast owned and run bike shops, which were still in the majority in the late 1960s, and more modern, conventional businesses.

Downstairs were lines of new and second hand machines – all of which were vastly beyond my budget. Upstairs were the offices, stores and more second-hand machines but, once more, there was nothing which I could even dream of owning with my available capital.

Across the road from the main shop was a storage area and this next bit of the story might well induce a tear or two. Old bikes had been piled inside – quite literally jammed in and heaped on top of each other without regard to damage.

It would make a more dramatic story if I could say I remember seeing some exotic, pre-war Brough Superior which is now worth £250,000 but it wouldn't be true. My only memories are of old bikes, unwanted and valueless, some of which had funny flat tanks and silly levers to change gear by hand. What a waste of space when what I really wanted was a Triumph Bonneville or Thruxton Velocette.

Apparently, every so often someone at Froddies would ring the scrapman and the old bike store, or maybe even stores, would be cleared out to make space for more rubbish – any bit of which is now worth a fortune!

*****

I have just said that I lusted after a Triumph or Velo and this is an interesting observation in one respect. As history is being re-written in the light of the current interest in retro bikes, there is a myth developing that the cunning Japanese sneaked into Britain covered in jungle camouflage and stole the British motorcycle industry by guile and deception. In fact, nothing could be further from the truth.

I can give you a couple of examples. This is a story I heard on several occasions from different people, so it might well be true.

Honda motorcycles were first imported by a company called Hondis. The Hondis' sales representative had an uphill job because there was a strong anti-Japanese sentiment in the country at the time. It is important to remember that 1960 was only fifteen years after the appalling atrocities carried out by the Japanese in Burma – a level of cruelty and inhumanity the equal of any war crime committed during the conflict.

So, even working for a Japanese company was considered to be a close relative of treason. The way in was to find very small dealers who were selling deeply undesirable machines such as Jawa, CZ, James, Cotton and the like.

The rep duly arrived at one such dealer, a one man-one wife business, which should have been a prime target for selling the superb little Hondas. Unfortunately for the rep, the proprietor had served with Orde Wingate's Chindit troops in the Burma campaign and had fought the Japanese through-out the length of Burma. He had also seen, at first-hand, the Japanese treatment of Allied prisoners of war.

He set about the Hondis rep and gave him what, in the Warrington vernacular, could be described as a "right good hiding" – in broad daylight and with an audience.

The rep was taken to hospital for treatment – it was that bad a beating – but the Police had no interest in taking any action because a Jap collaborator had got what he deserved. That's how hard it was to break into the British bike market!

However, it wasn't always this difficult. In December 1959 my long time sponsor, Eddie Crooks, established what was going to become one of the greatest Suzuki dealers in the world: the legendary Crooks-Suzuki based in Barrow-in-Furness, right on the very end of the Furness Peninsula in the far north-west of England.

Eddie had served in the army, with the motorcycling mad Captain Eddie Dow, as a National Service conscript and was British Army Trials Champion in 1953.

In fact, virtually the whole of his time in the army was spent with bikes and so when he returned to civilian life he naturally wanted to be part of the motorcycle industry. Eddie worked for a few bike dealers before setting up his own business in a terraced house in Crellin Street, right in the centre of Barrow. Planning permission was not an issue in the 1950s!

Eddie had a Jawa agency which was only marginally better than nothing. Somewhat surprisingly, Suzuki were imported by AMC – the parent company of Norton and Matchless - who clearly saw which way the wind was blowing. The Japanese imports were based in the James' factory, another AMC brand, in Greet Street, Birmingham.

Fred Miles, who was the Suzuki sales representative for the North-West, arrived at Eddie's deeply unglamorous little shop with three bikes on a trailer. Fred did not attempt any hard sell. On the contrary, he just told Eddie and his Service Manager, Frank Whiteway, to take the bikes and try to break them. Eddie and Frank took the 50s and an 80 on to Walney Island and rode them flat out. The little bikes ran faultlessly and Eddie became an instant fan. That's the truth of how the Japanese destroyed the British motorcycle industry.

I will add one more anecdote to the story of what the Japanese did to, and for, motorcycling. Just before I began teacher training, I wanted a bike to use as a commuter vehicle because all my available cash was tied up in my race bike and van.

I bought a second-hand Honda S90 – a little 90cc, single cylinder sports bike. It was in nice condition but not pristine. For three months, I hammered the bike ruthlessly – literally flat against the stop, all the time and on every trip.

On one beautiful Spring day, I decided to do a trip round Wales – a couple of hundred miles through the mountains. I rode the little Honda like a GP bike, with it wailing away in every gear – and it never once missed a beat. Better still, or worse from the point of view of the British bike industry, the S90 was also incredibly light on fuel. It handled well, was fast, frugal and beautifully finished: that was the reality which killed off the British bikes – not some oriental subterfuge.

I once had a conversation about this with my dear friend Fred Barlow who had been an apprentice in the BSA Competition Shop. He told me an interesting anecdote. The BSA Comp Shop had been sent a Honda Cub - Honda's ubiquitous 50cc, do anything, scooter cum bike. They were told to strip it down and report to the BSA Board regarding the machine's quality.

Brian Martin, the BSA Competition Department Manager, told senior management that the Comp Shop would have difficulty producing a single, hand built race bike to the standard of the Cub – a machine which was pouring off the production line in Japan by the tens of thousands. Yet still, we did nothing.

*****

The Suzuki dealer in Warrington was Bill Pope Motorcycles, a family owned business which was almost a modern dealership. The premises were pretty well state of the art for the time. Bikes were displayed well, in good light, and at the rear was an excellent workshop. In fact, with some appropriate branding and point of sale material, you might well have thought that you were in a 21st century dealership.

There were also two other shops in the Warrington bike trade and both of these were rather quirky. At the side of Tetley Walkers' brewery was Freddy's – a bike breaker. In the 1960s, breaking bikes for spares was a boom business. There were a number of reasons for the popularity. First, there was a huge degree of interchangeability between models. For example, a 350 Matchless and AJS were virtually identical machines. Even with Japanese bikes, parts could be swapped around quite easily from one model to another and sometimes even between marques - as with Mikuni carburettors. Finally, the machines were very simple. For example, even I – outstandingly one of the least competent mechanics in the world – could change a carburettor, a magneto, an engine or a gearbox. There were few special tools needed, and we lived in a world where every lad knew how to use spanners.

The problem with me and Freddy's is that I was never comfortable in the place. Freddy himself was known as a "character" and was too given to shouting for my taste. In fact, his mouth got him into trouble more than once and he made the *Warrington Guardian* court reports – always an extensive part of the newspaper – for jumping on the shoulders of a police officer, whilst absolutely out of his mind on drink, and attempting to pummel the bobby in the head. Not that the attack was very serious in practical terms, because Freddy was only a weedy little thing but nevertheless it was an indicator of his mind set.

The bits he sold were also strictly without warranty. Complaints were a total waste of time as was any expectation of customer service.

On the outskirts of Warrington, right next to the canal by Sankey Bridges, was a wooden shack housing Sankey Bridge Motorcycles. Despite its dowdy appearance, there was some high quality work done first by a big bloke called, not unexpectedly, Jumbo and, later, by a very talented mechanic, tuner and road racer named Colin Wilkinson.

*****

Supporting all these fine institutions was an engineering supply chain which meant that you could get anything done either, albeit rarely, as a legitimate job but invariably as a "foreigner".

The concept of the "foreigner" needs explaining. As I have said, I found stealing unacceptable and it offended me. Equally, I don't want to be all holier than thou because I was often a thief – of time or materials.

This is what I mean. When my racing became serious, I would often have bits made in titanium (ti) – at the time a very rare, exotic and expensive metal. These came from a variety of sources – but always connected with the nuclear industry in one way or another. The first port of call was the Cammell Laird Shipyard in Birkenhead which built nuclear submarines – boats as they are universally known in the submarine business. Ti is very light, extremely strong and it doesn't rust so nuclear boats have a lot of this metal in them!

In Warrington, Capper Neil were sub-contractors to the nuclear industry. Ti is unaffected by nuclear radiation, and doesn't corrode even in the harshest environment, so is popular in this industry. However, the top of the tree was Vickers, in Barrow-in-Furness, who were the biggest manufacturer of nuclear boats in Britain and right up there with the Americans and Russians.

If there was a few inches of titanium bar at the end of the job then it was possible to persuade a turner to make a bolt and nut rather than having the metal scrapped. The turner got a "drink" – either literally or metaphorically – and everyone was happy.

The same applied to having bits of welding done or maybe an exhaust cover fabricated from some stainless steel sheet. All these jobs were often done in lunch breaks or slack times during the day

Strictly speaking, this was theft – of materials and time – and was wrong. I, and the lads doing the jobs, justified this because everyone else was a thief too.

Teachers got free paper, pens and any confiscated contraband – and there was a lot of it. I never smoked so when I became a teacher, my super sensitive nose for cigarette smoke earned extensive booty during any playground duty that I did - all of which was happily passed on to my many colleagues who really did enthusiastically support the British fag industry.

Clerks used to put their own letters through franking machines instead of paying postage whilst the management ram-raided companies to a degree which was embarrassing. The fitter, turner or welder looked at his boss coming back from an afternoon's golf, a day at the horse racing or a very long, well lubricated lunch and thought, "Well, I'm entitled to a drink too…"

Unfortunately, the whole system fell apart because theft escalated to a galactic scale. The Ford car factory at Halewood, in Liverpool, was probably at the apogee because workers there were stealing complete cars – including body shells for use in rallying.

The bike world was also competing hard. For example, there was an unused Triumph Daytona engine advertised in *Motorcycle News* – every week! Now, either the lad selling the motor was extremely unlucky or…

Parts from the BSA plant at Small Heath were lobbed into the Grand Union Canal which ran at the back of the factory, to be recovered later, whilst the BSA Competition Department was known to be as leaky as a worn out sieve.

I put the blame firmly and squarely on the management. If you establish good, tight, fair management exercising the same standards from top to bottom, the workforce will come along with you. Without such managers, anarchy will result - and Britain in the 1960s really was anarchic.

*****

Warrington was also surrounded by major dealers – some of whom I knew quite well and others which I avoided.

In the beautiful Cheshire hills above Helsby was Hector Dugdale Motor-cycles – and this was an interesting place for a number of reasons. The business began in 1919 and it was woven into the motorcycling community with Hector sponsoring riders, playing his part in event organisation and becoming Chairman of the Cheshire Centre ACU – our local branch of the organisation which governed all motorcycle sport at the time.

Hector became one of the very first Yamaha dealers, when Mitsui Trading were the importers, and developed a reputation as one of the world's leading Yamaha racing dealers. His sons Alan and Gary also worked in the business which was housed in a light, airy, open plan building right in the centre of the village of Alvanley. Alan was a good, national class rider and his brother was a superb tuner. At the time, they had every base covered and, on Sundays, the whole area was jammed with riders either making the pilgrim-age to Dugdales or returning from a visit.

I met Hector on a number of occasions and he was always the epitome of courtesy and enthusiasm.

In the 1970s, when British trials bikes were worth little more than scrap value, I almost bought an ex-works AJS from him. The bike was in lovely condition and Hector wanted £55 for it. He was so desperate to get rid of the thing that he loaned it to me for the afternoon. I played around with it in Delamere Forest and on nearby Fox Hill. I really did like the bike, which ran beautifully, but I didn't actually lust after it. Hector and I had a bit of a haggle and he offered it to me for £50 but I stuck at £45. Now, a bike with a provenance like that is worth a solid £15,000. The benefit of hindsight...

*****

Another major player in the road racing scene was Bill Smith Motors in Chester. I didn't like the dealership because it was very grown up and a bit intense for someone as far down the social order as me. Much later, I got to know Bill Smith himself rather well and came to admire him on many levels.

First, he was a fine rider – absolutely top class and, except for building his business with fanatical determination, I think that he was the equal of superstars of the day. Perhaps he wasn't quite at the level of MotoGods like Mike Hailwood, Jim Redman or Giacomo Agostini but he was certainly a GP winner.

Bill's strength, and weakness, was that he was the ultimate wheeler-dealer and stretched the envelope of what was possible to the furthest edges of the outer limits. At one time, he imported Bridgestone motorcycles from Japan – and what fabulous bikes they were too – and then he developed a very interesting group of dealers who bought new Hondas directly from him – and in huge numbers.

All this success made him a bit too much for someone of my status, who knew next to nothing and was penniless.

A little further away, in Liverpool and Manchester, were more major dealers. Victor Horsman, in Liverpool, was another example of the rider/tuner/enthusiast who dominated the British motorcycle industry at the time. Victor had been a top rider on the legendary Brooklands concrete speedbowl before the war and he carried this reputation with him into his bike shop. Horsmans were main dealers for Triumph and BMW but, once more, they were a bit posh and upmarket for me.

A few miles away, in Great George Street on the edge of Liverpool's Chinatown, was Bill Hannah Motorcycles. The shop specialised in second hand bikes and new Ducatis. My personal experience was that they were ruthless to the point of being cruel. When I eventually scraped sufficient money together to, barely, afford the Velocette Venom I had always dreamed of, I was exploited with callous contempt. I am not vindictive by nature but I do hope that, somewhere deep in the bowels of Purgatory, the salesman who milked me dry has to eat a bucket full of rotting HP forms every day as a reminder of his cruelty.

At the other end of scale, about as far away as it was possible to get from Bill Hannah, was Fred Spann at Sandiway. Fred repaired bikes, and sold spares and a few second-hand machines. He was a fine scrambler, on his Matchless Metisse, and a top class trials rider until he suffered a freak accident when a tree branch poked him in the eye.

Fred was kindness and warmth personified, and probably helped out 90% of the starving young motocross riders in the area with discounts, good second-hand spares and, most of all, a smile and an encouraging comment. I don't think there was ever a kinder person in the bike trade.

I hope that Fred is the angel feeding Hannah's salesman the HP forms but, if he is, Fred would probably be giving him a hand to eat them - he was such a good person.

So, this is a brief glance at the bike trade through my eyes – but it will be a biased viewpoint. I saw what I needed and wanted to see. Richer riders – and everyone else really did have more money than me – would tell a different story, and scooter fans would hold yet another view.

The key thing was the vibrancy of the bike trade because motorcycles were mainstream and acceptable, rather than being the increasingly niche activity which is prevalent now.

The people in the motorcycle business were, largely but not entirely, also motorcyclists themselves. Very often – in fact, more than very often – they had raced or had tuned competition bikes. They loved motorcycles and bike racing was also a part of everyday society. I'll try to give you a flavour of just how much bike racing was woven into the fabric of normal life in this next chapter.

Chapter Ten

"Racing is life. Anything before or after is just waiting..."

Steve McQueen

I still ride at race meetings because I love the sport. As long as my body and mind hold up, you'll find me squeezing into leathers which seem to get tighter every year, and lining up for practice with racers young enough to be my grandchildren. These days, although I enter real races you won't find me putting my body on the line for the sake of passing anyone. No, I amble round and have a wonderful time because, as Steve McQueen said, "Racing is life. Anything before or after is just waiting."

Racing is now very different from when I first became an addict as a seventeen year old. I was at an ordinary club event last year and walked past the team of a youngster who was riding a modern Superbike. The group were rather better organised than most of the paddock but, even so, it was a shocking experience probably because on this day I actually took notice of what I saw.

First, there was a huge Mercedes van, kitted out with living quarters at the front and a garage at the rear. The van had towed an immense, luxury caravan. The bikes lived in a giant tent complete with an industrial plastic floor. There was also a really posh heater, TV, whiteboard for messages and a tool chest about the size of our kitchen.

I seem to remember that there were three pairs of wheels, clearly with tyre warmers powered by a monster generator. Spare screens and fairings were mounted on a beautifully manufactured rack.

Dad, and a mechanic, worked on the pair of bikes whilst mum and girlfriend established a "Hospitality Centre" to one side with a little table for nibbles. There was a large display board giving recognition to sponsors.

The rider sat on a folding chair, eyes closed and headphones on, getting into the "zone". It was all very interesting, and somewhat odd, for someone whose ambition had been to have a bike with a four speed gearbox - and which would last a whole race without blowing up!

*****

When I sent in my first entry form, even World Champions of the day looked like entrants to the Amateur Night Competition at the Bury Palais de Dance, compared with current, half-decent club riders. However, none of this detracted from the fact that the Cheshire Centre, of which Warrington was a part, was a hotbed of racing at all levels. Every form of motorcycle sport was within an easy ride of our house and I could have taken any direction with my obsession to race.

The truth is that I really wanted to road race. In Tripoli, the highlight of my week was finding a stray copy of *MCN* with the race results emblazoned across the front page. It's interesting that the lead stories were often about racing because bike sport was vastly more acceptable than it is today. If you can find a young man now who actually does race it will be a rarity, whereas in the late 1960s it was extremely common to take part.

The problem I faced with road racing was that it was vastly, hugely outside my budget – and also my mechanical ability. Would-be racers who were short of funds could fudge the issue with cleverly prepared bikes whereas I lacked all but the most basic skills with spanners, and had very little technical or mechanical empathy. I could change engines, gearboxes and the like but only with great effort because the discipline of putting nut "a" on bolt "b" was always alien to me.

Even if I couldn't afford to race, Oulton Park was on our doorstep and the chance to see the greatest riders of the day was impossible to miss: impossible, but still very challenging.

The reason that the great riders appeared at a British circuit was because of the way Grands Prix were organised in the 1960s. Now, the top riders live in a cossetted world. Nine times World Champion Marc Marquez's basic wage from Honda is nearly £10 million - and there is another £3 million or £4 million from personal sponsorship. If you even got to see Mr Marquez, except on the track, you would feel very blessed. We once saw most of Valentino Rossi's arm, and his whole hand without a glove, when we were guests at a MotoGP round: that was the highlight of the weekend!

But it wasn't always like this. In the 1960s, GP promoters exploited riders in a quite callous way and it was appalling. With the support of the FIM, who controlled motorcycle racing internationally, even works riders were paid only minimum start money and the least possible prize money, despite attendances regularly in excess of 250,000 – and even more than this at Sachsenring in the old East Germany.

In fact, the situation was sometimes utterly bizarre because at any GP behind the Iron Curtain, Eastern Bloc currencies were not convertible so riders took van loads of Russian champagne and Practica cameras back over the border to trade in the West.

The very best riders were paid a lot of money by the top factories, so World Champions like Jim Redman, Phil Read and Hugh Anderson earned a very good living from Honda, Yamaha and Suzuki respectively but for riders just one layer down from the best, life was hard.

The solution from the manufacturers' point of view was to let riders compete in whatever international meetings they wished because different rules applied for these events. If a promoter wanted to have a star studded entry, which would pull in the crowds, then he needed to pay the going rate both in terms of an appearance fee – known as start money – and also good prize money.

Marc Marquez is contractually forbidden to participate in any race except the twenty MotoGP rounds but stars in the 1960s rode in as many meetings as they could, to earn the maximum money.

Tommy Robb was a top flight GP rider and rode for Bultaco and Honda, but this was his life as a professional racer. We were chatting once at a classic event and this is what he told me:

"The one thing which strikes me every time I watch MotoGP on TV, is how riders can walk away from crashes. Most of the circuits we raced on were public roads and if you crashed then there was a high risk of serious injury – and a fair chance of dying. Racing was dangerous and our earnings did not reflect this.

"We also expected to look after ourselves. Except when I rode for Honda I worked on my own bikes, booked my own hotels and drove my own van to meetings. I'll give you an example.

"I always liked the Easter meetings in England because I could make good money - but it was tough. I would leave Belfast on Thursday and catch the overnight ferry to Liverpool. I didn't bother with sleep and I would get straight off the ferry and drive directly to Brands Hatch. Liverpool to Brands was 250 miles and in the early days there were no motorways.

"I would race all day at Brands – and every race was tough with a lot of works bikes and top riders. Throughout the meeting, I would be working on my own bikes and snatching what food I could throughout the day. There was no team catering and no-one to help me!

"Immediately after my last race, I would be packing the van and then hopefully collecting my prize money. Even whilst the racing was continuing at Brands, I would be leaving the circuit and then driving the 100 miles to Snetterton (near Norwich, in the far east of England).

"Snetterton was a faster track so I had to change the gearing and carburation first thing in the morning and then race all day – again, hard races against hard men. As always, it was just me, so we riders had to be really handy with the spanners and able to work under pressure.

"The moment I could, the bikes were loaded up and I drove overnight to Oulton Park (in North West England) – another 220 miles but this time without any motorways at all.

"I would arrive at Oulton at maybe 4am or 5am, snatch an hour's sleep and then have another day of hard racing.

"If everything had gone well, I would have earned a decent wage from the three events but if it didn't then I wouldn't. You either made your money on your performance - or didn't, and there was no safety net.

"If the GPs fell wrongly then the going was really tough too. I once drove from Barcelona in Spain, to Imatra in Finland, in one go. That was nearly 2,300 miles and the only sleep I got was on the two ferry crossings.

"You need to remember that I didn't feel special or treated badly. This is what we all did. It was hard for me but it was hard for everyone. It was just life as a professional racer and that's what I was.

"If it was a good trip, with a bit of spare time, I would call in and see friends in different countries on the way to and from GPs. That was great. It was tough but I wouldn't have swapped my life with anyone."

The manufacturers also provided second-string works bikes, and spares, for their contracted riders to use at these events – obsolete factory machines which had been superseded by some newer models. This was a key part of their overall payment package.

It wasn't only mainstream road races where you could find the stars. In 1968, Mike Hailwood rode a Honda 6 at the horrendously dangerous Monte Generosa Hillclimb in Switzerland - and for just a few hundred pounds start money. Having ridden there I can confirm that it really is bottom clenchingly scary even now, when the event is supposed to be a demonstration rather than flat out racing.

Mike crashed, breaking his collar bone, as the bike slid sideways on the railway lines which cut through the road. For the avoidance of doubt, there were – and still are – railway lines running right across the track and they are at the bottom of a savage, downhill drop. Imagine Marc Marquez on a works Honda doing the same thing now!

GP riders trying to earn a bit of money on the side wherever they could, explains why I was so fortunate being able to see the best riders in the world battling it out on the 2.8 miles of Oulton Park's ferocious climbs and descents.

The problem was getting into Oulton – and any other big meeting for that matter too. There were two issues – the first one easily soluble and the second much more difficult. Attendances at Oulton for the big events were huge. 73,000 fans came to see the first Bob McIntyre Memorial Event and the queue to get in from the north began at Sandiway traffic lights, a full four miles from the circuit.

In order to see practice, you had to be at Sandiway by 8am at the latest – and 7.30am was preferable. It was then a four mile battle until the last glorious run up to the Bailey Bridge entrance. Now, all the parking is inside the circuit but the crowds were so huge in the 1960s that bikes and cars parked all over the sandy common land surrounding the venue. I always liked putting my bike there for two reasons. First, it made getting out of the circuit vastly quicker and second, I could walk in.

As I have already said, I am uneasy with dishonesty at any level but I also understand the mind-set of people who are desperate. Getting into Oulton without paying was roughly my equivalent of those poor refugees stealing a handful of rice from an aid convoy – wrong, but perhaps comprehensible.

And blagging your way into Oulton without paying was virtually an official Olympic sport in our area!

There were a number of tactics and they all worked - to a greater or lesser degree. At the bottom of the pile in terms of sophistication was the misuse of passes. This was epidemic, with a melee of people leaving the circuit to recycle passes to their well-connected mates. It was fine – but way beyond my status because I couldn't even imagine knowing anyone who had an official pass.

Better, if only for the danger element, was hiding people in vans. I regularly saw six or eight bodies crammed, refugee style, into the back of a small Ford Thames van plus, of course, two bikes and everything necessary to go racing.

I have seen vans stagger into paddocks with their bellies almost dragging on the floor, there were so many illegal bodies inside - and then watched them unload like one of the Benny Hill films, where a couple of hundred people come out of a telephone box.

The fit, brave young men climbed over the wall but this was dangerous because there was glass on the top. It was also a good seven feet (2m) drop to land on the other side and, very often, the welcoming committee was either Cheshire Police or Oulton Park Security.

Then there was my method which required no physical skill at all – just the ability to stay calm under pressure and have a clearly thought out plan for the whole operation.

This is how it was done. The ticket booth was on the far side of the Bailey Bridge, inside the circuit. All that was required was to walk slowly and calmly up to the booth, taking care not to push or shove. Being totally normal, relaxed and utterly unremarkable was essential. At the booth, I'd look behind at someone a bit older than me and say: "He's getting 'em…" and then just walk through: no rushing, no tension or anything which smelled of dishonesty.

The key thing was that there was just one poor bloke taking the money – and about twenty zillion people wanting to get in. Usually, absolutely nothing happened and, by the time the penny had dropped, I had melted into the crowd.

Occasionally, he tried to leave his post and was almost buried by the wall of dishonest spectators making the best of the opportunity. Once or twice, he tried shouting the Oulton equivalent of "Stop, thief!"

At this point, I would stare fixedly at some older lad, and preferably a gobby one, who had clearly been trying to gain dishonest access to the track.

Then, quickly but without rushing, I would fade into the crowd – just another faintly scruffy, wax cotton jacket clad youngster clutching a faded khaki cloth gas mask bag.

Once inside Oulton, I was in heaven – quite literally transported to a world of colour and sound and smells which were from another part of the Multiverse. I abhor noisy road bikes, and I strongly feel that motorcyclists should be good neighbours with the rest of community, but the militancy which is now felt against noise in racing seems to have pushed the pendulum too far in the other direction.

When I stood at the bottom of Knicker Brook, and heard the calico-tearing wail of the four cylinder works Hondas, or the sibilant whispering urgency of a factory Suzuki, my soul was lifted. The snarls and defiant growls of the British, single cylinder Grand Prix bikes from Matchless, Norton and AJS penetrated deep inside me with all the emotional intensity of an opera fan listening to Wagner's Ring Cycle or Handel's Messiah. The only difference in the experiences is that, generally speaking, motorcyclists can't articulate the majesty of what we feel whilst those with interests in the more traditionally middle class arts can.

At the end of every visit to Oulton, or Mallory Park – and the same admission system worked there too – I would come back a changed young man, ears ringing from the cry of the mythical warhorses I had seen in battle. The scent of their Castrol "R" imbued bodies clung to me when I returned to the grey and magnolia hued prison of my everyday life. What I saw and heard wasn't the way out – but the images were indelibly painted on the far horizon of what could be possible if only…

*****

Road racing wasn't only the sport in the Cheshire Centre – very far from it. One of my favourites was grass track racing because the area was an absolute hotbed for "grassers", attracting huge crowds and very high class entries.

I was recently talking to John Cox, one of the North-West's top grass track racers and a true international superstar. He said: "Racing in the Cheshire Centre was some of the best grass tracking in the world and a normal 500 final was more like a World Championship than Centre racing."

Grass tracking is a sibling of speedway but rather than being run on smooth, prepared tracks inside stadia, a grass track can be staged anywhere there is grass and some space. Some grass tracks are run on billiard table smooth surfaces but others have going as rough as a motocross track. At one end of the scale, a track might be an almost perfect oval with wide, sweeping corners, whilst others can consist of two straights linked by a pair of hairpin corners.

A few grass tracks are even run on hills. These are known as mountain grass tracks and provide spectacular sport for both riders and spectators.

Grass bikes are cousins of speedway machines but with minimalist, rubber band suspension, just enough to deal with the worst of the bumps. The top machine to have was a Hagon chassis – a proper, grass racing product – powered by a 500cc JAP 4B engine. The engine was an ancient British design, dating from the 1930s but was still very effective on grass tracks right into the 1970s.

The JAPs ran on methanol, an alcohol fuel derived from wood and universally known in grassing as dope – and, remember, marijuana hadn't reached the vast majority of the population in the 1960s! A dope burning engine runs on a very high compression ratio – JAP 4Bs needed 15:1 – and produces immense torque at low revs. A standard JAP engine made around 45hp at an astonishingly low 5,000 rpm and powered the ubiquitous Hagon chassis. A Hagon JAP weighed only 200lbs or so, 90kgs – and was capable of warp speed acceleration.

The fastest JAP engines in the world were produced right near to us, in Frodsham, by Jimmy Rawlinson – although southern based tuners would dispute his primacy! Jimmy's motors were making almost 50hp. He sponsored some of the finest riders in the country such as Peter Collins, who later became World Speedway Champion, and the legendary Chris Pusey - both of whom were regular entrants in Cheshire grass tracks.

The great Baybutt brothers – both multiple British champions - came down from Wigan and Terry Owen and Frank Pottenger headed north from Wales for many Cheshire Centre events.

Of them all, the greatest was Chris Pusey who rode grass bikes with a flair and verve which was breath-taking – imagine George Best or Diego Maradona on two wheels! Chris was also a gentle, courteous, kind person who I got to know well and liked tremendously. Tragically, alcohol dominated his life and he died of liver failure in 2002 – a calamitous waste of a God given talent.

I later became quite a decent grass track racer – but racing a motocross bike. I'll come to this a bit later in the story but for now I would like to take you to a typical grass track of the time.

The first thing that you would notice is the informality of the event. Once you have either paid your admission, or blagged your way in as a "friend" of a rider, every part of the event is open. In the paddock, you will see even the great riders of the day working on their bikes, chatting to each other or to friends and spectators. The atmosphere is hugely egalitarian and welcoming.

The bikes are everywhere in the paddock and there is no VIP parking or reserved areas. The thoroughbreds are the Hagon JAPs, with both 350cc and 500cc engines. 250cc BSA engines, again running on dope, are the dominant power plant for the smallest class.

The best bikes are well prepared but never immaculate, showing the scars of battles fought in the mud and dust.

You will hear the same sort of braaahhh, braaahhh, braaahhh of racing singles being warmed up but the notes will be softer than those made by the Manx Nortons and Matchless G50s at Oulton Park. Dope engines run on straight, unsilenced pipes but the methanol softens the edge to their cry.

Tucked away somewhere, you might even see an odd motocross bike ridden by those of us who liked competing on the grass. Perhaps Jim Meadows will be there with his immaculate, red Matchless Metisse or Johnny

Done, come to take prize money home with his 250 Husqvarna. There might even be me and my beloved works BSA – hoping for a fast start and the chance of keeping the grass bikes at bay for six laps.

Everywhere will be the sweet smell of methanol fused with castor oil: dope and Castrol "R", the intoxicating perfume of grassing!

Spectator viewing is incredibly good with only a couple of ropes separating you from the action. The 500 final comes to the start line - which is an elastic tape pulled drum tight across the track and released by a pin from a post in the centre.

Riders jostle for position on the start line, and waves of bellowing snarls from the barely restrained JAP engines rampage across the track. Everyone is tense, hunched forward on their bikes to keep the front wheel from lifting, eyes fixed on the starting pin in the centre of the line.

Revs are kept at a constant level for a few seconds and then the pin is released by the starter. Before his hand has fully pulled the release rope, riders have dropped the clutches on their Hagons, pushing back the elastic tape whilst desperately trying not to break it which would cause the start to be red flagged, stopped and re-run.

A wall of sound and a wave of grass cuttings sweeps over you, as the JAPs launch off the line and you cheer on your chosen rider to pitch his bike later, braver, more skilfully into the first corner - which is jammed with twelve ferocious riders.

The sliders like Johnny Cox run wide whilst peg huggers, such as the cerebral Dave Baybutt, ride a more technical race and then, through the middle charges the immortal Chris Pusey. Chris has made a bad start because he didn't get a good position on the start line. When he should have been in the collecting box, getting ready to go out to the line, he was working on a clubman's 250 BSA and had forgotten about the big money final. This is why he arrives at the corner mid-pack.

The cheers of the crowd bounce off the natural arena as Chris lays his Hagon down almost on its side. His forearms are bare, with his polka dot patterned leathers flapping around. A tattered scarf streams out from his neck. There is no mistaking Pusey in all his war gear glory.

He tears after the leaders and, on the second corner, drops his Hagon even harder into the loose surfaced bend. Now, he's hanging off the bike – right arm tight against his body, stretching the throttle cable almost to breaking point – left arm straight, fighting the immense slide.

The JAP engine snarls and Chris' Hagon rears up like a stallion ready for battle. The bike is still laid over at an angle which must result in a crash but Chris climbs forward and out over the machine, balancing the roaring, bucking, 200lbs of metal with the delicacy of an ice skater in a final pirouette.

He charges through the field, achieving the impossible for the five remaining laps and then finishes with an enormous wheelie, to the delight of the huge crowd baying their approval.

"Racing is life. Anything before or after is just waiting . . ."

Chris Pusey – one of the great motorcycle racers of all time – in a Cheshire Centre meeting with riders of my humble calibre. What could be better?

$$\ast\ast\ast\ast\ast$$

We weren't in one of the prime areas for observed trials in the country. The epi-centre of these tests of balance and throttle control was further east and north than us – in the rocks and bogs of Yorkshire. Nevertheless, there were a lot of trials events and I enjoyed watching some of them.

My favourite was the Northern Experts Trial which was held high in the Pennine Hills above Macclesfield. In a trials event, competitors have to ride through very rough sections of rocks or mud without stopping or putting a foot down.

Now, what can be done with a trials bike is simply incredible. No, even this word does not do justice to the unbelievable athleticism and physical courage of the riders as they clear immense, vertical climbs or ride over rocks which would defy the bravest mountaineer.

Things were very different in the late 1960s with the tests, called sections, being very difficult but still comprehensible to a rider of my ability – whereas I look at a modern trial and thank heaven that I'm not riding!

Trials were also very egalitarian. Many road racers took part in trials during the winter, for fun and to keep fit, and some were very good. The greatest of all these multi-talented riders was Sammy Miller, who rode for FB Mondial in road racing Grands Prix and then dominated both British and European trials as a works rider for Ariel, Bultaco and Honda.

Sammy was also responsible for the immense changes which were taking place as I sat on the rocks above Dane Bower, watching the end of one era and the beginning of the next. There were some of the dinosaurs still competing, in the form of the chuffing, panting, siblings of steam engines. These were the British big singles produced by AJS, Matchless, Ariel and Royal Enfield. Riders guided these great carthorses over the rocks and up the climbs, more in a spirit of co-operation than domination. Their exhaust notes were soft and anthropomorphic, and the scents of baking mud and steaming grass seemed a wholly natural part of the Pennine environment.

But these creatures were on their last gasp. The future lay in the lightweight two-strokes from Greeves, Dot and Cotton along with their younger, athletic riders who forced their nimble machines through sections with an aggression which could never be achieved on one of the big, single cylinder four-strokes.

In their way, even the British two-strokes showed their past – rather than pointing to the future. They were, universally, powered by modified versions of the Villiers 32A road engine – a crude thing which even found its way into Bond mini-cars.

By contrast, when Sammy Miller finally left Ariel to join the Spanish

Bultaco factory he developed a proper, thoroughbred trials machine – the Sherpa. This was the bike to have.

The problem with trials for me was two-fold. First, I lacked the riding skill. I could ride well off-road, and, later, I did win a few trophies but I was better at racing than the mind games which are so vital in trials.

There are no start lines, roaring engines or adrenaline rushes in trials – simply intense concentration and self-discipline and, when it came to motorcycle sport, I was somewhat lacking in both departments!

*****

Motocross, or scrambling as it was sometimes known at the time, was far more to my liking. I wanted to be involved in elbow to elbow battles, and the sheer intensity of racing left me keen to have a go. With the touching naivety of the really, really simple minded, motocross also looked easier than trials and the bikes were much cheaper than road race machines - which was really what I fancied doing most of all.

Motocross was on the cusp of seminal change as much as trials. The two leading British factories were the Manchester based Dot works and Greeves down at Thundersley in Essex. Of the two, Greeves were by far the larger and had developed their own engine to replace the motocross version of the Villiers 32A power plant. The Challenger, as Greeves called their new bike, was far more advanced than the models it replaced but the chassis was still outdated.

The bikes to have were purpose built models from Husqvarna and CZ – marques which dominated World Championship motocross. Bultaco and Montesa were also actively selling proper racing machines. By the end of the 1960s and beginning of the 1970s, motocross and off-road sport in general had reached epidemic proportions – the desire for new dirt bikes was insatiable.

I want to divert from the main story at this point with two anecdotes which are indicative of the mess the British industry was in at the time.

Nick Nicholson, who was Greeves' sole importer along America's west coast, could not satisfy the demand for bikes and was also conscious that the machines he was selling were falling behind the opposition. In particular, Husqvarna had the west coast off-road market by the throat.

He offered to fund a brand new Greeves model in its entirety with an initial order sufficient to pay for all the design, development and tooling: everything! Greeves would then have a competitive machine to sell to the rest of the world without needing to make any further investment. The reaction of Bert Greeves was that the Thundersley factory would have needed a complete re-organisation to cope with the additional work - so thanks, but no thanks.

The company closed in 1977, albeit following a fire, but in reality it was because no-one wanted a Greeves by this time.

I had a similar experience. By the time I was twenty-one years old, I was working for three American magazines and had achieved some degree of fame – although I could never have imagined this when I was painting shelves and standing outside the Odeon waiting for K.

My editor forwarded a letter to me from a West Coast entrepreneur – the action really was California based – who wasn't in the bike trade but wanted to buy 200 dirt bikes, cash up front and in one order.

I knew the Dot (Devoid of Trouble) factory in Ellesmere Street, Manchester, quite well - and on many fronts. It was a strange place, arranged on four floors – or maybe even five – of what, I think, was an old cotton mill and was located right in the city centre.

Dots featured an interesting leading link suspension which actually worked very well for the time. In fact, I would have happily ridden a Dot when I first began racing – and I could have had one of the best specification machines on an interesting form of Hire Purchase. I was introduced to a lad who worked in the Dot stores and he was stealing a complete bike, bit by bit, every day - or every few days if it was a difficult week. The idea was that I would pay for each part as it arrived in Warrington, and eventually I would have a complete bike.

I didn't have the money for the project but, even if I had, this was real, unequivocal theft – not re-cycling some scrap bits in exchange for the much loved "drink" – and I wouldn't entertain it.

The whole Dot operation was hugely under-funded and amateurish in the extreme. I remember being given a tour of the R&D department on one visit to the factory. The centre piece was a frame with the top loops cut out so that an engine could be bolted in quickly and then run up on a crude work bench.

The company was owned by a man called Burnard Scott Wade who had joined Dot in 1932 – and had ideas firmly rooted in 19th century England. I phoned Dot and, with the utmost courtesy, pitched my idea to Mr Scott Wade. I could get full retail price, not a trade deal, for 200 Dot scramblers and out of the £200 selling price I wanted £5. I was still at college so £1,000 would have been a huge amount of money, bearing in mind that a nice, detached bungalow in a posh area of Warrington was somewhere around £5,000.

Equally, my reasoning was that my £5 commission was coming out of the retail, not trade, price and Dot were still going to get an additional £4,000 over and above what they would have sold the bikes at themselves.

Burnard Scott Wade went into low earth orbit and said that I had no right to expect anything at all and that I should be honoured to give Dot, a proud British company, the business. Further, at my age, I should show respect for my elders and betters.

The truth is that I was proud to be giving Dot the deal and I was equally happy that they should do very well out of it. But I was starting to grow up and part of this new found maturity was that I wanted some reward for my initiative.

I also resented receiving a lecture. If Dot had been half switched on, they could have put three bikes in a van and driven up the Pacific Coast Highway, visiting Californian dealers, and sold 10,000 machines. But they didn't and so it was left to me to put a deal together – and, student or not, I wanted a reward for my proactive efforts. The end result was a stand-off: Dot didn't get the order and I didn't get paid - something which has always struck me as a stupid outcome from something which could have been beneficial all round.

*****

I need to mention sand racing - a form of motorcycle racing which was concentrated in the North-West of England and which, later, was to play a seminal part in my life. It was very popular at the time too.

As the name implies, sand racing was held on the beach at low tide when the sea was, usually at least, a long way from the track. I loved racing on the beach for a number of reasons – the speed, the joy of power sliding the bike around the two oval corners which linked the long straights, but most of all for its militantly egalitarian ethos.

Everybody in our area rode the sand on one bike or another. The beaches were really hard packed when the tide withdrew so my friend Sammy Green could race his standard, road going, 200cc Ariel Arrow complete with road tyres.

Serious competitors preferred road racing machines and these were the fastest, particularly on the long straights of the mile oval at Ainsdale. They lost out to the motocross machines on corners and so it was a fascinating battle of compromises. The usual winners were hybrids – motocross chassis with dope burning engines.

I won a fair few races on the beach because I loved the speed and was good at sliding a bike. The sand gripped a knobbly tyre beautifully and it was tremendous fun to have the back end hanging out on a motocross bike, Chris Pusey style.

But winning anything was a long way in the future because the only way was up from the start of my competition career – and very slowly too!

*****

Because motorcycles were so much more mainstream they had a level of acceptability, from every part of society, which isn't here today. Things were also generally more easy-going. On one occasion, I was taking my motocross bike across the other side of town, to a lad who had a range of springs for the Norton Long Roadholder forks which the bike used. There were three sensible options. The first would have been to borrow the springs and then play with them in my garage at home or, alternatively, take the fork legs to him for his expert advice. Option #3 was that I could have loaded the bike on to the trailer and transported it this way - but then I would have had to fix the puncture in one of the trailer wheels, which would have been a lot of mither for a four mile trip.

Of course, the one thing not to do would be to ride it there – so, clearly, this is what I did. I duct taped the number plate from a BSA Bantam which had briefly passed through my hands, to the rear mudguard and a different plate from some other bike to the front forks, because two identification plates were still needed at this time.

The final, and very token, nod towards road legality was to Jubilee-clip a speedometer, salvaged from some old wreck, to the cross brace on the handlebar. I added a bit of knackered cable and tucked the loose end away, out of harm's way, beneath the fuel tank. Et voila - a fully illegal road bike!

I did ride sensibly – no manic wheelies or excessive speed – and so, at 8am on a Sunday morning I hoped to slip through the centre of Warrington unnoticed. It was a forlorn hope. Outside the National Westminster Bank, right in the centre of town, a Police Triumph Speed Twin, in the universal maroon colour beloved by every force in the country, pulled alongside me and motioned me on to the kerb.

The officer, who clearly knew his bikes, took a walk round my fake road machine – and I tensed myself for the onslaught. He was particularly interested in the all alloy Tiger 100 engine.

"Nice bike…"

"Thanks, I'm just taking it to have the forks done."

"I raced a Tiger 100 in the Manx."

"Wow! That must have been great."

"Not that great actually. It threw a rod and I ended up sliding down the road after Ginger Hall."

He took another tour and, without doubt, was totting up the errors and omissions.

"Look, you ride carefully and get home as soon as you can because I don't want to see you again.

"Got that?"

I nodded vigorously. "Yes Sir. Thanks Sir. Thanks."

He grinned: "I like scrambling so I'll keep an eye out in case I ever see a bike like yours racing."

In fact, I did take the gypsies' warning and rode the bike back home along the canal towpaths, as many motorcycling miscreants of the day did, safe in the dark and blessedly thick fog which was so common in Warrington winters.

*****

Shortly afterwards came an incident which reached legendary proportions amongst Warrington bike racers, so much so that people actually visited the spot where it began. I did - just to get the full flavour of the epic tale.

I have already mentioned Warrington smog and on this evening it was a real pea-souper. The thickest of these blankets fell along Warrington's many canals and the River Mersey.

On this occasion, "Jim" had been enjoying a drink, or five, in the Saracen's Head. Interestingly, the pub is just across the road from the site of Veratinum, the busy Roman port on the banks of the River Mersey. I know this because I did a dig there when I was a history student and found a very large Roman nail, which is my total claim to fame in the archaeology business. In the normal, and accepted, management style prevalent in the 1960s, the dig supervisor took many extended breaks from the hard work - in the Saracen's Head! However, back to the tale of derring-do.

When the story was retold, Jim always insisted that he wasn't drunk - and remember that, at this time, the drink driving laws were much more liberal than they are today - but he did admit that perhaps he was not at his Oulton Park, starting grid sharpest.

He crossed the road from the Saracen's Head and made his way carefully down Wilderspool Causeway into town. It wasn't the easiest task in the dark and thick fog, along with six pints of Greenall's finest bitter adding their own layer of obfuscation. Although the river had long since been diverted, just where the ancient ford to Veratinum used to be the mist hung particularly densely.

At the side of the road, having a fag break in his brand new Ford Anglia Panda police car, was "Steve" – another bike racer.

Panda cars were state-of-the-art police technology at the time. They were all basic cars, like the Ford Anglia or the Morris 1100, and stood out because they were blue, with a big white stripe down the centre, across the roof and down over each front door: hence the colloquial name of Panda. The aim was to raise the visibility of the police wherever they went and so deter criminals. Steve was obsessively proud of his factory fresh Panda – and delighted that he was no longer pounding the pavements on foot or panting to the scene of a crime on his police issue bicycle.

Jim was driving an ancient Triumph Herald – one of the more mediocre examples of British automotive engineering. The vehicle had two interesting design features which are particularly salient to this story.

First, all Heralds were constructed from paper thin steel which could be dented just by looking it aggressively. The cars were also very prone to rust. Jim's Triumph had been heavily attacked in this way, reducing the strength of the under engineered steel even further.

The ventilation system was also dreadful, with a weak dribble of air always failing to remove any mist from the windscreen.

So, Jim is edging his way into town, steering with one hand, and wiping the fog from the inside of the windscreen with the other. In fact, Jim insisted that he was still in full control when he rammed the off-side of the shiny new Panda car.

With one mighty bound, Steve leaps out of the Panda car, truncheon and handcuffs at the ready, so that he can arrest the foul felon who has smacked his pride and joy.

Then he's faced with his race mate...

A damage assessment is made. The Herald has taken what appears to be a real hit with the left-hand wing well and truly walloped but the Panda car, in all its pristine Ford glory, has merely had the rear lights whacked in and an extended scratch along the side. In fact, nothing that would stop anyone from going racing the following day if it were towing a trailer. Critically, there is a healthy line of bright red Herald paint smeared down the side of the Panda car.

A hurried conference follows. Steve explains that he is going to investigate a very suspicious noise at the rear of the houses which back on to the old River Mersey. When he returns, he will report the hit and run accident on his car.

They don't do man hugs, or anything like, because these haven't been invented in Warrington yet, but there is a very hurried handshake and the promise of a drink at the next race meeting. This is proof positive, if proof were ever needed, of the bond which exists amongst racers.

Steve heads off down towards the river and Jim gets back into his Triumph and pulls away ever so slowly. Jim lives on the other side of town but the fog is getting thicker by the second so it's just a question of trickling down Wilderspool Causeway at walking pace, over the bridge and then getting the Herald out of sight, under a tarpaulin sheet, until it can be sorted out much later. Truly *The Great Escape*, Warrington bike racer style.

Steve returns to his cherished Panda car, gets on the all-new in-car radio, and reports the incident to Warrington Police Station. No-one has much hope of catching the culprit but all the boxes have been ticked. With one seriously good deed being done by one racer to another, Steve lights up another fag and practises the story he's going to tell the lads back at the Station. As the fog gets ever thicker, the strength of the tale increases in its credibility and the job is done.

Meanwhile, Jim is properly stressed out with the collision, the ever thickening fog and the not wholly helpful fact that the Herald's weedy demister has now packed up altogether. Together, these factors lead to real navigational challenges, and when he drifts into the centre of the road the problems hit peak proportions because now, neither pavement can be seen.

The attack on the Panda car had not gone wholly unnoticed. Two members of the thin blue line are on their first ever shift in a gleaming new Ford Transit Police van – still with that lovely, super-new plasticy smell inside and no bits of dead sandwich in the footwell. They are parked up at the bottom of Bridge Street, just the other side of the river from Wilderspool Causeway, when they pick up the message about a potential hit and run driver not too far away from them.

In a flash, well, quite a slow flash because they can barely see the Trannie's bonnet in front of them, they grope their way over the bridge and bear left, in front of the bus depot, and head up Wilderspool Causeway towards St James' Church – which is almost precisely the point Jim has reached, driving with his left hand whilst attempting, and failing, to clear the mist from the windscreen with his right.

In fact, he is still trying to see through the almost completely obscured windscreen when he whacks the right hand side, front wing of the gleaming new police Transit – this time with a proper belt.

England's finest leap from the Trannie in a state of considerable angst and then see said red Triumph Herald, not only with what's left of the right-hand side front wing hanging off but also the left side dinged.

T' job's a good 'un. Out come the handcuffs and off Jim goes to Warrington Police Station whilst the Fire Brigade are left to clean up the mess.

Back at the Station, Steve momentarily catches Jim's eye – but not a word is said. In fact, it's better than nothing. The six month driving ban handed down by Warrington Magistrates takes Jim right into the start of next season, so Steve acts as chauffeur for the first half dozen meetings – and for free. How good was that?

Chapter Eleven

Onwards, Upwards, Sideways and Backwards

Before I could go racing I had to climb the very steep, rocky and dangerous mountain path of getting some money, and my record in this respect wasn't brilliant. However, things were about to change.

Everyone is an expert today and, with access to a Twitter account, you can become an instant world-wide celebrity. I'm not bright enough to say anything of value in the length of the average Twitter message, which is 33 characters, except "Yes please," when Carol offers to make a cup of coffee so I guess that I should be excluded from having an opinion on anything. Regardless, I will take a chance in this book if only because the voice of the ordinary person is so rarely heard in today's frenetic cacophony of special interest groups.

I think that when I was growing up it was far easier for a very ordinary person to break out of the social group into which they were born and raised, and do something different – and maybe even better.

Now, we even have a shed full of highly paid Social Mobility Commissioners, but in 1965 all of the available help came from kind people who saw something in me that not even I recognised. Despite my family background, my shyness and social ineptitude there must have been some dim, yellow spark barely visible in the black background of ordinariness which made me worth a bet – even if it was a 1000:1 long shot.

I wonder now if the same chances are available to equally ordinary kids who are not members of any special interest group or minority, and don't see the only way out as an appearance on Love Island or Gogglebox.

But that is now – and I was lucky.

I don't know how I realised that I had a business brain but somehow it dawned on me that a profit could be made from selling second-hand bike bits. Remember that I was living on £5 a week so 50p profit was a lot of money – and I did start to acquire a steady flow of ten bobs (50p).

I was a particular whizz at selling the Villiers engines which powered a lot of the smaller British manufacturers' bikes, and soon I had accumulated £25 capital.

The next step was equally important. I had a bank account with the Midland, right in the centre of Warrington and near to the infamous Army and Navy Store. For a kid from my background, the next step was unusual: I went to see the manager at the Midland Bank. I can't imagine why I did this because I had never met a bank manager in my life and these people, whoever they were, had to be so important that they descended daily from Mount Olympus! Regardless, I made an appointment and duly arrived in my tweed sports jacket and tie, and freshly brushed Hush Puppy suede shoes. Then I made my pitch directly to the branch manager himself. What a difference from today where a computer scores every overdraft! In those happy days, a keen young person could appeal straight to someone who could use their personal discretion to make a reasoned decision and then help, or not, based on merit.

I asked for a £15 loan to go with my £25, to enable me to buy a BSA Gold Star scrambler - and still live whilst it was being sold. At the time, £15 was an awful lot of money to lend to a young person with no credit rating, no business experience and, for that matter, no business either! Regardless, something must have touched a chord and so I was given my loan.

Just as important, I was also provided with an invaluable lesson in fiscal and business responsibility. The manager explained that the £15 was his money, not mine, and that I was to spend it only on financing this one deal and nothing else. I did not have his permission to do anything else with it – only to buy the Gold Star and then return his money to him in his bank.

To make the loan so personal was such a wonderful lesson to a baby businessman like me. I had been taught, right from the outset, to borrow responsibly, spend responsibly and pay back responsibly too. What a shame the same help isn't available today.

In fact, I bought the "Goldie" for £35. I sold its racing gearbox for £25 and the engine for another £25. Within a week, all the other bits had gone too and for a further £20. I had repaid the bank and, by still watching every penny, I now had £50 capital – and an overdraft facility.

I also had a stroke of luck meeting Sam Green – who was a bit older than me, much more grown up and had a Honda twin. From the outset, Sam was kind to me and even let me ride his Honda - which was a startling experience because the bike was so much more sophisticated than anything I had ever tried before. Intellectually, I thought that the Honda was breath-taking but it couldn't possibly be any good because it wasn't British: that was the mind set prevalent amongst a lot of us at the time.

But it wasn't the Honda which impressed me most – not by a long way! Sam lived with his dad in a rather posher council house, in Orford on the other side of Warrington. This had a wash house - a brick outbuilding attached to the back of the house, designed for the woman of the house to do all the family's laundry. When not being used for their intended purpose, wash houses were pre-history versions of today's micro start up units and lots of businesses were launched from them.

I had use of Sam's wash house free of charge, and this was an immense help to my newly born enterprise.

*****

The tiny business not only provided useful additional income but it also helped me find myself – and on a number of levels too. Perhaps the most important discovery was that I didn't fit into any of the conventional slots that I should have occupied.

A centre for young people to meet in Warrington was the Hoagie Waggon - a catering van selling burgers and coffee. It was located by the Ritz Cinema, next to the River Mersey. At the time the river was so polluted that falling in would probably have killed you! The Hoagie sold basic, cheap food, played music and attracted both motorcyclists and scooter riders.

I visited it on a few occasions but found nothing attractive there. It should have been home ground for me, being with people of roughly my own age with apparently similar interests and of a social class which was similar to my own.

The problem was that I didn't fit in and always felt like an alien visiting a new planet on the Galactic Grand Tour. Yes, I was bike bonkers but I had also developed an almost equally strong passion for Charles Dickens and, when I wasn't reading *Motorcycle News*, you would have found my nose buried in *Great Expectations* or *A Tale of Two Cities* - and chatting about books like these was not likely to be easy at the Hoagie.

It is worth making another observation which is, sort of at least, tied into the Hoagie Waggon. With the current interest in the Retro scene, and particularly the association with motorcycles, there is a wholly erroneous view being developed that motorcycling in the 1960s was a mass of leather jacketed, badge bedecked Rockers - all riding café racer style bikes.

The truth was very different. There were a few, a very few, café racers running around but there was a lot less faux anything in 1960s Britain. People like me lusted after real road race machines, not pretend ones made from dull bikes turned into café racers. When you had seen Mike Hailwood battle the elements on an unrideable MV Agusta then a 350 Triumph with "Ace" handlebars and a pretend cooling disc, held on to the front hub with bits of wire, looked exactly what it was: fake.

Another thing which was missing was the animosity between Mods, who rode scooters, and Rockers who had motorcycles. I was never bothered, not in the slightest degree, that someone rode a scooter. For sure, I couldn't understand – not for a second – why anyone would want to ride something with two wheels which was slower and handled worse than a bike. But that was their choice.

It has now become fashionable to hype up the Mods versus Rockers battles of 1964 but in truth they were minor affairs, concentrated around the south coast of England. A few hundred kids rode down from London to Brighton or Margate a couple of times, ran around the town shouting and making a nuisance of themselves and there were some nasty scuffles - but that was all.

The anti-Vietnam War protests were on a vastly bigger scale and much more violent. If you want to see a proper riot have a look at the peace protests

- a somewhat ironic sobriquet, in view of what happened outside the American Embassy in Grosvenor Square.

In France, the protests got so bad that the government thought there was going to be a civil war. By contrast, a handful of silly Mods and Rockers really was only a small helping of poppadums before the main course of civil unrest arrived – which, because we were British, it never did.

There was some talk of a northern version of the rocker riots and this was going to be held in the pretty seaside town of Rhyl, on the North Wales coast. I only heard about this third hand but apparently there were not enough rioters to make a decent team for either the Mods or the Rockers so they all sat around, having chips and drinking coffee on the seafront. That was the reality of the Mod/Rocker/Café Racer culture.

There were biker pubs in Warrington and I tried these too. This time the choice was even easier. As a seven or eight year old, I remember standing on the pavement outside the frosted glass window of some pub or other, whilst my mum and dad had a screaming row inside because she had no money for food.

With this experience firmly rooted in my psyche, being on the inside drinking pints, buying "rounds" and shouting a lot held little attraction.

Another blind alley was Warrington Motorcycle Club. This was a big, important and well organised club which met in a large, wooden community building at Appleton, on the outskirts of Warrington. The club was so mainstream, sensible and bike focussed that it should have been home ground for me – but it wasn't.

The idea of someone organising things on my behalf did not sit well with me. I remember that one night we had a talk from a representative of Hepolite, the huge British piston manufacturer. It was really interesting, and afterwards I wanted to ask questions – a lot of questions – but was allowed just one. At the end, the Hepolite bloke was ushered away to talk to the grown-ups on the committee and I found this irritating, and - that trigger word of all trigger words for me - unfair.

I am not blaming the club or its officials for this, because what they did was very reasonable and sensible – and even fair! But being controlled and restricted was not what I wanted, or needed for that matter because, like some alien hoard, there were ideas growing inside my head at an exponential rate.

Another part of club life which was an utter failure, and again the fault was entirely mine, was the club run. Someone decided where we were all going, how fast we should ride and where we should stop. All three of these caveats were an utter anathema to me. I hadn't got my bike licence just to be told by anyone where to ride, for how long and at what speed. Bikes made me free and that freedom wasn't for sale simply to become part of a group – any group.

Things sort of came to a head when I conducted a particularly spirited series of passes dropping down into Ruthin on the A494. In Ruthin, when we had all stopped for a comfort break, one of the club hierarchy took me on one side and, with considerable tact and some kindness, suggested that perhaps club runs didn't suit me.

I was delighted to have been sacked and rode back to Warrington - by heading in the opposite direction, through the Clocaenog Forest and then back home along the A5. Riding in completely the wrong direction to where I was supposed to be going was, perhaps, an apt metaphor for my life at the time.

Strangely, it wasn't club runs, or wanting to be heard, which finally concluded my life as a clubisti. Rather, it was the club notice board. My spares business was going very nicely and Warrington Motorcycle Club had both a substantial membership and a notice board which carried ads for spares and bikes for sale. In my eyes, it was a dream combination.

Things were even better because, invariably, the ads were dire. For someone with a love of words, they were mind numbingly dull – and then some. "For sale. BSA primary chaincase. Will fit BSAs. £5. Ask Jimmy."

I wrote little vignettes about lonely Villiers pistons who wanted a new daddy, and cylinder heads so beautiful that the Queen really wanted one for her jewel collection. I also wrote satire – not great material but good practice for my later life. In short, my ads stood out as being miles better than the opposition – and this was not good.

This time, I was actually summoned before the committee and had my first formal ban – for placing what was considered to be commercial ads on a noticeboard reserved for club members. I should have taken a photo or secured some other memento, because getting banned was going to become a very regular occurrence in the rest of my life but I just shrugged and walked away. If getting banned was the price to pay for being cleverer than everyone else, and working harder, then so be it. I was fed up with club life, with all its constraints, because I wanted to be a racer.

★★★★★

Wanting to race does not describe my state of mind at all well. You might want a cup of coffee at break time or an early dinner if you are starving. Perhaps you might fancy a new, posh leather jacket or seeing Jim Redman with his Honda 4 at Oulton Park. Moving up a gear, you could dream of a date with the lovely S, having just received a bonus for burning RSJs successfully all week. All these are wants.

Racing wasn't like this – not at all. I wanted to race so badly that I used to go to sleep, fitfully because I have never slept well, with the snarl of race engines in my ears. I would brush my teeth accompanied by the scent of Castrol "R", not minty gel, and stand patiently whilst some boss or other berated me for whatever sin I had committed that hour/day/week and see not an angry face but a chequered flag. In short, I was a hard core addict before I had even sent in my first entry form.

The problem was that if a list of ten attributes for a prospective racer were drawn up then, in March 1966, I wouldn't have had even one of them. I lacked knowledge, riding experience, mechanical ability and I had no friends or contacts who knew anything about motorcycle sport. But I did read *Motorcycle News*, and I had been to local scrambles meetings and seen my heroes Johnny Done, on his little 250 Dot, and Brian Nadin with his mighty 650cc Triumph engined Metisse, battle it out - and that looked a lot of fun. From the trackside, there seemed to be little reason why I couldn't do just as well, if not better. Isn't that what all addicts think when they're sure that they will be the one who can manage to take drugs safely?

The first issue was a bike – and with almost no budget. During lunch break, one of the fitters said that his mate owned a BSA scrambler which had been built from a B33 road bike. I could have this fine steed for a mere £15.00. I was near to tears with delight. There were only two slight snags. First I could only buy the bike from the farm where it resided after 10pm, and second, he had mis-laid all the registration documents that went with the BSA, careless person that he was.

So off I chuffed on the AJS, along to the farm where the GP-bike-in-waiting resided. The farmhouse lay near to the East Lancs Road, one of North-West England's top areas for the redistribution of goods liberated from the cities of Liverpool and Manchester. The bike was underneath a large piece of sacking in the barn, and my guided tour of it lasted all of three seconds. A quick flash of the torch revealed a knobbly rear tyre – so I knew for certain it was a genuine ex-works, Gold Star scrambler worth at least £300 – then the sacking was returned and I was relieved of my money. Straight afterwards I was given a hand to push my AJS down the farm track for 200 metres before starting it, so as not to wake my new friend's elderly mother of course. And no, I wasn't even vaguely suspicious. Delivery was promised in the very near future.

In fact the service was excellent. When I woke up the next morning, there was my shining new racer lying on its side in the front garden of our council house. Only it wasn't new and it wasn't shining and it wasn't a racer either! To be exact, it was an iron engined BSA B33 road bike with a prehistoric 3.50 x 19" Dunlop knobbly on the back wheel as its sole concession to off-road use.

Perhaps the most amazing thing about the whole story is that I wasn't even very disappointed. It had a big 500cc engine and one knobbly so it couldn't be very far off a racer could it?

A month of total celibacy, and a lot of scrounging, transformed the BSA into a pretend race bike. I met a lad who had been racing a Greeves Hawkstone for a year and he knew everything there was to know in the world about racing off-road. Truly, in the world of the blind, the bloke with a bit of goggle not covered in mud is king!

My new expert mentor explained the importance of fitting an air-filter – previously I had not even a glimmer of an idea what its purpose was – and I had bought a lightweight, steel BSA Bantam tank for five shillings (25p) in a Villiers spares deal. Being employed at Burtonwood – I try to avoid "work" in the same sentence as my period of employment with the Air Ministry – I now had nearly £5.50 a week to spend. This meant that I could also afford a real racing seat and a pair of alloy mudguards – which I mounted high like the trick ones on the works Dots that Northern youths worshipped at this time.

Best of all, one of the fitters at Burtonwood promised to set the timing on the BSA magneto for me so that the bike would start somewhat more easily. However, since he wouldn't come to our house I had to get the bike to work for a lunchtime tuning session. Lacking a van or trailer, this might well have caused a problem, except for the fact that January and February in Cheshire are both very, very foggy months. A route was plotted which took me largely through the back alleys of our housing estate and then on to the towpath of the Sankey St Helens Canal. This in turn led to the rear entrance of Burtonwood Air Base and left only a quick, one mile dash along a public road to get to the site where I worked. Clearly, the joys of CCTV on every corner had not been visited upon us in the Swinging '60s.

It was only a matter of days before a real pea-souper fog, straight out of Sherlock Holmes, hit the Warrington area and the seven-mile journey was completed incident-free – despite the open exhaust pipe. Of course, it did mean sitting outside the hangar until six o'clock on the return journey since the fog had lifted and I had to rely on total darkness for protective cover - but being wet, cold and hungry was no big deal compared with the chance of advancement in the world of racing.

There were still two unresolved issues, one of which I was aware and the other not. The first was a front tyre. Ignorant though I was, even I had managed to work out that an Avon SM road sidecar tyre, so badly worn that it was as smooth as a modern racing slick, was not entirely suitable for off road racing. Here, an interesting anthropological factor arises: is scrounging genetically inbred into racers or is it a case of rapid behaviour modification?

Whatever the cause, I hit the local tyre depot with my first sponsorship sales pitch and they hit me back with a Goodyear Grasshopper 19" front tyre. This example of the worst of American high pressure exporting techniques was originally designed as a lawnmower tyre. It became notorious for inducing speed wobbles – an impressive feat in vehicles with a top speed of 5mph.

I also came away with a powerful ally. The cheap deal came through the good offices of a slightly older lad by the name of Ken Bromley. Ken had a van, some money and he wanted to be a scrambler too. Incredibly, he had even less knowledge and experience than me and was prepared to offer me a lift in his Thames van in return for acting as team manager, secretary and mechanic.

I genuinely worshipped Ken and for a rather strange reason. Although I could sort of drive a car, I didn't yet have a licence. By contrast, Ken drove around in a cloud of ice crystals he was so cool. His favourite method of driving was to slump forward with his elbows through the steering wheel. Forget Carnaby Street, the Kings Road and all the other allegedly hip things. Ken could drive with his elbows through the steering wheel – now that really was cooler than absolute zero!

I did my best to prepare the B33 for the battle ahead but my best was not very good at all. For example, I knew nothing about setting the gearing on an off-road bike. How the bike is geared sets its top speed, acceleration and ability to claw through tough going off road. All motocross bikes are geared very low so that first and second can be used at very slow speeds. Unfortunately, I knew nothing of gearing and my B33 road bike cum pseudo scrambler was still on its original road sprockets, which would give a top speed of 75mph – just a shade high for the average club scramble. Of this, more later.

Ken had bought a Villiers 200cc 9E engined Dot with a genuine 4 speed gearbox – lucky devil having such exotic machinery – so nothing stood in our way. Entry forms were sent off for the Oswestry Club's opening scramble of the 1966 season.

Before I could race, I faced another clothing challenge – two in fact. The first was protective trousers. In the period, bib and brace race jeans were quite popular but real leather ones were mind numbingly expensive and way beyond my wildest dreams. The answer lay in a back street dealer's window in Chester. As I have noted, racing was very much mainstream at the time and so it wasn't bizarrely unusual to find scrambles clothing in the window of a road bike dealer. I think that these jeans must have been a sample, or just forgotten, because one side had been sun bleached to quite a light grey whilst the leg which had been in the shade was still in its original black colour.

Still, I wasn't a fashion icon and the price was good at £5. A fiver for a pair of leather jeans, even multi-hued ones, would have been a steal had they been the product of a cow, or even a sheep. Unfortunately, they weren't any form of leather but PVC – the sort of thing normally worn by boxers who need to shed weight immediately before a fight, or by followers of a particular life-style.

Even so, £5 was really cheap.

I knew that I couldn't race in my ex-dispatch riders' gloves so I scrounged a pair of worn-out work gloves from one of the fitters at work which would do, would have to do, at a push.

My fireman's boots were fine and a work shirt would do for upper body protection, so now I was fully kitted out and good to go.

*****

As I have said, it was dreadfully foggy when we arrived at the hillside course above Oswestry. The whole track was covered in a dense mist and matters were further complicated by an incessant drizzle which fell on to an already soaked course.

Being one of the first competitors to arrive meant that we could have a prime spot right next to the track on some nice, soft ground. The next hour was spent digging the van out and parking it on a timber raft made from fencing to prevent it from sinking out of sight forever!

Scrutineering went ahead without any hitches except for one comment to the effect of, "You're not going to race that!" Since I was very proud of my BSA, I saw no reason not to race it.

After some thought about tyre pressures, Ken and I decided that around 20 psi front and back would be about right since this worked pretty well on the road. Everyone else chose 5psi, the received wisdom for muddy motocross, but what's the problem with being 400% wrong? Ken and I were now good to go racing.

Even now, I can still remember that course better than anything I have ridden since. There was a narrow, off-cambered straight which led into a sharp little right-hand climb. From there, the track peeled off left into a dip, followed by a steep climb of about 50 metres. I don't know what the rest of the course was like since I never did get to see any of it!

With all the confidence of the truly stupid, I burnt off the start line in the first practice session in real GP style. In fact, I did actually lead the pack into the first corner confirming my impression that there wasn't much to scrambling really and that the sport was about to witness the emergence of a new megastar.

I held the "lead" round the first corner and hit the descent with plenty of throttle in first gear. Had I pulled off this manoeuvre on road gearing, I would have been winning prize money that day. Unfortunately, the 385lbs (175kg) of B33 spat me off like a flea when we clanged into the bottom of the drop.

Undeterred, I pushed the BSA back to the paddock in only twenty minutes for, if nothing else, I was razor fit in those days. By this time, I was ready for the second session of practice and a perfect repeat performance. I achieved the hat-trick by managing the same feat in the last session.

By this time, I had actually only ridden the BSA for 300 metres on the track but I was considerably leaner, fitter and more exhausted than three hours earlier. I was also developing a consciousness of having something akin to very strong personal body odour problems, judging from the way marshals were avoiding me.

It would be nice to say that, in the racing, everything came right. However, the truth was very different. I did manage to clear the bottom of the hill on one occasion, only to have the BSA flick me off going up the climb and then hit me on the way down again. And, I might add, a passing swipe from a B33 is not to be sneered at!

An analysis of the day's racing revealed the following. Three practice sessions: three crashes. Total distance covered (on bike), 300 metres. Racing: three starts, three crashes. Total distance covered, (on bike), 325 metres. Front mudguard bent beyond recognition. Hand cut. Leg burnt from BSA rolling on rider. Lost approximately a stone in sweat.

Arriving home, my mum's first words were, "What was it like?" "It was great Mum, really great. And the week after next, we're riding at Whitchurch and I bet I make the final."

As I said, enthusiasm counts for an awful lot and, most importantly of all, I was now a real racer.

Chapter Twelve

Sign on the Dotted Line

I suppose all adolescents have fantasy dreams. The strange limbo state between being a child and a fully-fledged adult is so stressful that the mind inevitably seeks some comfort in escapism. Like other lads of my age, I too used to fantasise - but not of smiling, helpful versions of K. Not even of a Velocette Thruxton with K clinging tightly, and a bit passionately, to me as we swept into Oulton Park, my wallet bulging with sufficient funds to not only pay for the admission but also two bags of chips after practice. No. My dreams were of a four speed gearbox.

One of the greatest obstacles I had to overcome on my way to becoming a super star racer was a rabid enthusiasm which absolutely annihilated all and any common sense. However, the problems associated with scrambling an all iron B.33, complete with lawnmower tyres, had finally managed to impress themselves even on my brain – and that took some doing in those days!

Yet even at this very early stage, the first foetal signs of the racer's cunning were beginning to make themselves felt. After the great Oswestry disaster, in which I had managed to ride all of 300 metres, all day, aboard the great iron carthorse, it became apparent that I needed something lighter and more raceable. So I managed to sell the BSA at a vast profit to my best mate, whose van I also shared. After all, what are mates for? In fact, I almost doubled the value of the bike and came away with a killing, amounting to some £10 – very well worth having at the time.

So, now I had £25, Ken had the BSA - and the world was my oyster. Well, at least my baby mussel! The next step in the exercise was to buy a bike at a good price and leave myself with a cash surplus. Ken had heard about a Dot which was for sale, and offered to take me to see it in his van so that the prize could be recovered instantly if we decided to make the purchase.

Immediately I saw the bike, I fell in love with it. As may be seen, I had a very distinct hormone imbalance. My glands were all working flat out making some secretion which made me weak-kneed at the sight of a Dot scrambler, rather than attractive young ladies.

One would have to be very deeply in love to admire this particular bike. Originally, it was a mid-1950s model, powered - although this is a gross over-statement - by a 197cc, three speed, Villiers 8E engine producing something in the region of 5 or 6 bhp when crisp and fresh and markedly less in the knackered state of this particular specimen. But, and this was the big thing, it had the latest front forks, as used by the works Dots.

Please believe me when I say that I saw nothing strange in a tired old bike having brand-new, works type forks, nor did I make any connection with the fact that the owner's cousin was a stores-assistant at the Dot factory. Not even the present incumbent's furtive glances, and his frantic willingness for me to remove the bike as soon as possible, raised the slightest suspicion of any potential problems. In fact, I congratulated myself on being a real ace wheeler-dealer in having beaten him down in price from £25 to £20. Had I realized how close Manchester CID were to making an arrest, I could have probably got him to pay me to take the bike away. Nevertheless, I now had a new bike – a real racing one too – and a £5.00 surplus. Life was looking good.

The Dot was a vast improvement over the BSA, particularly in terms of handling. For the first time, I could actually go downhill without babbling prayers and because of its extremely light weight, probably some 200lbs (90 kgs) less than the BSA, bumps could be tackled in safety. The drawback was the power, or rather the lack of it. Even now, I can clearly remember the way that revs crawled up to a peak of about 4,000 at which point, the snail-like acceleration ceased altogether and the motor began gasping for breath. A gear change then had to be made so that the next crawl could begin, and the momentum continued. The major snag in this exercise was the three speed gearbox.

The gear change itself was ponderous and inaccurate, making any but the most leisurely of changes totally impossible, but the really insurmountable obstacle lay in the huge gap between first and second. The decayed state of the motor prevented sufficient rpm being built up in first to enable second gear to be engaged and thus allow the bike to pull away, nor was there sufficient torque for second gear to be used without the engine screaming. To put things into perspective, 5bhp is less than a 50cc scooter. Only when the surface was absolutely flat, or better still downhill, could second be used effectively, after which third gear was no problem since it lay comparatively close to the ratio beneath.

The team's next outing should have been at Crewe but as we were loading the B.33 into Ken's van, it slipped and the solid bar footrest bit him on the leg – and quite badly too. The injury not only prevented him from driving the van but also kept him off work for a week.

Since the BSA was a sensitive beast, we were sure that it had taken umbrage at being sold and was now going to wreak vengeance on both Ken and me. These competition thoroughbreds are very highly-strung animals and cannot be treated with too much respect!

Two weeks later, we were on a beautiful, grassy circuit at Whitchurch. When I picture that course in my mind, I always feel sorry for modern racers who have never known the pleasure of competing on rolling grass. They miss a real treat since it is one of the best surfaces of all to race on – especially when, as in the case of Whitchurch, it had been mown really short by a flock of sheep.

It soon became apparent that not only could I complete a lap but I could also manage several laps in succession: stardom here we come! What was even more amazing was that I could, almost, race other no hopers who were wobbling round at the back of the pack. Thus, the prospect of not only finishing a race, or perhaps even several races if good fortune shone upon me, but also of not finishing last, became a very real hope.

The problem – and throughout my racing career even when I have ridden Internationals there always has been at least one – was the hill just before the finishing line. To be quite honest, it wasn't much more than what, in modern parlance, would be called a double jump but sat on the bottom, astride a 200cc Dot with a three speed gearbox, it was inarguably a fully grown hill.

Worse still, it was absolutely the wrong length and angle to fit the power and gear ratios of my Dot which I thought was a very unreasonable act on the part of the organizers. Given the unbelievably low maximum rpm of which the Dot was capable, first was far too low and because of the complete absence of power, second was too high. The only solution was to use first gear and foot vigorously, like a Tour de France cyclist without pedals.

Using these tactics in practice proved not only that I was one extremely fit young man, but also that I was not going to stay healthy for much longer if I insisted on legging the Dot around whilst wearing the PVC jeans. Little wonder they were cheap: at the end of a race, I could literally pour sweat out of them, and my weight was dropping discernibly each time I rode.

Not only that, but even as the callow, insensitive youth that I was, I did begin to notice the way other people were edging away from me in the paddock and began to wonder why. A little thought would have revealed the answer. The combination of several pints of perspiration, liberal spray-ings of sheep excrement and two-stroke blow-back from the Villiers carbu-rettor, was leading to a personal body odour problem which could not have been stopped by the highest of high tech, modern deodorants.

Still, that was a problem for the future and today's challenge was to beat a puny bespectacled youth who looked about my standard: that is utterly inept, but who enjoyed the dual advantages of riding a full 250cc Greeves and of having a four speed gearbox. Could Omar Khayyam dream of anything more desirable?

The first two races were real fights to the death with Mr 4-Speed-Greeves and me battling it out for last, or next to last, place with the verdict always going to my arch enemy.

The snag was the hill before the finish. I could beat him around the rest of the course but on the last climb he always zoomed past, leaving me thrashed both on the track and in my mind. Well, to be more accurate, he more putt, putt, putted past - but my frustration was certainly the genuine article.

My moans and groans and pleading for a four speed gearbox eventually attracted the attention of one of the more mature riders who, in a vain attempt to get some peace and quiet, decided to try to help me. With infinite care, he explained that the clutch could be slipped for very brief periods to maintain the revs, thus allowing second gear to be held for the whole climb and securing that coveted, next to last place. At last I had the answer. Victory would be mine!

And so it turned out to be but, as my Grandad always taught me, "Nowt's for nowt." The race followed the same pattern as before, with "4-Speed" taking an early lead in about 33rd position but gradually dropping back until he came within my grasp. I would pass him on the downhill sections by the simple expedient of withdrawing the clutch, since the Dot went faster coasting than it did under power, and "4-Speed" would re-pass me on the uphill climbs. Little did he know of my master plan for the final lap.

Steam was issuing forth in clouds from the PVC pants as I led into the last rise with "4-Speed" hot, or at least lukewarm, on my shoulder and ready to adopt his normal passing line as my Dot expired. But this time, as the motor gasped its last breath, I withdrew the clutch and the revs soared to somewhere around 4,100 rpm and I paddled for all I was worth towards the chequered flag and the first rider I had ever beaten.

Whilst I was personally delighted with my success, I didn't expect much of a reaction from the flag marshal and the other riders, but they too seemed to be ecstatic. At least, they were certainly very animated and gestured desperately at the clutch side of the Villiers engine. They had good reason, for there was an uncommon amount of smoke pouring from the primary chain case.

Ken removed the oil filler plug to investigate whilst I sat astride the bike, basking in the glory. We both made tactical errors! Given access to fresh air, the merely white-hot, cork lined clutch plates soon began to blaze merrily and the flames licked purposefully up the leg of my PVC jeans. No amount of huffing and puffing could extinguish the blaze and I began to wish that my mentor who had taught me the art of clutch slipping had also mentioned the dangers inherent in the exercise.

Once the elation of beating "4-Speed" had worn off, I began to evaluate the cost of the win: one dead bike and, almost as bad, one pair of only slightly used PVC jeans with the left inside leg most definitely charred. My racing career was at an end.

Then the God who looks after the witless and naïve made a quick sally and presented me with a saviour in the form of one of the local experts who was campaigning an Alpha-Dot, a real hot-shot scrambles machine at the time. He examined the virtually brand-new forks on my Dot with a knowledgeable eye and offered me £25 for them and the chance to keep the rest of the bike. The forks were off before he could get his wallet out.

Better still was that Ken and I off-loaded the rest of the Dot for £7 10s (£7.50) on a "sold as seen and approved" basis to an even greener noviciate than me. That's the beauty of playing down amongst the dregs of the racing world. If you look hard enough, there's always someone who is even less knowledgeable than you.

This maxim was proven by the fact that I also managed to pass on my little used, PVC scrambles trousers, "Only used once..." to a would-be star for £1. In doing so, I also learnt that everything has a value to someone. It's just a matter of matching product and purchaser.

By Monday, the final score revealed a breath taking next to last place, £26 in cash and the end of a far from beautiful relationship with a pair of plastic health hazards.

Now to greater things!

*****

After the traumas of the 8E engined Dot, I was determined – absolutely dead set – that the next bike I raced would be a full 250 – and it would have a four speed gearbox.

Non-racers might consider this grimly determined lust to be slightly odd. After all, to a rider with my minimal talent, it mattered little whether I was racing a three speed Dot or a factory BSA. I was still going to be a disaster.

In fact, it was not the pathetic slowness of the Dot, nor its utterly reliable unreliability, or even the humiliation of it bursting into flames as I crossed the finishing line, which fuelled my desire for a proper, four speed 250. No - the motivating factor was that, for the first time, I had actually beaten someone. Racers, by their very nature being of a somewhat strange mental complexion, are capable of building the most grandiose fantasies from the flimsiest evidence. My internal reasoning went something like this:

1. *I have beaten someone (albeit for 35th place) whilst riding a decayed wreck of a Dot. Therefore, I clearly have vast reserves of talent.*

2. *If I have a full 250, I will beat everyone. This must be the case since I am obviously so immensely talented.*

3. *Brian Martin, BSA's competitions' supremo, will then immediately offer me a factory BSA ride and I can give up work and become a full-time racer.*

4. *Once aboard a works BSA I will become World Champion, very rich and famous and will never have to paint shelves, brush up floors or do any of the other humiliating activities I presently have to suffer.*

5. *I know all this to be true because I have thought it out, in great detail, whilst undertaking said brushing up, and the evidence is conclusive.*

If you think I was of a particularly dreamy frame of mind, just talk to a modern racer and you will see that I was completely normal, or abnormal, as the case may be.

I was also faced with the dual burden of wanting a bike instantly, at the same time as needing a rip-roaring bargain in order to purchase anything at all with the £26 which represented my total working capital. Still, luck was on my side. Scanning the *MCN* small ads, I found a Vale-Onslow Dot for sale in the picturesque village of Bunbury, not very far from Oulton Park. Bunbury is still very Olde Worlde and was very, very upmarket even in those days, before it became the haunt of the Cheshire executive set. This factor was to prove of critical importance.

Unless you happen to be a real Dot or Villiers expert, it is unlikely that you will know the Vale-Onslow Dot since it had only a very brief working life. It was the brain-child of Len Vale-Onslow, OBE, at the time head of one of Britain's biggest motorcycle dealers and, like many of his generation, deeply involved in motorcycle sport.

Len saw that lots of riders who owned 200cc Dots would feel much happier if their engines were full 250s. Sensing a nice little market, he commissioned the German two-stroke genius, Hermann Meier, to design a conversion for him. Meier did a very clever job, producing a really powerful - by 1960's standards - short-stroke barrel which bolted straight on to the 9E's crankcases.

The only fault that both parties made was casting the barrel in iron, no doubt for the sake of economy. The result was a real "fast-while-it-lasts" motor and, in this case, the lasting used to be about ten minutes before the piston seized on the large exhaust port. However, compared to the dreadful three speed 8E, I felt sure that the bike would be amply good enough for me to win the Cheshire Centre Championship – as a minimum!

Inevitably, the standard problem of cash arose but since the advertisement had said "£40 ono" I felt that £25 was a sufficiently "or-near-offer" for me to become the bike's new owner. In fact, the vendor proved to be a really miserable toad, the sort of chap who wouldn't give a drowning man second-hand breath and, from the outset, the chances of him releasing the bike seemed slim. His idea of the nearest offer was going to be £39 19 and 6 (£39.97½ p). In fact, I don't know what he was doing with it in the first place since, to hear her talk, his wife seemed to be at least first cousin to the Queen.

Still, since we had come thirty miles to see the bike, the least I could do was to have a test ride – even if I wasn't going to buy it.

This wasn't a problem since at the back of his mansion sized residence he had an equally enormous paddock, a good acre in size, running uphill in a pleasant bank: ideal for a spot of practice.

Now, whilst the tuned exhausts were beginning to appear on the latest bikes towards the end of the '60s, the Vale-Onslow barrel had been manufactured a long time before expansion chambers were even a twinkle in Herr Doktor Walter Kaaden's eye. As a historical note, Herr Kaaden invented the modern two-stroke engine in the late 1950s and, more particularly, the exhaust system still in use today on any form of two-stroke – racing or commuter.

Instead of a Kaaden developed expansion chamber, the Dot had a short, widely splayed megaphone exhaust, about 14" (350mm) long. From this instrument came the most unimaginably loud bellowing. At fifty yards distance the noise was actually painful and at a mile, it could still peel the paint from door frames. Truthfully, a two-stroke running on a megaphone exhaust is the ultimate in anti-social motorcycling.

Not that this worried me unduly or, for that matter, at all. If I couldn't have the bike, at least I could enjoy the sheer delight of having enough power to actually accelerate uphill and a range of gears sufficient to negotiate any hazard which I could imagine.

What I didn't realize was that my Saturday afternoon practice session was not going down at all well with the local gentry, whose quiet gin sipping in garden bowers was being somewhat disturbed by my efforts. As a result the 'phone lines were getting hot! The outcome was that when I came in from the second session, the owner was under strict instructions to get rid of the bike at any price – and the Queen's cousin insisted that it had to go there and then – instantly! So, yet again the Great Protector of Imbecilic Racers looked after me and we departed with a real four speed 250 for only £25.

That Dot taught me the rudiments of racing – at a price. For the first time, I had a bike which would more or less do the things I saw real scramblers achieve on their bikes. It would jump properly and power slide – although the terrifyingly short wheel base made this manoeuvre distinctly hazardous when undertaken by a keen but clumsy pilot. Best of all, it would genuinely accelerate so that I could just about pass another no-hoper on equally uncompetitive machinery. In short, it was at least the essence of a genuine race bike and it permitted real racing - but only sometimes.

There were two main groups of faults with the bike - both of which caused me considerable grief. The first of these was, quite simply, a design error. The Dot's chassis had been conceived around a very low-powered 200cc motor and even when new it was hardly adequately braked. Keep the same brakes, subject them to ten years' wear and tear, and then double the power of the engine unit and you are asking for trouble. I got it - in large doses and with almost boring regularity, since applying the tiny "tobacco tin" brakes on the Dot had virtually no effect on slowing it down. Dragging my ex-W.D. fireman's boots along the track was at least twice as useful as a method of retardation and not bothering at all, but relying on youthful courage and determination, was even better.

Unfortunately, cannoning into riders, marshals and chestnut fencing was doing my embryo reputation no good at all and after torpedoing an experienced rider on a Metisse – who was lapping me at the time – I was given a straightforward warning. Take care – or else! And the "else" was not going to be an invitation to the Matchless factory's next Christmas party.

The problem was largely solved by the bike itself. Whilst it was in sound running condition when I bought it – which is more than could be said for any of the racing bikes I had sold to date – its inherent fragility and my fondness for practising soon wore it out. This was the second major problem. No part of the motor, from the ignition to the clutch – and everything in between – had been designed for racing and, as a consequence, everything got very upset when stressed.

I have already mentioned the barrel's propensity for nipping up but in a way that was almost a secondary problem. Much worse was the way the clutch drum spread under load and the flywheel magneto's fondness for flying off at high rpm. There was also the gearbox's desire to find a false neutral - and then positively refuse to budge until every single rider was out of sight. Overall, it was a mechanical war zone.

Gradually, I got the motor sorted. I found out that by brazing two steel bands round the clutch drum, it would no longer spread under load. However, what was of more importance was that I discovered the power of barter. I positively enjoyed sending for regs and making entries but I soon discovered that I was in a minority. Thus, my clerical labour skills became a marketable commodity in return for ten minutes of a welder's dinner time. He got his entry filled in and submitted easily and correctly, and I got my clutch drum tuned. Racing was doing more character building than school had ever achieved and it was also teaching me a far more useful set of skills.

The second major discovery was that I had become a celebrity – albeit an extremely minor one. As a racer, I began to enjoy the first hints of privilege. Warrington's major motorcycle dealer, Jack Frodsham Motorcycles, quite rightly treated my friends and me like first cousins to some primordial algae. However, gradually the word trickled down to the storemen that the twitchy, nervous youth at the counter was, in real life, A SCRAMBLER. Not that this had any financial benefits but when I came in for Villiers parts – an all too frequent event – at least the tassels of a very faintly pink carpet were rolled out.

The most immediate result of this was that I was allowed to sort through the Villiers' spares box for "good" contact breaker points. The ignition system on the 9E was grim by any standards and its only concession to racing was Villiers' manufacture of a "sports" ignition cam. Compared with today's infinitely variable electronic advance and retard units, and ignition timing which is tuned with a laptop, the 9E's demand of 1/8" before tdc looked to be something that Moses had brought to the paddock written on a tablet of stone.

Not that Villiers' recommendation regarding the timing had much to do with real life, since the dreadful Wipac points were of such abominably poor quality that the two sides often skidded across each other almost at random, rather than opening and closing with any degree of precision. But there were most definitely "good" and "bad" sets of points and, as a real racing man, I was given the opportunity to do my own quality control investigations.

Over the next couple of months, I began competing for places in the bottom third of the field – but not last, he said proudly and somewhat defensively - rather than racing with the absolute plonkers.

As each meeting went by, I fell more and more in love with the sheer joy of racing – to the detriment of everything else. Not only was I doing a job for which I was grossly over-qualified in academic terms but because the work was extremely easy, both physically and mentally, it left me in prime condition to race and I was as happy as a sandboy with no further ambitions in life.

✶✶✶✶✶

The meeting which Ken and I had both been anticipating eagerly was our first race at Hatherton Hall – at the time, one of the most famous tracks in Britain. I was beside myself with excitement and this led to an archetypal racer's mistake: the last minute test session.

Giving the Dot a last blip round our practice track I seized it solid, breaking the piston ring in the process. To say I was distraught was the understatement of the year. At 5.00 pm the day before the race, there was no chance of a rebuild. Well, almost no chance.

One of Cheshire' star riders at the time was Johnny Griffiths. John was one of the best riders in Britain and, had he ever taken the sport half-seriously, a near certain world champion. He was also one of the nicest people you could ever meet. Johnny always had lots of motocross bits for sale and, as luck would have it, he did have a Vale Onslow barrel in stock.

I rang John at 5.30 and he agreed to open up first thing in the morning and let me have an exchange barrel, already bored, and a new piston for £7 10s (£7.50) and when I perceptibly blanched at the cost, he added, "And you can pay me when you've got the money." Somehow, dealers aren't like that today but perhaps customers are different too.

We arrived at John's nice and early, and the barrel and piston were waiting for us. Fitting it was a half-nothing job – ten nuts, including the carburettor, and within fifteen minutes we were on our way.

The only problem lay in John's severe warning of the importance of running the piston in properly, since, with a new bore, the already temper-amental barrel was a certainty for seizure if it was not thoroughly bedded in. Running in a racing two-stroke on a Sunday morning is a lot easier said than done but in the true spirit of British initiative, a solution would be found. It was too. We would run the bike in, balanced on a stand inside the back of Ken's van, whilst we toured South Cheshire! It was as simple as that.

We reasoned that if we opened the windows of the Thames van, and left the rear doors slightly ajar, the forced draft from the front windows would push the exhaust fumes out along with the noise. Well, the theory was sound.

The noise was truly horrific and the dense clouds of Castrol "R" mixed at 20:1 gave a very good impression of a fierce fire burning inside the van. By the time we got to Nantwich, we realized that even by racing standards, this behaviour was just a shade over the top so when the police pulled us in at the entrance to Hatherton Hall we had our answers all neatly polished and ready to hand. Yes, undeniably we had seen a maroon Thames just like ours and of course it was making a terrible racket but it was full of Rockers, not nice, clean-living lads like us. Not only were there Rockers in the van but they had long hair and were probably going to a pop concert as well, which provided clear proof that they were hooligans.

I don't know whether we were believed or not but for whatever reasons, we were waved through and on to Hatherton's hallowed turf. There were over 160 riders entered and I would love to finish this episode with a tale of how I finally won fame and glory, but the truth – or at least as much of it as is printable – must out. On the first lap of practice, I came a real cropper dropping down to the river. The bike lay on its side with the engine revving its guts out, until the Amal monobloc finally ran out of fuel. Then it seized solid.

I was going to have to review my relationship with two-stroke motorcycles.

Chapter Thirteen

Happy As a Mongrel With a Bone

The saviour came in the form of my mum. She often did her best for me, and with some kindness, and on this occasion she really bailed me out. There was a Tribsa advertised in *MCN* and it was a top quality bike. Tribsas were built from a BSA rolling chassis, powered by a Triumph engine. They ranged in quality from loosely converted road bikes with iron barrelled Triumph engines, to really trick things like the bike in the ad.

This Tribsa had the full checklist for a top quality special. The BSA frame handled well normally but this one had Norton "Long Roadholder" front forks and a little alloy Norton front brake. The rear hub was from a BSA Gold Star and there was even the correct BSA "SCT" gearbox – again from a Gold Star. Power came through a properly tuned, all alloy Triumph Tiger 100 engine.

There were also lots of really nice touches, courtesy of the much loved "foreigner" system. The lad who had built the bike had been a mechanical fitter at GKN, and he had fabricated some lovely bits which made the bike more than just a cheaply thrown together mongrel. The bike on the front cover of this book, with me grinning like a dog with a bone, is the Tribsa.

It was still a lump of a thing for someone of my size, weight and riding ability but it was a proper racing bike and would change my life vastly – and in many ways.

*****

The first time that I rode the bike was at Pott Shrigley – a lovely, rolling hillside course, set up in the Pennines near Macclesfield. I had practised on the Tribsa, using the ample space along the Sankey St Helens Canal where the piled up dredgings made some excellent hills, but I hadn't raced the bike before.

It was a lovely, hot day and I always rode better in these conditions but the problem was learning how fast my new bike was – and a properly tuned Tiger 100 engined Tribsa was seriously quick. It was a steep learning curve and being able to accelerate up the steep climbs at Pott Shrigley and pass people left, right and centre was a shock – and a real joy. Of course, I showed absolutely no sympathy for the poor souls struggling up the inclines on Greeves and Dot machines – and why should I? If I was faster than them, they should have got their mums to sponsor them too.

Even with so little experience I was already a demon starter. One of the reasons for this success was my speed of reaction but the other was that I was already learning the intellectual side to fast starts.

Before my heat came to the start line, I had watched the 250cc class and studied how the starter behaved. In those days, races were started with a long length of elastic which was secured in the centre of the track with a release pin on a metal pole. A rope was attached to this pin and when it was pulled hard the pin shot out, the elastic twanged to each side at high speed - and the race started.

Most riders stared at the elastic in front of them and dropped the clutch the moment it disappeared from their view: I developed a more refined technique. Strange though it might seem, the first thing was to work out the character of the starter. Some officials were anxious and/or keen. They wanted the riders brought to the line, kept static for a moment and then set off. In their view, the less time riders were waiting the better. This often led to ragged starts because cunning riders would hang back from the elastic and would already be accelerating when it flew back. This was called a "roller", as in rolling up to the start line - and I later became a master of this black art.

A different approach was taken by starters who were meticulous and professional. I always enjoyed riding with them. We came to the line, everyone was brought to a proper halt and then the elastic was released. Starts like this were fair to everyone – and safe.

Finally, there were those who enjoyed their moment of power and kept riders waiting an inordinate length of time. These officials often had bad starts because impatient riders jumped the start, broke the elastic and everyone had to make a u-turn and begin the whole procedure again.

The actual position a rider took on the start line was critical too. As a beginner, I was shuffled out to the end of the line and this had two problems. First was the obvious one. Even super strength elastic took a long time, relatively, to migrate to the very end of the start line and this was not helpful to quick starters like me.

The other issue was much greater. The best position was right next to the starting pin. When that moved, you banged in the clutch and away you went.

The better clubs refined the procedure by having the pin masked but it was still possible to beat the system. Level one was to watch the rope which was attached to the pin. When this was fully tightened, the race was on.

I moved on even from this. Once I had established what sort of official was in charge, it was possible to see his arm tighten half a split second before he pulled the rope – and I was away.

But I could do better still – and did! I would look behind and watch the starter's eyes - a final, quick check that the line was formed, and three seconds later the pin would be out.

If the starts were timed to perfection, I could actually push the elastic without breaking it - and this did result in a flyer. Over the years, I was often criticised for these lightning starts but my view, and I think that it was an accurate one, was that if I didn't break the elastic then it was a fair start.

With the Tribsa, I really had a bike which would get off the line competitively – and then the trouble came. The biggest issue was that I was neither big enough nor sufficiently strong to manage a 370lb (170kg) machine. There were other riders of my build who could handle similar machines but they had a greater skill level. Fast starts and a lack of strength and skill were a toxic combination.

In the first race, I made an absolute flyer of a start and was somewhere around eighth or ninth place in a field of maybe 35 starters – a galactically impressive performance for me. The Tribsa romped up the steep Pott Shrigley hills with ease and by lap three I had only lost a few places. One section of the course ran alongside a small stream and the track there had formed into deep ruts. Some poor muppet, not unlike me, had stalled his bike in the optimum rut so I pulled out to cross into the next slot and pass him, missed a gear and the bike came to a halt in the slime. I rocked the bike back for another attempt, someone ran into the back of me and that was that: the engine coughed to a halt and I fell into the mire. Gosh, goodness me and bless my soul were just some of the expletives which ran through my mind!

I had fallen from my best ever position. Now it was a matter of getting the bike going again and then battling my way back into a half-decent finishing position to qualify for the final: then things went really wrong.

Unusually, the medical cover at this event was provided by the Red Cross rather than the normal St John Ambulance Brigade. As I was frantically kick-starting the Tribsa, a couple of marshals grabbed the bike and dragged it off the track whilst a whole gaggle of Red Cross medics surrounded me and insisted that I accompany them to their medical tent. No matter how much I protested my fitness they were having none of it until I had been signed in and my "injuries" recorded.

Once I had been logged in, everyone lost interest in me and my protestations that I was fit and well were fully accepted. Now, all that I had to do was retrieve the bike and then sit in a sulk when the 500cc final was run – thinking that I should have been in it.

The situation was all the more strange because, even in my brief riding career, I had learned that medical care at race meetings was very relaxed. Okay, properly dying was a bit of an issue because the body had to be dragged off the track but anything less than this – broken legs, arms, concussion and so on – were considered to be mere flesh wounds.

The back story to my incarceration was that, according to paddock gossip, the Red Cross cohort in charge at Pott Shrigley were in some sort of competition for the most casualties treated during a season - and motorcycle race meetings, rather than church fetes or pony club events, were considered to be the motherlode in terms of building up casualties – hence the desire to get me logged in and recorded, followed by a marked disinterest in treating me.

I still hope that they won and are suitably grateful for my noble contribution in sacrificing my first ride in a final to help them.

*****

I rode the Tribsa almost every weekend and got better with every outing. Then came a life changing moment – and it still affects me today.

My starts were bringing results which put me regularly in the top dozen or so at local motocross meetings, and this attracted the interest of a local car accessories' firm who had given me a bit of discount on things like oil.

The owner expressed an interest in sponsoring me to a greater level – and, maybe, even buying a bike for me to ride.

Like a lot of amateur sponsors, he talked the talk and was full of getting the ultimate motocross machine of the day for me – a 250cc Husqvarna. The Husky was a real Grand Prix replica and would have been wonderful because it was tons lighter than the Tribsa and just as fast. When he came to see me ride, I was determined that I would put on a good performance.

I entered the next Cheshire Centre meeting at Hatherton Hall and my prospective sponsor said that he would come and watch me race. The day was hot, dry and dusty and I always rode well in these conditions. Maybe it was the scarring from wallowing around in the mud at Oswestry during my baptism of slime - but I liked rock-hard going and enjoyed the heat which put off a lot of riders.

I qualified well and in the final I made a blistering start in a good quality field and was maybe fifth, or so, on the first lap. I can still remember what happened next with pellucid clarity. I hammered the Tribsa down the hill towards the river which intersected the Hatherton track and caught the front wheel in a rut. If I had been stronger maybe I could have held on but I wasn't, and the handlebars were snatched out of my hands.

It was a big accident, and the bike cartwheeled down the track snapping off the front forks. I followed the Tribsa, head over heels in full, Olympic gymnast style. One foot caught in a rut, I pivoted round it - and felt my knee tear apart: it hurt!

The injury had snapped the medial ligament and this meant that my knee would never – could never – be stable again. Since then, five decades ago, I have not been able to kneel down without my knee dislocating - and nor am I able do normal things like kick a ball or jump from even a low height, for fear of my knee collapsing when I land.

The full extent of the injury wasn't diagnosed at the time and I could be bitter or angry about this but I'm not, because the reason for the error was simple – and completely understandable.

When I arrived at Warrington Infirmary I was treated by a young doctor who spoke only very poor English and was under immense pressure – as the NHS has always been. If you think that the NHS crisis is a 21st century phenomenon you should have seen Warrington Infirmary in the 1960s – with patients stretched out across chairs, slumped in corridors and determinedly dying at every opportunity. It was a chaotic scene of mayhem which, had Pieter Bruegel still been painting at the time, would have been a centrepiece for one of his epic artworks.

I was dirty, smelt rank with dust-encrusted sweat and was lacking in confidence. Except for not being blind drunk, I was the sort of archetypal working class patient who cluttered up Warrington Infirmary on every Sunday evening of the year. I was sent for an x-ray, which showed no broken bones and that was that. I had crashed a motorbike and paid the price. What else was there to know?

The following day I was discharged and drove myself home, using one of the hospital's crutches to depress the clutch pedal on my van. With my very high tolerance to pain, it wasn't that big a problem.

Writing books is a strange exercise in some ways. Most importantly, a professional author wants to entertain his or her audience and, hopefully, persuade some of them to actually buy a book! However, books also cause deep reflection - particularly if they are autobiographical in nature like this one.

As I am typing now, sat at my desk, my knee is causing me some discomfort, as it has all my life. I've also regretted things that I could not do, especially when my daughter was young. It would have been great not to have to think about my knee collapsing when I was playing with her in the garden and to enjoy bouncing around on a trampoline with her.

Against this, I have still been able to race – and with some modest degree of success. I became a half decent skier, yacht sailor and enjoyed a host of other strenuous physical activities.

In fact, my knee was often a side issue compared to other racing injuries. When you hear two medics discussing your imminent death in the back of an ambulance and sirens screaming on the way to hospital, you know that you've been hurt rather badly.

So here is the big question. Would I have swapped a fully intact body for a life without racing? The answer is an unequivocal no. I got hurt because I made a mistake. Note that I made the error. It wasn't a team mate, a support group telling me what to do, some government regulation forcing me into some form of action or my dad being drunk. I chose to race and take the chance of getting hurt - I made the mistake and I paid the price. This is how I would want things to be. As I have said before, I believe that racing motorcycles is one of the purest forms of human endeavor. The obverse side of the coin was that I was about to feel the joy of success - and the same criteria apply. Racing is a hard mistress but a joyous companion too.

But there was the problem of my Tribsa, which was as badly wounded as me. The first task was to get hold of Sammy Green and get him on to sourcing some good second-hand front forks for the bike. To his everlasting credit, Sam came up with a pair of Norton forks and we began re-building the bike so that I could make a racing come-back at the earliest possible opportunity. Whatever the problem with my leg, it couldn't possibly be permanent could it? So the Tribsa had to be race ready as soon as I could walk.

*****

I had all the determination and health of a super-fit eighteen year old and the fact that my knee kept on folding beneath me wasn't that big a deal. As well as riding motocross, I started entering grass tracks and soon found that I had a knack for this sport.

It is an inescapable fact that a decent grass track rider, with a competitive machine on a proper track, will always beat a motocross rider. Not nearly always, but absolutely 100% of the time - without question.

A grass bike has more power than a motocross machine and it's lighter too. Sliding round corners, it will be faster through the bends and accelerate quicker down the straights.

Given this set of circumstances, entering a grass track race with a motocrosser would seem to be an utter waste of time but the odds start to shift when any of the parameters change.

For example, grass bikes ideally need a smooth surface, where their limited suspension is not taxed to the limit. They can't deal with tight corners well either because they have minimal brakes. A decent grass bike will run up to 70mph easily and if the maximum possible speed for a corner is half this, then there is a problem in slowing the bike down. The fix is to lay the bike down and scrub off speed as it slides round at a sharp angle to the direction of the track. This will slow the machine down but immediately raises another issue, because the bike has to be accelerated out of the corner again and this is not straightforward with the rear wheel spinning.

But there is always a caveat in any sport and, in this case, it was that a minority of grass track courses were quite unsuitable for proper grass machines. The tracks might be so rough that the restricted suspension of a grass bike couldn't cope or, because of the nature of the available land, there could be very tight corners which required heavy braking thus causing real problems for grassers.

As I said earlier, I always ride better in nice weather and the June sun was beating down on a lovely grass field, south of Oswestry, when I pulled into the paddock.

The Welsh grass courses were often what might kindly be described as rather ethnic, and this one was as good an example of sheep pasture as you could hope to see. The track was the shape of a Norman knight's shield with a fast, broad curve at the top, leading downhill to an ultra-tight point. The two linking straights were pock marked with sheep scrapes, where the animals had dug holes to shelter against the bitter, winter winds.

Best of all, the start was downhill so none of the grass track bikes could go flat out and be totally committed into the tight first corner - for fear of over shooting it.

After practice, I knew that I was in with a chance of being in completely unknown territory. I could actually make the top four in a race! Why was this important? Prize money was paid all the way down to fourth place. It was an impossible dream. The kid who hadn't completed a single lap in his first race, and who had to run alongside his bike to finish his second event, was now looking at prize money!

I rode well in my heat and qualified for the final. The elastic tapes flew back, I launched the Tribsa off the line - and led into the first corner.

It was a strange place to be and more than a bit unnerving. Having a completely empty track in front of me wasn't a new experience. In my first few races, I had been so far behind that there was often no-one else in sight. But this was totally different. Fifteen seconds after the start I still couldn't see another rider – but the roar of the Jawa and JAP grassers on my shoulder told me that the rest of the field was well and truly there!

There couldn't have been a religious fanatic anywhere in the world babbling more prayers as I tipped the Tribsa into the first corner. Please God, don't let me fall off. Please God, don't let everyone pass me so I end up last. Please God, don't let me make some other horrendous mistake which I can't quite conceive but which will ruin this wonderful moment. P-L-E-A-S-E G-O-D!!!

To be competitive on a motocross machine in a grass track you have to "ride the pegs". This means that you ride right up to the edge of the white, track boundary marker pegs so that there is no room for a grass bike to slide up the inside and then out accelerate you on the exit to the corner.

However, if you knock the pegs over – they are only tiny wooden stakes no higher than a jar of coffee – you will be penalised. The knack is to ride with your foot actually over the pegs but the left-hand side of the bike still a tiny distance from them.

I placed the Tribsa to perfection and the grass bikes had to swing wide, way round the outside of me. The result was not only that I led into the first corner but out of it too. I was beginning to like this!

On the climb uphill, the grass bikes with their huge power and weight advantages simply pulled away and left me in a lonely fourth place, a good distance behind the leading three but with the same gap over the other eight riders chasing.

The yellow and black flag came out to indicate the final lap and I concentrated as I had never done in my life. Not exams, writing, job interviews or being sacked could match what was running through my mind.

I sat outside myself and talked to the riding Frank constantly. Brake just there. Tip the bike in here. Ease the throttle on now. A touch of opposite lock to correct the tiny slide. And then the chequered flag came out and I had finished fourth.

I rode through the paddock and back to my trailer recklessly fast and dived into the car for the paperwork for the event – the "regs" (regulations) as the entry forms are known. Yes, it was true! There was prize money paid down to fourth place in the 500cc final. I had won prize money! I had lost my amateur racing virginity and was now a paid rider! I sat back against the trailer in a daze and took deep breaths. This is the world of the amateur racer, where success is an unusual experience.

The next stage in the process was almost as hard: I had to collect my prize money – and I was a virgin once again.

After the last race, I went across to the Event Secretary's caravan and stood in line. All the stars chatted informally with him and took their little brown envelopes with a coolness which made the North Pole look like a sauna.

I shuffled nervously up the line until I was by the window of the caravan. The secretary was busy checking the results with the girls who did the lap scoring.

The wait was interminable and I felt a burning desire to visit the toilet. How bad would this be? I was going to wet myself with fear, waiting to collect my first ever prize money.

The Secretary looked up: "Yeah?"

Gulp. Swallow saliva - in desert dry mouth. "Frank Melling. I finished fourth in the 500 final."

Silence.

The silence stretches into infinity whilst he consults his results' sheet.

Now a deafening tinnitus is roaring in my ears. Has there been a mistake? Perhaps I wasn't fourth. I must have been lapped and couldn't remember. Maybe I had knocked a peg over and they've excluded me.

I know - it's all a dream and I'm still painting shelves in semi-darkness, watching the minutes tick crawl by until I can clock-off!

Oh God, please don't let me die. Not now. Not here. Not with ten shillings prize money on offer. Please God.

"Here."

He slides a small brown envelope to me. On it is scrawled "Melling 4/500" in blue biro. In the envelope is a crumpled, pink ten shilling note – 50p. I have won prize money! I am a professional rider! My life is complete! It is a seminal moment in my life – and I still have that very same ten shilling note.

That ten shilling note also swung open a huge door - and what that revealed initially took me by surprise. Motorcycle racing is an intensely selfish activity because it is a truly naked place to be.

Make a mistake and you will get hurt - as I knew all too well. The injury or death you suffer will be a result of your own error and you will pay the price.

Ride well and the success will be yours too. Yes, at the highest levels you will need a good team behind you but in the area of the racing universe I inhabited, there was no support.

I prepared the bike. I loaded it on to the trailer. I drove to the meeting. I made the good start and I had won ten shillings.

It would have been wonderful to have my mum or dad, or someone who had been impressed by my hand-holding skills in the Odeon cinema, standing track-side sharing my success - but they weren't and so I made my own way and stood, or fell, by my own efforts.

What this showed to me is that I could change my life. I didn't have to be tied to my family background and a council house. I could rely on myself to make things different and this was an immense shift in my mind set. From now on, I was going to become a player in life's game – not a spectator reacting to circumstances which were thrust upon me.

This is the purity and joy of racing. You either win or lose on your own merits with your own skill, your own tenacity and your own courage. Or you don't win and this will be your responsibility too with no valid excuses and nowhere to hide. I loved the idea.

The lesson was a gift from God in terms of every aspect of my life.

Chapter Fourteen

"You're wasting your time here . . ."

In truth, I still wanted to road race. I had taken myself to see the Dutch TT at Assen and had become intoxicated with the sounds and smells and sights of the howling works Hondas, the aggressive screams of factory Yamahas and the sibilant whisperings of the 50cc, twin cylinder Suzukis but this dream was getting further away, not nearer, as every week went by. After Burton-wood, even I was beginning to get some idea that I could, or should, be better than a fitter's mate leaving dodgy bits of scrap in firmly sealed lockers and wrecking Avo meters in my spare time. I had to do better than this.

The next step was both very instructive – and, once more, life changing. Again, it pivots around just how highly regarded engineering was in Warrington and what a desirable occupation anyone who worked in industry had. I got a job with a small precision engineering company who made tooling for the huge number of manufacturers in Warrington. Tooling is not spanners or a hammer but it could be anything from the metal shape used to stamp out parts from a sheet of steel or aluminium, to the former around which tubing was bent. Even with the most modern machinery, without tooling you can't make anything and toolmakers were the industrial elite working to the very highest standards.

The owner of the company took an instant shine to me. I was polite, enthusiastic and – as always – could slaughter the jobs which the rest of his workforce found challenging: give me a pen and paper and I was well away. Unfortunately, my skill set was usually misunderstood – as it was in this case.

My boss decided that I was wasting my time as a gofor, and was capable of doing much better. So he shuffled me off to Warrington Technical College to learn how to be an engineer. He was getting on in years and his children had no interest in the business, so maybe he saw me as his successor.

The standards at Warrington Tech were incredibly high because its purpose in life was to produce the next generation of toolmakers and owners of engineering businesses. The best way to think of the college was not as one of the limp wristed, pseudo academic institutions that we have now but more like a religious seminary where the trainee priests were expected to be wholly committed to their calling. Being an engineer in Warrington was a serious business!

A bit like becoming a Royal Marines officer, or an SAS commander, engineering managers were also supposed to be competent tradesmen.

For one day a week, I attended an engineering course which was held either at the main technical college building on Long Lane or in some pre-fab buildings alluringly near to Warrington Library - where I really wanted to spend the whole day...

It was a tough regime and we worked at a brutal pace from 9am to 9pm. To be honest, it was a horrendous experience! The problems came at me from every direction and I had nowhere to hide. First, engineering has a lot of maths in it and, at the level I was working, a ton of physics too – and I found both subjects very difficult.

Moments of force, calculations of torsion and tensile strength taxed my brain to the limit. It's also worth remembering that this was in the days before calculators so the maths was either done with a slide rule or logarithmic tables.

I never did master a slide rule because it was a bit like watching a Druid do an incantation at the summer solstice. Outsiders, and I was definitely one, sort of know the purpose of all the dancing around and singing but what is actually happening largely remains a mystery.

In essence, the middle bit of the rule slid about between two fixed outers – hence slide rule – and numbers were read from it. The truly dire quality of this explanation indicates just how little the process meant to me. The calculations which could be done were utterly mind-blowing – truly unbelievable.

For example, the father of the modern two-stroke was a German engineer called Walther Kaaden, who worked for the MZ factory. Using only a slide rule, and presumably a fair few sheets of paper and engineering drawing pens, Herr Doktor Kaaden could, and did, calculate the speed and behaviour of individual molecules of gas as they exited the exhausts of the two-stroke engines he designed. The complexity of the calculations was so demanding that they are still hard work for modern computers - and yet engineers of the period were whizzing the results out, using bits of polished wood with numbers inscribed on them.

Note that engineers were doing these calculations: I wasn't.

Things were just as bad when it came to engineering drawing. You may remember that I had done only one year of Tech Drawing, whilst the rest of the lads on my course had been drawing since they left primary school. They were very good, very fast and also read the drawings in an interesting way.

With Margaret Thatcher, it became popular to sneer at engineering as "tin bashing" – a pejorative and wholly inaccurate comment, made by people who don't know the difference between a lathe and a llama. The situation is even worse now, with the BBC leading the fight against anything which involves actually making products.

When an engineer reads a drawing, he or she sees the finished part in their mind. I can't do this but I have seen how clever the skill is on many occasions. Instead of lines on a piece of paper, or now a computer screen, an engineer is able to visualise precisely what they are making and it is a wondrous thing to behold – and all this without any augmented reality from a computer programme.

By contrast, I could see virtually nothing – and understood even less.

Things came to a head when we were in the workshop one afternoon. We were given a spec. sheet to turn a tapered brass bush, with an internal thread, on a basic Boxford lathe. Almost before the smudged, blue Ozalid drawing had hit the bench, my colleagues had a length of brass in the chuck and were well on their way to creating a piece of metal working art.

By contrast, I couldn't read the drawing; or cut the piece of brass square because I was so cack-handed (what a wonderfully succinct and onomatopoeic expression) with the hacksaw; then I left the key in the lathe chuck (which was a true Court Martial offence because it could have flown out and killed someone) and, finally, I couldn't even use a pair of Vernier callipers to accurately assess the mess I had made.

No wonder my tutor openly prayed that had he been killed in the ill-fated WWII Dieppe raid, he could have escaped ever coming into contact with me!

Ironically though, not a single moment of this time was wasted. On the contrary, when I began writing professionally I did have a grasp of industrial techniques and, although in an embarrassingly incompetent fashion, I can weld and use a lathe. Most importantly, I developed a tremendous respect and admiration for engineers and, later, this was to prove hugely useful.

If only we could learn to admire what we can't do, or even understand, then Britain would be a happier and more successful place in which to live.

*****

The one part of the day which all my class loathed, and thought was an utter waste of time, was "General Studies 2" I never discovered "General Studies 1".

GS2 was an hour slot in the afternoon and was an interesting reflection on Warrington Tech's view of the engineers it was producing. Making things in Warrington was considered to be a high status occupation and the officer class which led the workforce was an elite. This was vastly different from the patronising, faintly embarrassed way you see the media and politicians talking to those involved in manufacturing today.

The tutor read out a piece of news, or a cue, on some current topic and we were supposed to write a 150 word précis. Then some students had to read out their work. I thought that this was heaven – in fact a bit better than being completely perfect. The ideas were easy to understand because I had an excellent level of general knowledge, and the words just flowed from my pen.

Now, instead of being the class idiot, I was the star. Producing a 150 word précis from a lecture was so simple that I had it done in the same time as it had taken everyone else to interpret an engineering drawing. This was great.

Things came to a head during a discussion about the police, and whether they were biased against working class young men and turned a blind eye to the well-connected and middle class. We were asked to define justice and the group came up with the normal range of: "Not getting picked on"; "Not getting done just because you've been on the pop" and "What's wrong with taking a bit of scrap home to do a foreigner?"

I wrote: "Justice is the perfect judgement of man by man." My lecturer made no comment.

At the end of the session, when the group was streaming out for tea break, my lecturer called me to his desk. He was blunt and demanded to know where I had "copied" my definition of justice from.

I explained that I hadn't but that it was my own work. He paused for a few seconds before saying: "You're wasting your time here. Get yourself out and into somewhere where you can use your brain."

And that was that: Careers' Guidance, Warrington Tech style.

Clearly, I was never going to be an engineer but what came next was infinitely worse.

Chapter Fifteen

A First-Hand Tour of Purgatory

Highly regarded as the trades were in Warrington, the loftiest aspiration for most working class families was that their off-spring would get a job where "You didn't get your hands dirty…"

To move off the shop floor and into the "office" was the dream for most parents and the normal way to do this was to become a draughtsman in the drawing office. Draughtsmen were the keystone to engineering because they took the designer's ideas, and often initial drawings, and made them ready for production.

This is how it might work. The designer draws a new spade. It is "x" long and "y" wide and has metal of "z" thickness and "w" hardness. That's the design engineering drawing.

Draughtsmen will then do production drawings. These will show the production staff how the spade should be made, its specifications and the materials which must be used.

First, there will be a drawing for the wood turner to produce the handle. There will be another drawing for the shaft and a third to show how the handle is pinned to that shaft.

Meanwhile, someone else will produce a drawing for the press tool used to stamp out the metal part of the spade.

This is an extremely simple example but it indicates how much work goes into taking something as complex as a motorcycle and making it ready for production.

From the drawing office, you might work your way up the chain to become a manager. This career path was a key problem for British industry where managers were either parachuted in via good connections or worked their way up through the ranks. Either way, they lacked professional management training so their skill in running companies was, at best, weak.

There was an additional challenge. As well as not being skilful managers, there was a woeful lack of vision when it came to big ideas. When I became a journalist, I was able to see many senior managers in the motorcycle industry close up and they were, universally in my experience, conservative and risk averse.

Finally the Public Limited Company system hamstrung any hope of creativity, which it sacrificed on the altar of short term profit in an endless drive to increase the value of a company's shares.

I firmly believe that it was neither the shop floor workers nor the engineers and designers who were at fault but the management. Every team needs leading and if that leadership is absent then the sort of anarchy I experienced at Burtonwood will result.

The proof of this still exists today. British designers lead the world in almost every field imaginable, from satellites to vacuum cleaners, and British factories make products of the highest quality. But, to do this, the workforce has to be led well – and it wasn't in the 1960s.

Clearly, with my engineering skill set I was never going to progress further than fitter's mate so I tried a different route – and it was a truly epic failure, of biblical proportions.

There was an advertisement in the *Warrington Guardian*, my nemesis yet again, for officers in the Post Office – then a state owned enterprise like the Civil Service. I got properly washed and dressed, brushed my Hush Puppy suede shoes and went for interview at Telephone House, in Manchester. I interviewed well and made a good impression – and why shouldn't I? My letter of application was of a very high standard and I was articulate, smiling and confident when it came to the interview. I knew nothing about the Post Office, except that my Uncle Frank worked in Warrington as a postman, and had even less knowledge of administration. Regardless, I must have looked like a good prospect and so I was offered a very attractive post as an Executive Officer – and with the promise of a good pension when I retired in only 49 years' time. What could be more attractive than that to a smiling, super fit young man bursting with ideas and energy?

*****

Even now it is difficult to articulate just how much I loathed the whole existence which being an Executive Officer involved.

My day began when I looked at my face in the mirror as I got washed. The eyes which stared back at me were haunted with the thought of what was to come: it really was that bad.

I caught the bus from outside the vicar's house and, if I was lucky, I got a downstairs' window seat away from the fog of cigarette smoke on the upper deck, and with the freedom to look out of my red painted prison into the real world.

The highlight of the trip was to jump off the back of the bus whilst it was still moving, just before it turned left in front of the National Westminster Bank. This strategy saved me several minutes and so allowed me to catch a very slightly later train and delay my daily sentence marginally – and hoarding the minutes of freedom became very precious to me.

I caught the 07.43 train from Warrington Central Station and I choked on the caged stench of the wage slaves, locked in the carriages on the way to their empty lives. The smells were not those of the old ladies sitting on the long seats at the back of the bus into town, but the empty, unified scent of a common tribe who had agreed to a life-long sentence of commuting in return for a safe job and a guaranteed pension five decades hence.

Their faces were a universal, sun-starved grey. The females tinted this patina with a sepia mask but still the greyness pushed its way out through pale pinks and whites, and oozed malevolently on to their dresses and jackets.

I looked at the faces a lot as we swayed and staggered in the overcrowded carriage, pushed into each other through the movement of the train whilst simultaneously being kept light years apart by the English obsession with privacy and personal space.

Their eyes used to fascinate me - darting, protective and quick to default to fight or flight when we pulled into Cadishead Station and more commuters jammed into the already non-existent space. Their faces were blank and empty, sucked dry of any emotion by the endless, mindless, repetitive strictures of life in a Manchester office where thought, and thinking, were punishable crimes.

The contrast between the tradesmen I knew and these wage slaves was immense. A welder might be an employee, working for someone else, but once he started a job he was the master of his own micro-world and beholden to no-one.

So I swayed and touched and swayed and parted and swayed until only my body remained in the carriage, and I was free - racing, reading and tapping away at my Adler. In this way, I stayed sane.

As I walked the half mile to Telephone House, my stomach churned at the thought of being locked into C5 – the fifth floor of this house of punishment. It sounds very melodramatic but that is how I felt.

In fact, I should have been ecstatic because I had one of the best, and most interesting, assignments in the building.

Because I had interviewed so well, I was given the job of dealing with discretionary leave. If you've ever seen that YouTube video of a chimp running round the guerrilla camp shooting a Kalashnikov, then you will have a pretty good idea of me looking after discretionary leave!

The system worked like this. The first step was that I was one of the very few officers who had a direct, outside line when the vast proportion of staff had to go through the switchboard. This meant that engineers could contact me personally.

There was a limited amount of annual paid sick leave at the Post Office but this was guarded jealously by engineers. I have seen blokes staggering into work almost dead rather than "waste" precious sick leave which could be used for throwing a sickie at key times – like away games, a long fishing trip or to extend a public holiday. Certainly, sick leave was far too valuable an asset to be used on such a trivial thing as being ill.

However, sometimes there was a need for additional time away from work as well as the generous holiday allowance and sick leave. This was discretionary, compassionate leave and was there for funerals, visiting sick relatives on their death beds and similar emergencies.

I hated the Post Office because it quite literally tried to suck my spirit from my soul. Every act, from visiting the toilet to the type of pen we used, was controlled. Every letter I sent out came from a standard file of approved documents. Other than the date, and the recipient's name, nothing could be altered or improved.

I sat five spaces in from the window and longed to see people scurrying about in the streets below, but I wasn't permitted to move because my work station was where someone in the upper reaches of Telephone House had decided that Discretionary Leave would be: five places from the window – from now until the end of time...

So, I actively loathed the Post Office and all that it stood for.

Added to this mindset was a breath taking level of incompetence on my part. I had a Clerical Officer assigned to me and the poor lady was driven to tears by my slapdash approach to administrative tasks. With each approved application, the recipient's name, work base, employee ID and a mountain of other data had to be recorded manually and then painstakingly transferred, by hand, to a master file.

Inevitably I would forget which information I should have gathered and, on the very rare occasions when all the boxes were completed, the data would be replete with errors and my poor Clerical Officer would have to try to sort out the mess. It was total anarchy.

Of course, word soon got out that the bloke in Telephone House was a soft touch when it came to leave applications and I was soon inundated with requests. On a philosophical level, how many grandmothers can you credibly have before anyone gets suspicious, and what sort of dreadful illness wipes one out every six weeks or so?

Gross incompetence was one of the reasons why I was so free and easy with leave applications but the other was an attempt to attack the heart of the Post Office. This was strange because although I have an immensely wide range of failures and character weaknesses, spitefulness is not one of them. I think that you need a small, petty mind to be mean and I'd rather have an argument openly with someone than do something underhand to hurt them. The Post Office however, was the one exception!

After six months I had become a legend in my own lunchtime in terms of generosity, and the poor clerical officer who was supposed to be helping me was in despair. The damage I caused was truly impressive and so I was summoned to see senior management.

I was called into a private office, on the floor above my workstation, and there a surprisingly kind and tolerant senior manager asked me if I was really happy in my work. I was incredulous. Happy? I hated even thinking about Telephone House, with a loathing which is normally reserved for war criminals who have committed mass murder!

However, I wasn't being shouted at or threatened or getting ready to duck in case someone threw something at me. Maybe there was a way out.

I explained that I really did love my job and really, really, really loved working for the Post Office even more but I found the daily travelling stressful. Me, who rode the length and breadth of the country for fun, now found the 30 minute commute too much to handle both physically and mentally!

The three wise men sat opposite and nodded sagaciously. Yes, it was a challenge travelling all the way from Warrington to Manchester and they could understand how this would affect the standard of my work.

Yes – nod, nod, nod – it was a real challenge – nod, nod, nod – but, even so, they were not quite wholly happy with my performance – nod, nod, nod – and so my position was, how can we say this, not as rosy as it might otherwise be – nod, nod, nod, nod - and a final nod.

Had I perhaps thought of other careers which did not involve all this dreadful travelling?

I could have fallen on the floor and licked their polished shoes clean, I was so overjoyed. Yes! I was going to be sacked. Greater joy did not exist in the world.

What was even better was that they were prepared, willingly, to avoid the truth. How about: "Melling, you are a mindless, irresponsible moron with the administrative skills of a bored gibbon.

"We are now going to beat you senseless and then sue you for the return of your wages."

But no, they were too civilised, too genteel and probably too kind as well. From their point of view, I had thrown away a brilliant job with paid holidays, a sick pay scheme and a pension in only forty-nine years' time. I truly deserved their every sympathy.

So I took Vol Res. - Voluntary Resignation; the Post Office equivalent of Seppuku - the Japanese ritual suicide undertaken by a Samurai who had dishonored his Master. I would be forever without a Lord – without company status or protection, and left to wander the world depending only on my own wits for survival. In fact, although I didn't know it at the time, I was going to be a freelance writer and what in the world could be better than that?

I quite literally skipped and jumped all the way to Manchester's Central Station with a smile which was positively manic.

The saga wasn't over though. I was given a reference, a real one on proper Post Office paper and signed. It was a master of obfuscation and ambiguity. Much was made of my happy personality and my willingness to help people. The fact that I was barely capable of signing a letter in the correct space at the bottom of the page was tactfully glossed over. I looked at the reference and was more than a little proud of myself – a fine case of believing your own PR!

Chapter Sixteen

Not Quite What I Had in Mind . . .

My lifetime at the Post Office did have some slight benefits because I continued to learn about girls – and goodness me I really was still at the pointing-at-the-words-with-one-finger stage of the "Big Boys' Book of Life."

The typing pool was on the way to the toilets. Lavatory breaks were not strictly timed but it was noticed, and commented on, if anyone was absent from their work station either too frequently or for an excessively long time.

I used to take the maximum number of toilet breaks that I could get away with, regardless of what my bladder said, and so had the chance to pass the typing pool quite often. The typing pool was an essential part of any big organisation because only trained typists could use a manual typewriter effectively. This sounds a rather strange thing to say now when everyone can peck away at a phone or iPad and get some sort of text out, but professional typists were nothing like this – absolutely nothing.

For a start, they all touch typed. This means they could hit the keys on the typewriter with total accuracy and without looking at them. In the typing pool, the skill was essential because the girls, and I never once saw a man, had a pile of letters on a shelf to their left and an enormous Olympia typewriter in front of them. They looked to see the very slight amendments which were needed to any standard letter and then bashed away, producing it without ever looking at the typewriter keys.

The girls were super accurate, blisteringly fast and completely reliable. Other than needing feeding occasionally, and a bit of sleep at nights, they were miles better than any modern artificial intelligence system.

Their speed needs noting. The best typists could knock out 80 or 90 words a minute – hour after hour after hour. This needs putting into perspective. When I started to write seriously I learned to touch type and I am writing these words now - quickly, accurately and without looking at the keyboard. In fact, for a journalist or author, I type quite well. How well? Around 40 words per minute - and with a correction maybe every 50 words – but, even in a 'flu epidemic, or an outbreak of war, I would have never been allowed near any firm's typing pool because I'm so slow and inaccurate.

As things turned out, 40 wpm is fine for me because I only have a 40 wpm brain – and that's only on a good day – so I can get all my ideas down without having any need to type faster.

*****

About a third of the way down the typing pool, quite near to the toilets, was a pretty little dark haired girl about my age. After a few weeks I caught her eye and received the hint of a smile in return.

It's worth noting the speed of the courting procedure at my end of the scale. In the interests of balance, it should be said there was a lot of free and easy sex at the time but this was enjoyed by what was almost a different race of people from me – those who knew about girl and boy "things" and what to do. By contrast, I was still on the first page of the manual – and at the top of the page!

One day, my new typing pool friend was wearing a tartan pinafore dress and, because it was hot, a very minimalist white blouse underneath. As she leaned forward to pick up the next letter I was in a position to look. She saw what had happened and I blushed intensely, but she never said anything. She just tidied her work and, as I made my excuse to leave, I got slightly more than my normal half smile.

Later in the week, I decided to pluck up my courage and make some progress – or not. The first thing was to check whether we were on the same lunch break. Not everyone took their lunch at the same time. Breaks were staggered throughout an hour and a half so that the relentless administrative behemoth which was the Post Office administration never ceased spewing out its letters and dicta. If money never sleeps, then certainly the ability of the Post Office to generate correspondence was a good precursor to this maxim.

We were blessed with good fortune because our lunch breaks were within five minutes of each other. In fact it was better than that because I actually started first so I could be the knight in shining armour, waiting down at the typing pool but well hidden from the laser glare of her supervisor, when she was ready to leave.

A short walk from Telephone House was Piccadilly Gardens, a haven in the grubby, noisy city centre. We agreed that we would have our sandwiches there together.

I quite liked Piccadilly Gardens. There were flower beds, bits of lawn and a fountain in the centre. The traffic wasn't nearly as dense as it is today so it was almost peaceful. Off to one side was the BBC studio and on the other side of the park, the main shopping area.

We talked about nothing and, clearly, there was no physical contact – of any kind – but I was suitably encouraged.

I was a couple of minutes late getting back to my desk, and got a look from my clerical officer which would have drilled holes in the hull of a nuclear boat, but I didn't care. I'd had a lovely lunchtime in the company of a pretty girl and the weather had been perfect. Anyone who applied for discretionary leave for the rest of the day was going to be on a sound bet!

The following day, suitably emboldened by our highly successful lunch-time tryst, I decided to go for broke and ask her out. She seemed to be quite keen but I need to clarify the adjective "keen" which is normally completely unambiguous. My new girlfriend-designate had a very strong East Lancashire accent. Now there's nothing wrong with this because I had a northern accent too. However, her diction was replete with short vowels and extended, soft rolling "rs" – a bit challenging to follow but somewhat romantic and even encouraging. I translated this as her being open to an offer. Maybe?

She suggested that I could take her to the Bury Palais de Dance for the Saturday evening show. To give you a hint of the communication problems, the Bury Palais de Dance was pronounced as Burrypallyd'dance – as a single word.

The Bury Palais de Dance was quite a famous venue in the North West of England but, with all my money going on bikes, I had never been there – although I did know of it.

We agreed that we would meet by Bury Station and I went back to my desk with a hop, skip and a jump. At that point, the romance train began its inexorable progress towards the blown up bridge.

I was desperate to show off my new girl conquering skills and couldn't wait to tell one of the few other lads of my age that I occasionally saw in my area of the 5th floor.

He knew my soon-to-be-girlfriend by reputation – and the Bury Palais de Dance.

"Bloody hell! Do you like fighting? She loves seeing fights and when the Scousers get there it'll really kick off. Then they put all the lights on and the bouncers come in and the bother really starts.

"Unless you're handy, you'll get a right good hiding."

This raised serious problems for me. I didn't like fighting, wasn't very good at it and the whole venture was going to wipe me out financially.

How much did I want the date? Not that much actually...

To my credit, I did make some lame excuse and from then on, whenever I went to the toilet we strenuously avoided any eye contact.

*****

All was not lost though, because there were sometimes seats on the train home, as distinct from having to stand up for the whole journey. Overcrowding on trains is now thought of as a modern problem but it was very apparent even fifty years ago.

Sometimes, I sat opposite a girl of my age who also got off the train at Central Station, in Warrington, so I knew that she must be a local girl. Once I was away from Telephone House, I had a nice happy smile and wasn't bad looking. Over a few weeks I smiled at her, she smiled at me and then we sat together on the train home.

To be honest, except for the embarrassment of chickening out of the Bury date and going down to the Palais de Dance, getting stuck into the

Scousers and ending up with a broken nose, I wouldn't have pursued the relationship.

I know that it is deeply politically incorrect to say this now, but the truth is that lads of my generation did like pretty girls – and this is fact. Maybe in 21st century Britain, young men have a wider, more thoughtful view of a potential girlfriend but in 1965 decent looking lads went out with pretty girls.

However, this wasn't the real problem. The major issue was that my new "friend" CN – she was very far from a "girlfriend" at this time – actually liked working in Manchester. She was training to become a manager in a big insurance company and was bursting with pride at her achievements. More than that, she actually took delight in the fact that her day was so heavily structured.

Like me, she had immutably fixed lunch and tea breaks but she thought that these were great because "You knew where you were…" By contrast, I loathed any form of routine in every way.

She too used standard letters and this was another wonderful idea in her eyes because it avoided mistakes. Her manager had promised her that, in only a few years' time, she would be allowed to compose a letter herself – and she was beside herself with excitement at the very thought.

She took great pleasure in the actual commute too. She knew when the train was due to leave Warrington, all the stops on the way and the precise time it took to walk to her office, which was off Deansgate.

Where I saw the train carriage as a constraining prison, she looked upon it as a place of safety, protecting her from the vagaries of the outside world. I wanted to escape rules, regulations, fixed lunch breaks and fly to freedom - whilst she longed for certainty, restraint, control and so, in her own way, to be free from the fear of the unplanned, unstructured and therefore unknown.

Very occasionally, I think about the chaotic, disorganised path I have trodden through life and wonder whether she was as happy with her choices as I have been with mine.

However, these were not my thoughts at the time: outside Central Station, under the bridge, I wanted to get to know her better.

She had the same idea and invited me to come and listen to some music at her house and, although I wasn't much of a music fan, I jumped at the opportunity.

The USP of the date was that she lived in old Orford - in a big, semi-detached house which her parents actually owned. Wow! This was roughly the equivalent of a visit to Buckingham Palace - or perhaps even better than that.

Her house was so posh, and so huge, that they actually had a real, brick built garage, a front garden, a back garden and – although this was difficult to believe – a front room where they all had Sunday dinner sitting together round the dining table. My head was swimming just thinking about the sybaritic luxury of it all.

She would ask her dad if we could sit in the front room, play music on her Grundig tape recorder and "Get to know each other better."

I need to say a little bit about the Grundig because, in this wonderful age of having every song ever made on your phone, the Grundig was a beast from a different galaxy.

For a start, it was a big lump – very Germanic, heavy, super strongly built and about the size of a toolbox – and not far off the same weight either. It came with a hard cover which protected the sensitive elements of the machine in transit and this was so tough that it would have stopped an attack from one of my cannons.

The music was stored on two large reels of brown, magnetic tape. The tape was pulled slowly from one reel to the other through a magnetic tape head at the bottom of the machine and away you went – a noise which could be recognised as a song crackled out of the in-built speaker. Overall, it was a brilliant piece of kit and I was truly envious that she had a Grundig of her very own.

One more important thing to note is that the actual tapes were very thin, extremely strong and there was a lot on one reel. A 30 minute tape was around ½ mile long which is an awful lot of thin strong material to have unwind uncontrollably.

The quality of the music was very variable because all the Grundigs came with a little microphone and this was how the recordings were made. The preferred method of acquiring the music was by putting the microphone next to the family's television at 7.35 on a Thursday night when "Top of the Pops" was broadcast by the BBC.

It's interesting to note that popular music was much more inclusive than it is today. I don't think that I could name three current pop stars now, and I certainly couldn't sing along to their songs. By contrast, everyone from grannies to little kids knew The Beatles, The Rolling Stones, Cilla Black, Dusty Springfield and even less famous bands like Gerry and the Pacemakers and the Beach Boys.

Because of this unified culture, the whole family gathered round the telly to hear the latest songs and it was no imposition to have the Grundig's microphone positioned next to the TV's speaker and record the songs which crackled out from it.

The quality was not outstanding. In fact that's not fair: the recordings were outstanding – outstandingly bad! This wasn't the problem it might seem however, because the TV sound was appalling too and tiny transistor radios were no better. Things were helped by the fact that everyone knew the songs, so the Grundig was there as a prompt, almost karaoke style, more than something used for serious listening.

I duly arrived on my bike at 7.30 – and was met by CN's mum and dad as she hovered somewhat nervously in front of them. The bottom line was that her father was not best pleased. I think that I must have been the first lad that she had brought home and he clearly had higher aspirations than a peasant in a Belstaff jacket, carrying a helmet in one hand.

My smile managed to thaw the reception, albeit very slightly, and CN's mum brought us coffee and biscuits, which was very nice and yet another sign of how upmarket this liaison was going to be.

We chatted and she was sort of reasonable company but still obsessed with succeeding in the insurance business. She had been to Warrington Girls' Grammar School and had two "A" Levels which was a heck of an achievement. Her parents had been so proud when she had joined the insurance company and saw a glowing future in front of her – safe, clean, well paid and with a pension.

Things progressed very nicely and as the last of her mum's rather excellent chocolate biscuits disappeared, there was some extremely consensual snogging – and I do need to stress that CN was a very willing participant.

She was just as encouraging when I tried to undo her bra. Now there is no argument that the error was mine but, by way of a defence, I only had the very vaguest idea about female clothing and how it fastened – or in this case unfastened.

Somehow I managed to pinch her and she let out a little squeal – only the tiniest squeak. Her dad, who must have been listening for just such an attack on his insurance-manager-to-be daughter, burst through the door and quite literally leapt into the room like a Berserker warrior with a hangover - and frightened me half to death.

CN shot bolt upright and I fell off the couch and on to the Grundig, knocking it over. Not that a mere fall was going to stop a machine of the Grundig's build quality. The reels continued their relentless circulating until my foot skidded over the top of the deck and several miles of tape entangled me.

CN's father was furious – not to say unequivocal regarding what should happen next. "Get out of my house you dirty bastard – get out now!"

Later, I thought that this was a somewhat harsh assessment of my character because his daughter had hardly been a reluctant participant. However, this was later. The immediate problem was disentangling myself from a synthetic spider's web of tape – and this wasn't as easy as it might seem.

Recording tape is properly strong and I was desperately trying to escape from its clutches whilst nobly avoiding wrecking CN's precious Grundig. A prompt exit was very desirable because CN's dad was a big bloke and I was certain that I was about to get a real bop round the ear – or worse. Maybe I should have taken the Palais de Dance option, which looked like a much safer bet at this moment.

Now the show reaches its crescendo. Mum has joined the scene along with CN's younger sister. The sister is really impressed, shrieks and covers her head whilst Mum has a jolly good scream. Perhaps shrieking was a well practised family skill.

Using the strength of the truly desperate, I snapped the tape, grabbed my helmet and jacket and escaped through the front door which was slammed after me. I sat on the wet front lawn, gasping for breath - but delighted to be out in one piece.

The door opened again, for just a second, and my pair of Army and Navy gloves hit the lawn next to me. That was the great delight of the English middle classes: they could always be relied on to be polite and honest.

The post script to this epic tale of failure was that when I saw CN on the train, a few days later, I got a white hot glare that gave me second-degree burns. From this, I gathered that I was off the invitation list for another listen to her Grundig.

*****

The one girl I never lost interest in was S. After bottling out of the RSJ burning job with the Irish lads, I had clearly failed to raise the immediate ante for a luxury, no expenses spared, chicken-in-the basket and two, not one, bottles of Babycham.

Despite the setback, I never lost hope. Even when my best offer was a potential punch up at the Bury Palais de Dance or an actual fight with a Grundig tape recorder, S was always there in the back of my mind.

Before my period of incarceration in Telephone House, I used to try to drive along one of the roads which S walked down when I knew that she was returning from work. Then, I would casually offer her a lift and we could talk for a short time. Sometimes, we would stop outside her house and we would chat for longer.

To be honest, S wasn't much better at the courtship game than I was and so we both blundered around, ending up in one social cul de sac after another as we tried to make sense of our new adult world. With the benefit of hindsight, I am certain that she was as keen on having a real boyfriend as I was a real girlfriend. She was a nice girl, as I was a nice lad, and she must have seen what was happening to the more switched on members of our respective genders – and wanted a piece of the action.

This is why she really did try to be helpful - so much so that she even came to a race meeting. This rather bald statement needs some further explanation. The first time my wife came racing she was instantly on board and loved everything about the sport. Not only did she understand the rules of motorcycle racing but almost instantly, and intuitively, she knew what was going on in the racers' minds. In short, she was – and is - a thoroughbred racer girl as much as I am a racer.

Some girlfriends that I have had actively disliked the noise, the smell and the pressure: that's okay too. No-one with half a brain would want to be involved with a bloke who thinks that putting his body at risk, by trying to ride round in circles a bit faster than a group of other equally dysfunctional nutters, is a sensible way to spend a Sunday.

Others have come along to be supportive, interested and kind. S was one of these. Instead of taking her on a real date to somewhere sensible like the cinema, or one of the zillions of rock concerts in the North West, we would go for walks round race tracks together. I am embarrassed writing that last sentence but it is actually true because racing was everything to me.

She really did try hard, and persuaded her dad to bring her to a meeting to watch me race. It was raining and the paddock was a muddy quagmire. I'm still mortified with what happened next. S had dressed smartly for me. She was wearing a cream jacket, lime green jeans and open sandals with little high heels. She had even put on some plastic Poppit beads, which were all the rage at the time.

I should have been grateful, and I do mean actually bursting with appreciation, that a nice girl had made such a big effort for me. But what did I do? Largely, ignore her - because I was having a bad day with the bike. This was brought to a head when the valve pulled out of the rear tyre's inner tube.

Having to change the inner tube just before the race was a real issue. Seeing a really lovely girl sink over the top of her sandals in the mud, wasn't. Eventually S's dad led her quietly away, bare footed and carrying her sandals, with her lime green jeans covered in mud: I'm still ashamed today.

I saw S in the week and said how sorry I was and her reaction was interesting. She was pleased with the apology and sort of understanding – but not in the same way as a real, thoroughbred racer girl.

Here's the contrast when you have a partner who loves racing: we once had a problem with our race bike in France. Things had been going from bad to worse all weekend and we had nowhere dry to work. Carol held a big umbrella over the engine and me whilst I sorted out the problem with the carburettors - and in the monsoon conditions you can imagine how wet she got!

Then she stood track side whilst I raced and only when the bike was back in the trailer did she get into some dry clothes. That's what makes racer girls special. They understand racing and racers, and anyone with a partner like this is beyond blessed.

S wasn't a racer girl and, in retrospect, never was going to be a member of this elite group. But she was pretty, and every time I was with her I felt like a different person. The feelings weren't just sexual. Eighteen year old boys have no problems with being sexually aroused by anything and everything. There wasn't a minute in the day, or night, when I wasn't excited by something, no matter how loosely connected with girls!

But with S, another door opened. The vast majority of my experience of women came through my mum, whose hands were rough through manual work and her face lined. She was never dirty but if I recognised any scent it was of carbolic soap or bleach.

I used to try very hard not to make eye contact with S for fear of her thinking that I was staring at her – which I always was. Her skin was tight and firm and wrinkle free. Her lips were pale pink and smooth, without any make-up, and there were lovely hints of delicate pink roses in her cheeks.

When I was permitted to kiss her, it was like entering another world of softness and the very essence of her womanliness. I could have spent hours doing nothing more than just gently touching her cheeks and wondering in awe at them.

When we held hands, it was a particularly wonderful experience. My hands were large and strong with callouses from work and racing. Her hands were small and soft, and fitted inside mine in a way which made me feel very protective and quintessentially male. She was definitely pure woman and, in my own baby way, I was beginning to feel equally manly.

There were many huge changes happening inside my adolescent brain, and so very fast that I felt as if was being tumbled upside down every time I was with S.

Eventually, I made some clumsy attempt to move on from kissing. She was angry and tearful but not crying. I still remember what she said: "You're like all men. You want to have sex with every girlfriend – but then marry a virgin!"

But I didn't want to have sex with S.

I wanted to hold her hand, and to meet her after work, and for her to ask me if I'd had a good day.

I wanted to stroke her hair, and tell her that she was lovely.

I wanted to walk with her round a race circuit, and for her to be excited about racing.

I wanted her to be my special friend, and for me to feel proud when I walked alongside her.

That's what I really wanted. Sex was not even on the wish list!

We drove home in silence, and exchanged the briefest of goodbyes outside her house.

It was a black day, so I went straight into my shed when I got back home and cleaned the Tribsa.

A bit later, my mum brought me a cup of coffee and a thick round of toast.

She also had the *Warrington Guardian* with her, folded over at the jobs' section.

"Have you seen this, Love?"

Chapter Seventeen

I Can Do This

Inevitably, my mum had found an advertisement in the jobs' section of the *Warrington Guardian*. This time, it was a rather odd one. The post was for an unqualified teacher to work in a secondary modern school, in Runcorn. There were no professional qualifications required, only an interest in English and a minimum of five "O" Levels. Clearly, I was on sound ground in both cases.

Tapping away on the Adler, I wrote a very literate letter of application and, with some very neat footwork, managed to edit my chaotic employment record – even the Vol Res from the Post Office. After Telephone House, I really was resting at home because my leg was still not up to manual work following the huge accident on the Tribsa - and the thought of a Mk II version of administrative work in a Post Office clone frightened me to death.

I suppose the story would read better if I said that I had always dreamed of teaching but that wouldn't be true. I knew about teachers because only two years earlier I had been sitting at a desk in front of them. I was also very aware of what I considered to be good teachers, ordinary ones and those who should never have been allowed near kids. All this I did know but as for how anyone became a teacher, what teachers did away from the classroom or anything else even vaguely connected with the profession, I didn't have a clue.

In this respect, I wasn't the only one. Let me give you a few examples. I taught for a head teacher who had been a sergeant in the Army Pay Corps during the Second World War. He came out of the army, did a nine month crash course in teaching and was appointed to a school by his uncle, who was chair of his town's Education Committee. The following year, he was promoted to deputy head teacher and the year after he was given his own school. Nine months training, two years' school experience - and away you go, holding the fate of a school full of kids in your hands.

Another head I knew was a corporal in the Pay Corps – perhaps this branch of the armed forces generated a lot of teachers – and he also became a head teacher at supersonic speed.

A third head was an ex-RAF admin corporal, and an educational psychologist I worked with, and a rather good one too, had done just a one year course - after spending most of the war as a very junior Navy officer making sure that all the ships at Scapa Flow were properly provisioned before they went out to fight.

In short, there was a desperate shortage of teachers in the 1960s.

It's easy to take a rather superior view of this state of affairs now - but we shouldn't. There were, allegedly, 600,000 kids being taught by unqualified teachers in 2018 and the current training situation where teachers "learn on the job" is a disgrace.

Would you want to rock up at your doctor's surgery and be treated by someone who had a biology degree or an interest in sick animals? In fact, would you want your car serviced by a fitter who had been laying tarmac the week before? Yet, graduates with degrees – any degrees – are now being trained as they teach.

As a professional teacher, I find this situation appalling. Later, I spent three hard, intellectually challenging years in full-time teacher training and I am proud of the academic and professional rigour of my course – but that was to be some distance in the future.

The *Warrington Guardian* came out on Friday and I wrote the letter of application the following day. I got an invitation to come for interview, by return of post, and found myself in a small, Victorian office, in Balfour Road Boys' Secondary Modern School.

My mum had checked that I was presentable, complete with my now standard interview war gear of Harris Tweed jacket and brushed Hush Puppy shoes, and I sat bolt upright on the edge of my chair, as I had been taught. The head's name was Edgar Parsonage and he was somewhat formal and rather brusque, but with an occasional smile which was sincere.

He wasn't an English specialist but asked me a few questions about my interests in literature. This was home ground for me and I could, and would, have talked all day about what I read.

The interview was interesting because I had stumbled, quite unintentionally, into a new world and one in which I was extremely comfortable. No-one had asked what I read when I was a farm labourer or a fitter's mate. Why should they? Literature had no relevance to what I was doing.

The same applied at Warrington Tech. Books contained information – specifications, plans, engineering drawings replete with data. Why would anyone want to read about stuff which was not true?

As for the ideas which books generated, these were an anathema for the Post Office. The role of officers was to execute the diktats of their superiors, not to think independently. Having ideas could only lead to trouble – as I had proved so effectively.

Now, someone was at least passingly interested in what I thought about Dickens, Philip K Dick or whether *The Day of the Triffids* was really credible. It was a new experience and I loved it.

Two days later I was appointed to the post of Unqualified Assistant Teacher in Balfour Road Boys' Secondary Modern School. I was to receive two-thirds of a qualified teacher's salary and the same holiday allowance as all the other staff. In fact, my mum had sold the idea of me becoming a teacher entirely on the basis that I would have lots of free time. As she so succinctly put it, "Think of the holidays when you can work on your bike and still get paid."

*****

I turned up for my first day as a teacher, hair combed, teeth brushed and wearing a nice white shirt which my mum had ironed for me. I chose one of the less flamboyant ties I owned and my mum had pressed my best pair of grey trousers so that, overall, I looked quite like the real deal.

I didn't have the merest hint of an idea what teachers should do or how they did it. I need to stress this point: I had not the merest hint of a clue what would happen when I walked up the steps, into the school and knocked on the door of the small staffroom.

To be honest, I didn't get the warmest of welcomes. It was a bit like those Battle of Britain films where the new pilot nervously enters the fighter squadron mess, and all the hardened aces can't be bothered even greeting him because he'll be dead and out of the way after the first sortie or two.

Unqualified teachers at Balfour Road tended not to last very long, or even a little bit long, and so there was no reason to roll out the red carpet for me. I would be gone in a couple of weeks at best – shot down in my first engagement with the kids.

I was nervous but not worried. I had been fired from so many jobs, and in so many ways, that getting the sack from this one would not have been anything but completely normal. Racing also helped – and hugely too. The naked, utterly unequivocal nature of racing did generate a strange sense of self-confidence. Racing was actually dangerous, as I knew from my many injuries, and you either faced up to this or didn't ride. By contrast, getting cold shouldered, shouted at or fired were all quite minor issues.

My biggest concern was falling prey to Franklin D. Roosevelt's immortal words: "The only thing we have to fear is fear itself."

I was given a tour of the school in the morning, and my smiling face and good manners thawed some of the staff. The school was small with around 400 pupils housed in a rather wonderful, although sombre, Victorian building.

The boys' building had a mirror image of it attached to the other end. This housed the girls' school. A high wall separated the two schools and boys were not even allowed to lean on this, let alone shin up it and see the unseeable who inhabited the mythical land of boobs and bums and bras on the other side. The separation was so meticulous and all-encompassing that in all the time I worked at Balfour Road I never - not once – saw a girl pupil, or a member of their staff, on our side of the wall. No "goings on" took place in well run schools!

After morning break, I was introduced to a battle hardened, veteran teacher called Jim Chadwick. Jim ran the Annexe and I was going to work there in the afternoon. The Annexe was a collection of light, airy buildings with huge windows, which at one time had been the Fever Annexe for the local cottage hospital. They were perched high on the hills at Weston Point, overlooking the River Mersey and pointing south and west with uninterrupted views right across to the Mersey Estuary. It was the most beautiful place that I had ever worked.

Jim drove me up to the Annexe and I thought I had arrived in Heaven. The sun was shining, the kids were playing in the quadrangle between the buildings and the Annexe teaching staff were so laid back that they were almost horizontal.

On the drive up to the Annexe, Jim quizzed me about my teaching experience. He had been hoping for someone who had at least stood in front of a class before, but he was resigned to making the best of what he had. His attitude was that I was better than having to double classes up – but only just.

We sat down in the staffroom and I was given a cursory introduction to my colleagues who showed very little interest in the new arrival. I think that the feeling was, just as it had been in the main school, I would only last a few days so why bother wasting breath on someone who wasn't going to be around?

Jim was busy with a million other things and so it was only as the lunch break came to an end that he turned to me and said: "You'll be taking 1B for English."

At this point, the full realisation of what was about to happen hit me. In a couple of minutes, I was going to be left with 34 eleven and twelve year old boys to control and maybe even teach – and, so far, I hadn't had ten seconds' training or even a single particle of guidance.

It was blushing time again. "What shall I do with them?" I asked Mr. Chadwick's back - as he marched out of the staffroom on his latest mission.

But Jim was long gone. Help came by way of Stan Williams, a truly larger than life character in the teaching profession who was also extremely kind to me. Stan gave me my first lesson in teacher training, scribbled on a page torn from a redundant exercise book.

"Look, here's how to do it. Tell them a story about getting shipwrecked on a desert island where there's buried treasure, and they have to find their way to it and describe what they see on the way – you know, marshes and jungles and wild animals and natives with spears and all that."

The miracle was that I did know and I did understand the "…and all that." And I didn't need any more explanation. Everything made sense instantly and, in a few seconds, I could see a lesson forming in my head.

Mr. Chadwick returned and Stan gave me a big smile and a pat on the back.

We walked across the corridor and into the wooden floored classroom, housing the neat lines of desks. Looking out expectantly was a sea of faces – anticipating, distracted, disinterested and, a few, even eager.

Jim spoke in his most headmasterly voice: "This is 1B. They'll be good for you. Won't you 1B?"

With that, he turned his back, closed the door and, true to his word, 1B really were good for me - and in many, many ways.

*****

I have been pondering about how to describe what happened next and this is the best metaphor I can provide. Have you ever seen a duckling or a gosling the first time they fall into a pond or a river as they follow their parents? They splosh into the water quite untidily and then, a few seconds later, pop up and start paddling away as if they have been doing this all their life. For me, teaching was just like this.

I stood at the front of the classroom and introduced myself. Then I explained the lesson and we began. The kids listened, I told the story of the shipwreck and the island well and with enthusiasm, and then we all got down to work.

I marked, corrected and encouraged like a born teacher and the kids wrote and drew for me. It was as if I had never been anything else but a teacher, it felt so natural and so easy.

After half an hour or so, Jim opened the classroom door, had a quick look round and then shut it without comment. Everything was peaceful, the kids were working well and, instead of trouble, Jim had a class who were quiet and gainfully occupied.

At the end of the day Stan was enthusiastic, smiling and encouraging, and full of questions regarding how the mission had gone. I was giggly with excitement and couldn't wait to tell him. Jim gave me a passing smile too and said that I had done okay.

For the first time in my working life, I felt happy. In fact, saying that I felt happy does not do justice to the absolute ecstasy I was experiencing. Here was a job I could do and I was good at.

More than that, I felt that I was actually achieving something positive for me and for the kids. I never thought of the situation in the philosophical terms of making a contribution to society but that nascent germ of an idea was there. Instead of ducking and diving, sneaking extended toilet breaks or struggling with physics and engineering drawings, I was as free as a bird in my own environment of words, ideas and explanations. It was as if the millions of words I had read, and thousands of ideas I had absorbed, were all there for me to use, naturally and easily.

Just as important, I had a gift for teaching which was God given. I knew, instinctively, how to pace a lesson, when to push and when to ease back. I felt when a kid needed a sharp tug on his lead or extra encouragement because he was struggling. I knew how to mark without being taught and most important of all, I loved the act of educating – the joy of teaching which, at its best, is a sublime experience.

At last, I had found my place in the world.

*****

148

There is a saying used by young squaddies who fall in love with army life: it's called army barmy. I had just the same feelings about teaching. If being on the train to Manchester and Telephone House was a trip to hell - then driving along the Manchester Ship Canal on my way to Runcorn was the road to Heaven.

I literally could not wait to get into the classroom in the morning and I hated going home in the evening.

My enthusiasm shone through in the lessons and the kids both liked and respected me. It was as if my whole life had been a preparation for teaching, and I had never been so happy or fulfilled. Here was something that not only could I do, but where my efforts were also valued.

I had a particular empathy with kids who struggled with learning and so I was given lots of opportunities to teach these children. The curriculum is now much more tightly controlled and regulated, so the opportunities for creative and enthusiastic teachers to share what they love are greatly limited. By contrast, I had complete freedom so that even the least able kid cleaned the imaginary pots along with Shakespeare's "Greasy Joan" and travelled to the centre of the earth with Jules Verne.

We read and wrote, spoke and played in the great sea of language that I loved and inhabited. And the kids did learn – they really did. I loved the act of teaching and I loved what I was teaching, so the kids loved learning alongside me.

Only a few didn't. These were not the ones who weren't very bright but those who objected to the frantic pace of work I set, or who were used to bullying other pupils – either physically or intimidating them with looks or comments. Having been on the wrong end of bullying, I abhorred it and so, for a very few kids, I was not good news.

Of all the things I have done in my life, working with children who had learning difficulties is the thing of which I am most proud. It's a long time since I have taught Set 4 English but I am extremely proud to still receive notes from my ex-pupils. One wrote to me a few months ago saying that he tells his children about a young teacher who taught him how to read when he was thirteen years old: one can't ask for more than that.

Chapter Eighteen

Not As Easy As It First Seemed

As well as being hyper keen and well organised, I had a USP which helped my relationship with the kids no end: I raced bikes. Once this information leaked out to the school, I really did have a head start in my desire to be accepted.

I was so enthralled with teaching that I actually stopped racing for a few months but then I woke up one morning with the urge to ride again. Although I was only earning two thirds of a fully qualified teacher's salary I had decent money coming in at the end of every month, and the spares business was ticking over nicely too.

I suppose that, more than anything else, it was my new found wealth which caused me to look at the Tribsa with critical eyes. One of the many challenges which clubman racers face is that – at least at the start of their riding careers - they really do believe that if they had the same bike as Billy Whizz who is doing all the winning, then they would beat him.

This line of thought has always been a fallacy but in the late 1960s, there was a germ of truth in the belief. The difference in performance between a real race bike, like a twin port 360 CZ or 250 Husqvarna, and converted road bikes like the Tribsa was immense. In fact, it was considerably more than even that!

I occasionally scrounged a ride on a 250 Husky and it was like riding a bike from a different planet. The Husky was light and powerful, with good suspension and brakes which worked. The Husqvarna engines pulled well too and made plenty of power. Even the gearbox and clutch worked properly. Best of all, the Husky was far more suited to my physique.

The bike was so good that Torsten Hallman won four World Championships on what were very close to production bikes, just well prepared at the Husqvarna factory in Sweden.

The problem was that Huskys were impossibly expensive – completely beyond me even thinking of owning one.

The 360 CZ was another bike I really liked. These machines were made in Prague, when the city was part of Eastern Bloc Czechoslovakia. CZs were a bit agricultural in terms of their looks, especially when compared with the beautifully finished Huskys but, again, the bikes could win GPs straight out of the box.

This was reflected in the way works riders were treated. Belgian Joel Robert, who won his first 250cc World Championship in 1964, took his CZ to GPs on a not very good trailer towed by a black Mercedes taxi.

Works support came in layers from CZ. First, you got a few spares free of charge via your local importer – but not many: maybe a piston half way through a season and a chain or some tyres. If you won, then you got a free, standard bike and a few more spares. Keep winning even more and a works cylinder barrel came your way, which gave a bit more power and a slightly crisper performance. Note that the rest of the bike was absolutely bog standard.

Finally, at GP level you would get a factory prepared bike, which was better than the standard machine, and a Czech mechanic. With this set up, you'd better be winning GPs on a regular basis or you were out.

In practical terms, this meant that anyone with sufficient funds could buy a bike capable of winning a British championship race, and finishing in the top ten of a GP.

Both the Husqvarna and CZ machines were reliable. They were built for racing and could take the hammering which motocross gave them, whereas bikes like my Tribsa were always breaking because they were a kit of road parts – and often well-worn ones too.

*****

As an arch patriot, why didn't I look towards a British solution to the Tribsa's failings? Well, I actually did – and got a good spanking for my efforts.

A theme I am forced to return to is the sanitising of history by commentators, professional and amateur, who simply weren't there. I suppose the problem is that if one looks at some immaculately restored machine, with paintwork better than a Rolls Royce and chrome so deep and lustrous that you could drown in it, there is a temptation to think that this was the norm for machines at the time: it wasn't.

If you then talk to the bike's owner, who has spent a quarter of his life researching the history of the Grimswitchdyke Flyer Factory, at the very least it is curmudgeonly not to be gracious. Since I have an unfortunate habit of telling the truth as I see it, I can assure you from multiple past experiences that being honest and candid is rarely a vote winner.

Further problems occur specifically for journalists who don't have the knowledge in the first place.

Finally, it's not a commercially smart thing to tell your readers that they are delusional and that their immaculate, concours winning, Grimswitchdyke Flyer was actually a load of sheep poo when it was new. Again, speaking from having been there, this is not an automatic way to win votes and influence people.

All writers are biased – it is impossible not to be. I am replete with bias because of my family background, social status as I was growing up, where I was born and – the obverse side of the coin – the quality of education I had at college and my innate intelligence.

I don't know what it was like to be a rocker at the Ace Café because I wasn't there, and therefore I can only comment with the bias which comes from second-hand, anecdotal information.

I don't see anything wrong with bias providing, and this is critically important, both the writer and the reader acknowledge that the bias exists and don't try to pretend that it doesn't.

Not that taking one side of an argument or the other is restricted to classic bikes. Jonathan Rea is five times World Superbike Champion and has the highest number of wins, pole positions and fastest laps of any rider in the championship - ever. Unfortunately, his sport isn't cricket, tennis, golf or some other activity which the BBC deems to be socially acceptable so Jonathan, and motorcycling, is snubbed.

Is this bias against motorcycling? Absolutely – but to address the issue would take a huge shift in attitude by the whole bike racing business – and, critically, the riders too. So, all that we can do is to acknowledge the status quo, shrug our shoulders and go riding.

My stories are all biased but, equally, they are as accurate and honest as I can make them. Yes, they are told through the eyes of a young man from an impoverished background but many others who were there would say the same things.

If I had wanted a British bike, what would have been the options? At the top of the list would have been Greeves but I'll come to this company last because their best bike had a big influence on my life.

Second to Greeves was Dot. The factory's flagship bike was the White Strength 250. The backstory to the White Strength soubriquet was the Daz soap powder TV ad which everyone could repeat verbatim in the 1960s.

The story went like this. A bloke dressed in a very, very naff suit of extremely fake chain mail and a cardboard helmet, rocked up at some housewife's door and, if she had a box of White Strength Daz in the house, gave her £5. If she was the proud owner of a giant box of said detergent, she was given a tenner.

Now £5 or £10 doesn't seem a lot but a fiver was worth about £100 in today's buying power so it was worth having.

In addition to the cash incentive, Daz's USP was its White Strength washing power so someone, and I can't imagine that anyone at the Dot management had anything to do with the idea, decided that their silver framed bike, complete with white fibreglass tank, should be called the White Strength.

The bike represented the absolute peak of Dot's racing design because the factory used an Alpha Bearings' bottom half, with a British Stefa ignition, mated to their own cylinder barrel and head. Transmission was via a Burman gearbox and the motor produced around 24hp, which was respectable for the day.

The White Strength Dot went very well but it was a real backyard shed special. For example, although Husqvarna and CZ were using tuned expansion chambers based on the well-known, and race proven, Kaaden principle, Dot soldiered on with a crude megaphone exhaust, the noise from which would kill deer at five miles: it was lethally loud!

The facts of the matter were that Dot had no budget for engine development and probably no inclination either.

The four speed transmission was never designed for racing and the hubs were road items bought in from Grimeca because Burnard Scott Wade had good contacts in Italy. The tank was fibreglass and this was bought in along with the mudguards. In all, the White Strength was a real parts' bin special.

The best part of the Dot was the leading link suspension which was designed and manufactured in house. The front forks were excellent downhill and Dot riders always made the most of this advantage. Against this, Dots were slow turning compared to the best bikes of the day and were, even with the introduction of the White Strength model in 1965, terribly old-fashioned.

Was there a fix? Yes – and no. As I explained earlier, the American market was on fire and there was the opportunity to trade off the back of this demand for dirt bikes, and produce competitive machines. In essence, this is what both Bultaco and Montesa did in Spain.

The problem for Dot was how to make the transition from being, effectively, a maker of factory produced specials to a full blown manufacturer. The factory lacked the management, design staff and manufacturing capability to do this successfully. The key indicator of these problems was how little of a complete Dot was made in the Manchester factory and how much was bought in from all over Europe.

The final incarnation of Dot race bikes were machines fitted with a German, Maico engine. These were satisfactory – but not brilliant.

I later became friends with John Griffiths, who was both a brilliant rider and very well connected in the motocross world. During the final days of Dot, in the late 1970s, John had sufficient capital to buy the Dot name and restart production but he told me that once he had begun a sensible due diligence process, every indicator warned him against the move. Dot was finished – out of ideas, out of date and out of time in the modern world.

*****

A factory which did have the manufacturing capacity, and an established dealer network in the US, was AMC – the maker of a string of machines under the Matchless, AJS and James brand names. The situation was even better, or maybe worse, than this because AMC bikes had a tremendous reputation after the war from winning endless championships in motocross and trials.

However, by the time I came to even think of a better bike I wouldn't have gone near a James Cotswold, which was AMC's lightweight offering and a good example of how not to make a 250cc class motocross machine.

I would have had the top Matchless bike of the day but it was way beyond my budget and, if the cash had been available, my money would have gone on a 250 Husky - which would have earned me a lot more prize money.

The top offering from AMC was the Matchless G85CS and, if it had been available ten years earlier, it could have been a really solid profit maker in both its race and road forms.

The heart of the bike was a walloping 500c, single cylinder engine which was a variant of the motors Matchless had been producing since the war. The G85's predecessor, the G80CS, was a lump of a thing and handled badly. Eventually customer complaints registered with the AMC board in Plumstead – and that was a world class achievement – and the go ahead for an all new, purpose built dirt racer was given.

The G85 engine was simply a development of the existing AMC single cylinder engines but this was okay. Reliability was improved by fitting a big-end bearing from the Matchless G50 road race engine, and a Norton mechanical oil pump was standard. The Norton oil pump was free to use because AMC owned this brand too.

Being a push-rod design, the engine was simple to manufacture and achievable - even using AMC's outdated tooling and machinery.

The cycle parts were given a total makeover. A brand new frame was built from lightweight tubing and the Norton Long Roadholder front forks, which I had on my Tribsa, provided the front suspension. They weren't the best but, in an earlier period, they would have been excellent.

There were also lots of very lovely and very British touches - like the slim, alloy petrol tank and the hand-made, alloy oil tank wrapping itself round a ginormous, 1½" (38mm) Amal GP carburettor.

The four speed Norton gearbox was a strong, reliable unit and a five speed cluster would have dropped straight in it – without any re-engineering or investment. The clutch was good too and the transmission was spoilt only by a weedy, accident prone, alloy chain case. Once more, fixing this was within AMC's budget and design capabilities.

The problem was the lack of will power and vision amongst management, which preferred cost cutting to taking anything approaching bold decisions for the long term good of the company.

The G85's front hub was a machined down version of the AMC road front brake and the rear hubs were using up stock from the G50 road racer. Instead of cutting corners like this, they could have looked at CZ or Husqvarna to see what was needed and cast some proper brakes in magnesium: everything was completely achievable, within AMC's budget constraints and technical capabilities too.

In all, the bike was very nearly there and, once again, with a management prepared to take the job by the throat, the G85 could have been the best motocross machine of its period – the 1950s!

The elephant in the van was that the bike was not launched in 1956 but 1966 - by which time it was a solution to a problem which no longer existed.

Yes, its 45hp engine was the most powerful of any motocross machine on sale but the G85 weighed in at a walloping 291lbs (132kgs) dry. Lining up for the start, with a full tank of fuel and a bit of mud, 300lbs was well in sight compared with 215 lbs (97kgs) dry for a 250 Husky.

If you haven't raced motocross, you might wonder what all the fuss is about for 75lbs (34kgs). To put this in perspective, 75lbs is the weight of a sack and a half of those potatoes that you see for sale at farmers' markets and those spuds have to be carried up hill, across ruts and over jumps. That's why weight was so important!

Having stressed all its failings, there was an obverse side of the coin which I saw first-hand. I rode at a terribly wet meeting high up in the Pennines, at a dismal place called Mow Cop which overlooks Congleton. It was sloshing down all day and the moorland track was turned into a quagmire. The master of the conditions was Dick Clayton, an AMC supported rider, who gave a master class on the G85. I can still remember the anthropomorphic snarl from the unsilenced exhaust as Dick lapped me, all crossed up but in full control. That was a bike which would have been a legend in the 1950s.

If missing the motocross boat with the G85 was a tragedy, there was a sister disaster attached to the saga. The G85 would have made a stunning, top-end road bike to rival BSA's legendary DBD34 Gold Star. The motocross frame would have been excellent on the road and the Matchless engine made as much power as a Goldie but was much easier to work on.

This is why we were frustrated with what British companies were offering us.

*****

Another company which could have changed the face of British racing was Villiers. This firm was huge and not only made motorcycle engines but also power units for a myriad of other uses. In 1957 they bought J. A. Prestwich Industries Ltd., makers of the J.A.P. engines – their only real opposition – to give them a monopoly on the supply of proprietary engines not only for British companies but manufacturers throughout the world.

Their position was so dominant that they had subsidiaries in Australia, New Zealand and Germany and associate companies in Spain and India – all eager to buy Villiers products.

In 1962 the company proudly claimed: "Jointly the two companies (Villiers and JAP) produce a vast range of two-stroke and four-stroke petrol engines and four-stroke diesel engines from 1/3rd to 16 bhp.

"These are the engines which power many of Britain's two-stroke motor cycles, scooters and three wheelers and the great majority of the motor mowers, cultivators, concrete mixers, generating sets, elevators, pumping sets etc."

Not only did the company produce engines but, as they said, again in 1962:

"The Villiers Group offers an extensive service to industry in the supply of drop forgings, castings, pressings and metal fabrications, spur, bevel and helical gears, and in the design and manufacture of Viltool special-purpose machine tools."

They also had economy of scale because their output was vast. As early as 1956, Villiers produced its two millionth engine - and duly presented it to the Science Museum: that's how big they were.

Despite their market dominance, Villiers engines were desperately unambitious and old-fashioned. The Villiers 34A engine, which had been supplied to all the smaller motocross manufacturers for years, was simply not fit for purpose. The gearbox and clutch were weak and the ignition system unreliable.

Further evidence that the 34A was useless, was that no-one used the standard barrel and cylinder head supplied by Villiers – not even right down at the very bottom of the motocross food chain. Rather, there was a booming business supplying tuned top ends from manufacturers such as Marcelle and Parkinson.

The answer was a real competition engine and this was the Villiers Starmaker, first sold in 1963. The Starmaker was a decent unit but, even at launch, it was backward looking. Instead of leaping ahead of CZ and Husqvarna, and starting off with a five or six speed engine, the Starmaker had four ratios. The engine was also air-cooled when MZ had already shown that the way forward for two-strokes was water cooling.

The points ignition unit was also old-fashioned.

Finally, the engine looked crude. The Japanese were already mass producing modern looking engines in the 1950s whereas the Starmaker looked very much like the old Villiers power plants. The appearance of the engine did matter because Villiers' direct opposition were making motors which looked more sophisticated, even if they weren't that different from the English products.

It wasn't as if Villiers didn't know what to do, or lacked either the capital or technical ability to make the best engine of its type in the world. Bernard Hooper, the Starmaker's designer, was very good and the Starmaker engine survived for many years as the AJS Y4 Stormer.

Villiers also made a six speed, road racing version of the engine, so they could have built either a five or six ratio gearbox for the Starmaker without any problem.

As always, the core of the issues rested with a desperately unambitious, short sighted management which, during the good times, had refused to invest in modernising Villiers' large Wolverhampton factory.

That same, dithering management team would have needed to commit to a proper, intense Grand Prix racing programme which would have shortened development time for the engine and raised its profile. Then, there would have been a chance at mass sales.

Even if the management had been first class, the Villiers' workforce was a by-word for militancy so maybe the fix was to move production to India where the jobs would have been welcomed with open arms!

It's not only me who thought the Starmaker was inadequate. Greeves, having promised to use the new engine, only put it in a few bikes after launch and then reneged on the agreement. Dot wouldn't go near it either, preferring to use their own engine for the White Strength model.

When Greeves did want to take the engine in 1967, Villiers belonged to the Norton Villiers Triumph Group (NVT) who, rightly and properly, wanted the motor exclusively for use in their re-launched AJS brand.

It was left to tiny manufacturers like Cotton and DMW to build the Starmaker into bikes, and companies like this did nothing for development or sales.

There were only two ways the engine could have succeeded – and the Starmaker missed both of them. If it had been dramatically better than a Husky or CZ engine then the posher end of the motocross machine buying market would have insisted on having it. The 20hp produced by the Starmaker at launch was pretty good – but not world beating. The same applied to the four speed gearbox which was yesterday's story.

Who would have built a world class chassis is a moot point, but maybe Greeves could have been spurred into action because, a little later, they produced the Griffon - which had excellent handling.

The other route would have been for the engine to be really cheap. Done this way, a host of smaller companies could have sold bikes which, although not as good as the best machines on sale, would have been okay for riders a couple of rungs above me on the motocross demographic ladder. An off the shelf racing engine would have had a world-wide sales base.

This second idea was highly achievable because Villiers had an Indian manufacturing partner already in place. The Indian government was desperate for technological investment, and Indian built Starmakers would have comfortably undercut even the Eastern Bloc produced CZs on price, and left Husqvarna for dead in terms of costs.

As things transpired, the Starmaker missed both targets until Norton took over Villiers and the AJS brand was resurrected. As an AJS product, tens of thousands of Starmakers were made - which proved the potential of the engine.

It would be a nice addendum to this story to say that I met Villiers' management, as only a little later I did with BSA, and laid out these ideas: nice – but a lie. I wouldn't have had the confidence, experience, nor a sufficiently broad world view of business to suggest manufacturing outside of Britain.

Another reason the idea would never have crossed my mind was because we held the view that Britain was the supreme manufacturing nation in the world. We had invented the jet engine, built the Spitfire, led the world in the production of nuclear energy and both conceived and built the Hover-craft. I, and many of my peers, simply could not understand what was going wrong – or why.

Although I didn't know it, as I was sitting in the Annexe staffroom surrounded by experienced teachers who liked me and kids who smiled when I walked into the classroom, my whole world was about to explode – but that was still to come. Eating my sandwich, drinking tea and reading *MCN*, all that I wanted was a British two-stroke which would get me into the finals at every race I entered.

The answer, apparently, was a Greeves – and what a mistake that was! The gate to this disastrously bad road was, unintentionally, opened by John Done who was the brother of Philip Done, a lad with whom I had become friendly.

The Done family had a large farm near to Pickmere Lake, the site of one of my less successful dates with S.

Johnny was sponsored by Greeves and kept his works bike in one of the loose boxes, on the right hand side of the yard.

Philip took me down there one evening and opened the top half of the stable door. It was like Aladdin's Cave with spare sprockets, chains and even a new, as yet unused, rear tyre: an absolutely incredible display of motocross affluence! The thought of having a complete, totally brand new tyre sat there, still carrying a Dunlop sticker and just doing nothing, showed wealth and success of unimaginable proportions.

I have to digress from the story for a moment to say a little bit more about John. He was a fine, international class rider and one of the nicest human beings on the planet. He was also a spectacularly successful car dealer, specialising in exotic vehicles. I saw him once in his little office on the car pitch, near the Manchester Ship Canal in Warrington. John looked like death warmed up –and not very warm either!

I asked him if there was a problem and he just smiled, patted the inside pocket of his sheepskin jacket and offered me a cup of coffee. The backstory to his black eyes was that he had been given a tip off about an almost new Ferrari which was for sale in Aberdeen, right up in the north of Scotland. The seller was going through a bad divorce and wanted to take some cash out of the marriage before the Ferrari became just another asset to be divided up.

John always kept a lot of cash handy. There was absolutely nothing dishonest or under-handed about this because a lot of business was done, to use the expression current at the time, with pound notes. It's wrong to think that the money which exchanged hands was trivial – like giving someone £25 for cutting a hedge. Large houses were purchased with cash, along with every other conceivable product and service.

What made John so smart is that he often underwrote the big deals. In this case, he had a very rich client in London who was looking for a Ferrari just like the one John had found. The problem was that the London buyer wanted the car instantly, the next day. The fix was to get an overnight train to Edinburgh and then on to Aberdeen, do the deal, drive the 600 miles to London and then get on another train back to Warrington.

I was no stranger to getting stuck-in to finish a job, but what John had done sounded more than a bit like hard work. I told John so and he smiled. "Yes, I was well knackered but a couple of thou' was okay, wasn't it?"

£2,000 was a truly astonishing amount of money because a nice, detached bungalow in Warrington would have been around £6,000 at the time. John had made a third of a bungalow for two days of tough travelling! Knowing what was in my wallet, I would have walked to Aberdeen and pushed the Ferrari all the way back to London for £2k!

John retired from international motocross but in the 1980s he made a comeback, and rode in the Tsubaki race team which I owned. It was a slightly odd experience to have my hero riding for me but John was the complete professional – respectful of my position, very helpful to the younger riders and the bedrock of the team. Sadly, he died at a very young age and I still feel very privileged to have known and worked with him.

But back to the Greeves…

A bike I could just about afford was a Greeves Challenger. This was Greeves' flagship race bike and was successful in both national and international events. To be fair to Greeves, and to me for buying the Challenger, the factory did have a stellar success record with Dave Bickers winning the 250cc European Motocross championship – the precursor of the World Championship, in both 1962 and 1963.

The problem was that the Challenger didn't suit me – not at all. There were three endemic problems – and a fourth brought about because of the peculiarities of the particular bike I owned.

All Greeves' machines had a very short wheelbase. This gave very good drive with the tyres of the day, which were prone to spinning in slippery conditions. The short wheelbase also allowed the bikes to turn more quickly. There was nothing inherently wrong with this way of thinking but it made the bikes very twitchy in a straight line and, coming from the rock steady Tribsa, I didn't like this trait.

The next problem was the unique Greeves' leading link forks. These featured a rubber-in-torsion system where a rubber bush, which is rotated slightly as the wheel moves up and down, acts like the steel spring in conventional suspension. These rubber-in-torsion forks were a derivative of the suspension used for the Greeves Invacar, which was the company's real money spinner.

Again to be fair to Greeves, their forks offered around 6" (150mm) of travel, when most machines could only manage 4" (100mm), but their action was very much an acquired taste. A secondary issue was that the 6" was controlled by hydraulic dampers which had to be in perfect condition. If they weren't, then the forks were very prone to tucking in under load, for example going downhill, and all that a clubman rider like me needed was an unstable machine in tough conditions!

Both these issues were exacerbated by the stiffness of the Challenger frame. Greeves had their own foundry and this meant that they could cast the legendary "I beam" front downtube. The main frame, which was steel, was located into this great lump of alloy and, as Bert Greeves insisted, it led to immense stiffness. However, there were three downsides – and that's too many in racing.

The first was that the alloy "I Beam" was heavier than a steel downtube. Secondly, there was no design flexibility possible because of the cost of changing the tooling for the huge alloy casting. The last was the most important. Contra intuitively, a good frame needs a degree of flex – and still does today, even with MotoGP bikes. With a genius like Eric Cheney designing a chassis, bikes could be built which had laser sharp, precision handling and yet had a slightly soft feel which made them very rider friendly.

So, the Challenger was absolutely the wrong bike for me – and that was only the good news. There was far worse to come. I could only afford a very early Challenger – a 1964 model - and this was plagued by terrible gear selection problems with the Albion gearbox.

My bike, in an attempt to keep it competitive, had also been tuned for more power. To clubman riders, the word "tuned" has the same value as "girlfriend" and "I'd really, really like to get up at 6am and go to Oulton Park instead of having a meal out" and "No, you need all your money for racing. Let me pay for the chicken-in-the-basket."

Sadly, tuned rarely translates into faster for muppet racers. Yes, tuned engines do make more power but what club riders need is an engine which is user friendly.

I later learned this lesson and took it to heart. I have won a few races over the years and all the successes, such as they are, have come on bikes which were, and are, docile and easy to ride. The simple truth is that I don't have the ability to deal with any challenges emanating from the bike and, to my credit, I have been bright enough to recognise this.

On the Challenger, I crashed a lot in circumstances where I really shouldn't have come off. This is a bad situation for a rider. With the peculiar way a racer's brain works, or more often doesn't, you can come to terms with accidents which are your fault. The big crash at Nantwich, which snapped my medial ligament, was 100% my fault – a result of ambition outstripping my ability.

Bike failures are also very similar. If a part breaks for no apparent reason, and an accident occurs, then it's possible to accept this.

The big issues come from when you are on the deck, wondering how the heck that happened. The Challenger was absolutely at the top of the tree in this respect. Viewed objectively, the errors were mine – but they were those of many other clubmen too. Greeves missed this most salient of points. It was amateurs who actually bought their products, not sponsored riders who were given them for free, and we needed a bike that we could trust not to let us down.

Top Greeves' riders, like John Griffiths and Johnny Done, could not only deal with the nervous nature of the Challenger but use it to their advantage – but club riders couldn't. On numerous occasions, I would make a minor mistake and that was that: down on the deck, hurting and the day's racing over. Never once did I feel that the bike was on my side.

Matters were exacerbated by the bike's power. As well as making motocross bikes, Greeves produced nice 250cc road race machines based very closely on the dirt bikes. A previous owner of my Challenger had tuned the cylinder barrel using the data from the road race machines, so there was little power right at the bottom end of the power band and then a big surge which caused wheel spin and unintended wheelies – or both at the same time, followed almost immediately by another short flight for the pilot as the bike spat him off!

Finally, there were always niggles with the thing – which spoiled the day. Sometimes, the gearbox would be sulky and it was a real embuggerance. Then the engine was prone to tightening – the precursor to a full blown seizure - and I would have to pull off the track and let it cool down.

The good news was that, thanks to my apprenticeship with rubbish, Villiers' engined machines, I had now become very sensitive mechanically and so never destroyed the engine, Vale-Onslow Dot style.

Even so, none of this was what I wanted to do when I went racing. Some riders, understandably, get a huge amount of pleasure from working on their race bikes, but for me, the act of competition was always more important than the preparation. It still is, which is why I smile at my good fortune every time I think of my wife, Carol, who really does have mechanical empathy.

*****

I didn't visit all the factories making motorcycles – but I did a fair bit of the Grand Tour and you might be interested to know just how basic they all were.

To give you a flavour of them all, here is a quote from Bert Hopwood - who later became Managing Director of BSA - describing his time as Chief Designer at Norton, just a few miles down the road from BSA at Bracebridge Street in Birmingham. I never saw the Norton factory working but Hopwood's words might give you an idea of British manufacturing in the 1950s and 1960s. Here's Mr Hopwood talking about his first day at Norton:

"Not even during the war time blitzes did I have to work under such difficult circumstances; the whole Norton building was such a slummy shambles sandwiched with machines and parts, and men and vermin, in a noisy conglomeration.

"My space was not too bad. After all, it was reasonably quiet and did not let in all that much rain."

By the end of the 1960s, when I first saw the companies, they were better but still light years' distant from modern manufacturing.

Dot, as I have mentioned, occupied what I think was an old mill building, right in the centre of Manchester in Ellesmere Street and less than a mile from the city centre. I never saw the whole building but the stores were on the second floor and the R&D Department, and that is truly being kind to the operation, was on the ground floor along with a large, open area for goods in and bits of projects which were on-going work.

I can't remember why but on one occasion I met Burnard Scott Wade at the Dot works and he showed me a ground floor storeroom with two little Guazzonis stood up against a side wall. He had imported them from Italy – one was a road bike and the other a cute little racer. This was before the huge argument we had over my £5 commission on the American dirt bike deal!

I was a keen listener and enthusiastic too, so Mr Scott Wade was happy to chat away, explaining that the Guazzonis were going to be part of an updated range of Dots, which would include a new trials bike. The Dots never appeared but it was interesting to see that there was already dissatis-faction with the Villiers' engines.

The bike assembly areas and offices were above the stores. I only saw these areas once and goodness me, they were basic. What lived at the top of the factory, I never found out.

Despite what you might read in the press and books these days, this was the reality of a small British motorcycle manufacturer – and Dot weren't even the worst!

Chapter Nineteen

Two Very Different Giants

To the north west of Dot, just ten miles or so up the road in Bolton, was CCM whose first factory was in Shiffnall Street. In fact, that statement is arguable because Clews Stroka bikes, the direct predecessor of Clews Competition Machines, were built in Alan Clews' large garage. Since Alan was building bikes in the garage, and selling from there too, maybe that was his first factory.

I wasn't fond of Alan, and he didn't much like me personally, but we did respect each other. I have limitless admiration for his vision and determination and I think that he admired my determination and integrity as a journalist. Certainly, this is what he said on a couple of the more peaceful times in our relationship. On other occasions, he described me very differently!

The factory in Shiffnall Street had been an old iron foundry, and then had been used for storage until Alan took it over and, with the help of his right-hand man Martin Hemmingway, transformed it into a proper little factory.

To say that it was totally unsuitable for manufacturing motorcycles is one of the great understatements of all time.

The works was impossibly cramped, with machines being individually built on little, angle iron tables.

The only reason it was possible to make bikes there at all is because almost every part of a CCM came from outside suppliers.

All the magnesium alloy castings were produced by a local foundry and there were endless problems with these due to porosity. The company was simply not used to making components to the very high standards needed for racing and it is a great credit to Alan that he got the results from them that he did.

If you ever come across an early CCM at a bike show, or a classic motocross meeting, have a look at the little bubbles in the castings and you will see what I mean.

The castings were machined at CCM, cheek to jowl with the machines being built.

The frames were made by Mick Eatough and came ready for assembly – and lovely things they were too.

Fuel tanks and seats also came from outside suppliers.

All this work took place on the first floor of the building and when the bikes were complete, they were lowered down to ground level on a hoist – really!

Despite the far from ideal environment, 42 Clewstroka/CCMs had been built by the end of 1972. This might not sound like a lot but the reality is that Clews managed to put together 42 complete bikes – with nothing missing – and this is a huge achievement. Building a one-off special is challenging but achievable by anyone with a mechanical inclination and sufficient determination. By contrast, 42 machines is precisely what it says: 42 cranks, 42 clutches, 42 gearboxes, 42 frames and so on. This is real manufacturing.

The one thing which was different about CCM compared to other small manufacturers is that Alan was, right from the start, very professional in his approach to making bikes. Whereas a lot of paper work was carried out on the metaphorical "back of a fag packet" by these micro manufacturers, Clews always kept a meticulous day book so that he knew what had happened, good or bad, why something had occurred and the measures that needed to be taken for the next step in the company's progress. This is why I admired him so much.

Perhaps Clews was thorough because he had a good engineering training. He once told me that he had done a limitless number of courses to avoid National Service. As long as you were in "education" you avoided two years in the armed forces - an idea which Alan thought was an utter waste of time.

CCM had engineering drawings for parts so that suppliers knew what they were making. This was the right way to go about the job. Instead of constantly relying on craft skills to make things fit, the part - usually at least - came from the supplier ready to use. Once more, I have to use the word professional for what Clews did.

CCM also produced proper, high quality parts books and even instruction manuals and this set them apart, well distant, from their peers and also explains why they could, and did, make so many machines.

With this vision came a ruthless determination – a really ferocious attitude. This is why we had cross words on occasions. By the time I first met Alan, I was writing professionally and had already developed a near religious zeal for telling my readers the truth as I saw it. Nothing, and no-one, was going to come between me and the duty of care I felt to readers, and my deep sense of privilege in being able to speak to them.

So, when I tested the very first CCM I had no problems saying that the chassis was too stiff and the engine too fierce for clubman riders like me. Alan became very cross and one of the more polite phrases he used to describe me was "You're a total w****r not fit to ride a motocross machine."

He may, or may not, have been correct in his assessment of my riding ability but I still wrote what I believed to be true about the bike – and would have done so if the Archangel Gabriel had been standing next to the CCM threatening me with a fiery sword: I was going to respect my readers and tell them honestly what I thought and that was that!

Although later I owned several CCMs, they always came in part exchange against another bike I was selling at the time. I rode a fair few but never liked any of them. For me, there was only one motocross machine to have – the Cheney: built by the man who I was incredibly privileged to call "Uncle Eric."

*****

I have a few real regrets in my life and one of them is not writing Eric Cheney's biography because I loved the man. He was everything, well nearly everything, I found interesting and attractive in a designer and creator, because he was a true eccentric and an utter genius.

The situation is even sadder because Eric had started to jot down bits and pieces for me so that we could produce a really good book – then he went into hospital for a minor operation and never recovered.

We got so close to doing the book it brings tears to my eyes just thinking about the lost opportunity. I was looking through one of my Cheney files, as I have been doing research for this book, and came across a letter from Eric. As with all his correspondence, it was written in rather untidy, blue capital letters. I had been constantly nagging Eric to let me write his biography and he replied:

"I HAVE THOUGHT OF DOING A BOOK ONE DAY I THINK I COULD CALL IT <u>MY FIRST 40 YEARS IN MOTO-CROSS.</u> WHAT COMMENTS ON THESE IDEAS. YOU MAY HAVE I WOULD LIKE TO HEAR. I COULD TAPE IT AS THE THOUGHTS CAME TO ME THEN PUT IT TOGETHER IN TIME & DATE ORDER.

I GUESS THATS ALL I CAN THINK OF AT PRESENT PLEASE CONTACT ME IS YOU REQUIRE ANYTHING ELSE.

ALL THE BEST

ERIC"

I was ecstatic that, at last, I was going to write the book I had been begging Eric to do for years and, a few days later, I sent him a detailed, five page outline for the book with 120 questions to answer. I still have the carbon copy.

As the years go by, people are forgetting what these two giants in the world of small British motorcycle manufacturers looked and sounded like, so here are my first hand memories of them both.

First, Alan Clews. Alan was quite a big man, not fat but heavily built. He had thick, almost black hair and a luxurious moustache. When I met him, and I did so on many occasions, he was invariably well dressed with a brown workshop coat or, in the office, a smart shirt and tie.

He was bright eyed and quickly spoken, with a strong Bolton accent, slightly harsher than the softer East Lancashire burrs of the surrounding towns.

Passion dripped out of every pore and he spoke in quick bursts with the last phrase tailing off before another machine gun sentence. He often stressed points with his hands, moving to and fro in his chair as he undertook explanations. At races, he was hyper focussed and intolerant of anyone who wasn't essential to winning.

In many ways, he was more modern than his times. Tie apart, one could easily imagine him running a big IT or tech company today, and being a media personality. I would love to have seen him interviewing some waffling, prevaricating candidate on "The Apprentice": it would have been a Roman amphitheatre blood sport!

The difference between Clews and Cheney was so great that one could easily imagine they had set out to be as different from each other as possible.

For me, the single greatest contrast between the two was that Eric very often gave the impression that he was somewhere else, a long way distant, when he was actually speaking to me. Clews was impatient, critical, enthusiastic, smiling and sometimes overtly bad mannered but, when he was addressing anyone, there was no doubt that they were the focus of all his attention – for a few seconds at least.

Eric was very kind and warm to me on a personal level and yet I often felt that only a small part of him was ever fully engaged in conversation. He was not well dressed and, with his hair swept over his bald head, he looked incredibly ordinary. Put him in a high vis jacket and he could have easily passed for a roadside litter picker or car park attendant.

Where Clews looked the epitome of rude good health, Eric was pale and thin with an angular face. This wasn't just a product of age. The old, black and white images of him just after the war show the same, gaunt appearance.

He was softly spoken, with his voice reaching peaks at critical points in an explanation and then drifting away again as most of his mind returned to more interesting challenges.

Eric also often almost closed his eyes so by-standers who didn't know better would see an archetypal paddock or workshop hanger-on, or gofor, rather than being aware that they were in the presence of a creative genius.

If Alan Clews was the focussed professional then Eric was the artist in metal. Here's how he worked.

In 1975, I went to see Eric in one of his workshops. I say one, not because he had many premises but rather that he tended to move about a bit. This one was in an old tobacco drying building, deep in rural Hampshire.

I have a very low opinion of the current obsession with Health and Safety, where you have to wear a high vis vest, hard hat and steel capped boots to mow the lawn, but Eric did operate rather towards the farthest other end of the scale. Gas welding frames in a tinder dry, wooden building with a dusty floor was perhaps not taking full cognisance of fire hazards. Regardless, no-one died, and the workshop didn't burn down, so things couldn't have been that bad.

Although Eric was born in 1924, he had the mind of an enthusiastic 21 year old. He had achieved great things with BSA engined machines – more of these shortly – but later was fascinated with the advantages of long travel suspension. With no BSA engines available in the early 1970s, Eric turned his attention to the Honda XL 350 trail bike engine - a light, indestructible power plant which could be bored out to 410cc. In fact, Eric got even more capacity from the engine and had a 450cc engine which made a fearsome power plant.

Although a whopping 100cc larger than Honda intended, the outside of the engine remained the same size and Eric shoehorned this into a sublimely neat frame. He then machined off alternate cooling fins, as he had done with some of his BSAs, which reduced weight and, allegedly, stopped mud clogging up the fins.

I don't know how well this system worked in practice but I do know that I used to get tingles in my loins just looking at the "porcupine" fins on my works BSA and the Honda had the same effect – and not just on me. Everyone who raced motocross, as well as many who didn't, used to go faint at the magical trickness of Eric's work.

Long travel suspension had taken over motocross by 1974, and Eric's interpretation of the concept was completely brilliant. Instead of a single shock, which was very expensive and still prone to fading at the time, Eric used a pair of over the counter suspension units which were both cheaper and more reliable. As I have noted, he simply thought differently from everyone else in the world.

By 1974, I had come to know Eric quite well – sufficiently to be able ask favours of him. This wasn't as easy as it seems because he could be very abrupt – or worse.

I pressed him to explain how he actually designed the frame and, using every atom of patience at his disposal, this is what happened.

There was a 350 Honda engine on the floor and Eric got one of the lads to hold it up against the wooden wall of the workshop unit. Then he got a piece of chalk and drew, on the wall, where the headstock was going to go, followed by the frame's spine and downtube.

He stood back a little way, rubbed out the headstock and ever so slightly altered the angle. Then he stood back again.

"Right that's it. Now, we'd cut the tubing and then make a jig so we could knock some more out."

I asked him how he could be so sure that he was right.

This time, he really was running the patience reserves out to the last drop in the tank. "It's obvious isn't it? Just look, can't you see that it's right?"

And, of course, the answer was that neither I, nor anyone else, could know how something as complex, subtle and finely nuanced as a motocross frame had got from Eric's head on to a chalk drawing on a wooden wall, and then into a three dimensional structure: that was simply innate brilliance.

The obverse side of the coin was that Eric was no Alan Clews commercially. Alan Greenwood, in La Jolla, California, was a Cheney fan and wanted all the Hondas Eric could make. In fact, that's the wrong verb to use. Eric could have made the Hondas – but wouldn't.

Probably, if Pope Julius II had offered Michelangelo the chance to do a second Sistine Chapel he would have been turned down. For creative geniuses, it is the act of creation which is the magic key – not making money from their God given talents.

Eventually, Miles Webb and Ralph Rustell – who were two Cheney employees - did make several batches of the frames and Eric said that they had produced around 125 kits – not that he ever counted, or cared for that matter.

*****

Perhaps I should write a longer story about Eric and his achievements, but in this book I want to concentrate on his character. I first came across Cheney machines at a British championship motocross meeting held at the legendary Hawkstone Park track, in 1965. I couldn't afford the admission ticket but I never paid to get in. If you were fit, and didn't mind a very long walk, it was possible to enter the circuit through the shooting school and, being both broke and not frightened of a couple of miles walk, I had free admission.

Eric was there with his Cheney Gold Star. This was a lightweight, comparatively speaking, 500 which used a Cheney frame with Ceriani front forks and a Matchless front hub. As always, Cheney had done a remarkable job in terms of the bike's weight and he got it a full 50lbs (23kgs) slimmer than a standard BSA Gold Star.

The bike was ridden by Jerry Scott, a formidably fierce competitor, who later went on to be a BSA works rider, before sadly getting killed at Boltby, in North Yorkshire, in 1966.

The Cheney sounded absolutely magnificent, with the straight and totally unsilenced exhaust snarling like some angry Minotaur as Scott hurled the big bike up Hawkstone's formidable hill.

There was another remarkable thing about the bike – and one which was totally unexpected: Eric had an artist's eye for what was appealing to motorcyclists.

Many great designers put function over form. Take Giulio Cesare Carcano for example, arguably the greatest motorcycle designer of all time. He produced the utterly amazing, eight cylinder Moto Guzzi GP racer - which is a technical tour de force. I have ridden this bike and I am in awe of its technical complexity and the masterful use of space.

Equally, the Guzzi "Otto" is as ugly a thing as you will ever have the misfortune to meet – graceless, almost crude and uninspiring.

By contrast, Edward Turner's iconic 1938 Triumph Speed Twin is a very ordinary piece of motorcycle engineering but looks stunning – svelte, eager and desirable.

Eric managed to have a foot in both camps. His designs were the best in the world and yet he had an artist's sense of how to make a beautiful motorcycle.

The bike he created for Jerry Scott was mainly polished alloy and nickel plated but was set off by blue anodising on the fuel tank. This was incredibly avant-garde at a time when any deviation from black was considered to be radical.

I never spoke to Eric at Hawkstone but stood, very shyly, at the back of the crowd admiring the bike. I was so far down in the social septic tank that I could never have imagined even being close to the great man and so didn't feel either neglected or hard done by. Kids from my background, with empty wallets and no contacts, stood at the back in silence because this was how life was – and should have been for that matter.

But things were to change for me – and Eric.

*****

If these stories were fictional or even just dreamed up from roughly what happened, I could smooth out the narrative so that everything followed in the correct order. You might notice how this is done in a lot of autobiographies. However, real life isn't that simple and so I have to jump about chronologically.

Now we're in 1972 – and a lot had happened since I was sneaking into Hawkstone Park through the shooting school.

I was a newly qualified teacher, which was my dream job, but additionally I was writing a huge amount for three American magazines. I was also very well thought of at BSA. I had been given a personal meeting with Lionel Jofeh, the Managing Director of the whole BSA Group and was sponsored by the factory on a full works BSA.

You can read these stories in detail in my autobiography, "A Penguin in a Sparrow's Nest."

I have often pondered as to why I should have been so highly thought of at BSA. In hindsight, I think that there was a range of reasons – and each one was important in its own way.

First, and most importantly, I was honest about my ability – both as a rider and a journalist. I have worked with a lot of world champions, and ridden with a few too, and it is difficult to describe just how much better they are than even a good clubman rider like me.

They are vastly, immensely, galactically more talented in terms of what they can do with a motorcycle and also how they think about racing. Last year I had a brilliant day at a small, club road race and finished second, three times, to a rider 40 years younger than me. I drove home with a smile which didn't leave me for a couple of days.

By contrast, a world class rider would have been quite literally suicidal at the thought of the second places. There is a saying in the GP paddock – and it is the same whether it's road racing, motocross, grass tracking or whatever.

"Second is first in the losers' race" – and top riders live by this mantra. Second is complete failure.

BSA had some of the greatest riders in the world on their books – double World Champion Jeff Smith, John Banks, Dave Nichol, Andy Roberton, the Lampkin brothers and many more. Nothing I had done at even my very best, in terms of racing success, could be compared to any of these superstars on the worst of their bad days – nothing – so there was no sense in pretending. The only thing I could do was to arrive at BSA and say: "Look, I'm only an ordinary clubman but I can ride a bike competently, I love racing and I love BSAs."

However, my very lack of ability gave me a useful edge over the best riders. I was truly one of the masses who actually bought BSAs with their own money, instead of being given the machines. The bottom line was that I represented, and accurately too, BSA's customers. I rode like a BSA customer, and I thought like a BSA customer because I actually was one – or could have been. What was important to me was also directly, heavily relevant to BSA purchasers.

What made me different from the vast majority of clubmen though was my ability as a development rider. I could report what a bike was doing, articulately and accurately, either verbally or in writing. This was an ace card which has proved invaluable all through my riding career.

Next, I was courteous, respectful and thankful for my privileged position. In terms of riding or technical ability I had no right to even clean up crumbs from the top table at BSA, so I let everyone who helped me in the factory, from the fitters to the senior management, know that I was grateful – very grateful indeed.

Finally, I was known to be scrupulously honest – even recklessly so. I was prepared to argue with the Managing Director of the BSA Group to put forward my readers' concerns about the quality of BSA products. I then wrote of my disappointment with the interview in two magazines – and didn't spare the criticism.

This should have resulted in me being excommunicated by BSA forever – but it didn't. My criticisms of Lionel Jofeh, who was unpopular at BSA, were considered to be fair and so my opinion, even though I was very young, was accepted and I ended up with a full works BSA for free, to keep communications open: that's how highly I was thought of at the factory.

On one occasion, I was asked to come down to BSA by Reg Dancer, who was the Head of PR for the whole BSA Group - including motorcycles, guns, machine tools, Triumph, Ariel and a myriad of other subsidiaries – and BSA Motorcycles' Works Manager, Al Cave – Mr Cave to you, young Melling. And don't ever forget it!

BSA never sold engines, or parts, to anyone and so it was an enormous shock when I was asked whether it would be a viable proposition to make 1000 B50 motocross engines, and parts, to supply to Eric Cheney and Alan Clews.

Mr Cave's office was a glass panelled structure, right in the centre of the ground floor of the factory and no-one went in there without a very good reason. Reg sat on the edge of Mr Cave's desk whilst he held court from behind it. I was put on a cheap, plastic chair.

The conversation was surreal because everyone involved in bikes knew, for absolute certain, that it was impossible to buy parts from BSA – absolutely out of the question. The fact that the factory was even considering the move showed what an utter crisis the company was in.

I was asked whether I thought that the project was viable and still, to this day, I am proud of being as scrupulously fair as I was. Bearing in mind my personal friction with Alan Clews, I could have either been overtly critical or, just as bad, damned him with faint praise.

I did neither but said what a good job he was doing with CCM and the number of bikes that was being produced. Then, because I knew that it would impress Mr Cave, I told him about the spares' lists and the day book.

Finally, I said that he would be a good commercial partner. This is what I meant by being meticulously honest, as far my knowledge and beliefs would permit.

When the subject of Eric was raised, I had to be fair to BSA in my judgement again. As I have said already, I worshipped Eric but I told BSA that he would not be reliable and, for sure, he wouldn't make 500 BSA engined bikes.

Cheney was well thought of at BSA and he had an ace card which Clews didn't. One of the great doyens of the BSA Group was Ken Heanes, who was a multi-gold medal winner in the International Six Days Trial with Triumph bikes and one of the world's biggest Triumph dealers. He was also a very near neighbour to Eric.

Heanes really did have VIP access to the deal makers at Triumph and so they hatched a plan for Eric to make the Heanes Thumper. This would have the truly superb Cheney JBR frame – the best motocross chassis of its time by a giant margin – with a BSA B50 engine, BSA B50MX hubs and front forks, and Girling rear dampers.

And that was only the visible bit of the iceberg in what was a spectacular deal.

Heanes was also going to fund the whole project, right down to the last detail. He would pay BSA for the kits of parts and buy the Reynolds 531 tubing and extra welding gas for what would be a genuine series production run. He would then sell the bikes through his shop and even deal with niggles such as HP finance and part-exchanges.

What could possibly go wrong?

Of course, for anyone who knew Eric, the answer was staringly obvious. After 20 bikes, maximum, Eric would get bored and that would be that – and it was.

I have read several reports saying that the reason the project failed was because BSA could not deliver the kits on time, and this is simply wrong. In fact, with Triumph Adventurer using the same hubs and forks as the B50MX, there were plenty of parts available.

Further, after BSA officially closed, spare parts were made into the Triumph TR5MX and around 200 of these bikes, badged 1974 models, went to Sweden. More, reportedly, went to the US so there would have been ample for Eric.

No-one – not even Eric when I asked him – knows how many Thumpers were actually made and anyone who does claim to have an accurate figure is not being honest. My best guesstimate, from talking to Eric about the subject on a number of occasions, was that he made around 125 Thumpers – and fabulous things they are too. However, remember that Eric might have just been telling me what I wanted to hear and he knew that I felt he should have been a real manufacturer, like CCM. It could credibly be that the 125 figure was on the high side and I wouldn't be at all surprised if Eric descended from heaven and whispered in my ear that the real figure was 80 or 90 bikes

I have a Thumper, with a factory specification engine, and the bike took me to my only national championship – the 1994 Vintage Grass Track Championship. Winning the championship took an awful lot of travelling and neither Carol nor I enjoyed the constant points counting - but beating all the top classic grass track bikes on a motocross machine was a lot of fun.

*****

When the BSA competition department closed in 1972, the factory's top rider was a brilliant giant of a man called John Banks. His relationship with Eric shows the other side of why I loved Cheney.

Another ex-BSA man, Dave Nichol, got Cheney and Banks together following the end of season Fox and Hounds meeting at Newbury. They met in a pub and the most ambitious plan in the history of Grand Prix racing – of any sort, bikes or cars – was hatched.

Cheney would provide Banks with £1,000 to seal the contract, six bikes and all the spares he needed. In return, Banks would compete in all the Grands Prix and the British 500 motocross championship. In less than an hour, the deal was done. There was to be a further £1,000 for Banks at the end of the season when bike sales had paid for the year's racing. Banks negotiated his own sponsors.

In 1973, £1,000 clearly had more buying power than today but, even so, it wasn't a lot of money. I checked the conversion rates and £1,000 then is worth about £11,000 currently so Eric signed one of the best riders in the world, for less than any top quality rider is paid per GP round today.

Remember also that at the time, Banks was earning between £300 and £500 in start and prize money from a single French International race. Nevertheless, both parties were ready to go out and win the world championship: this was no token, half-hearted attempt.

Combined with BSA's push-rod, 499cc B50MX single, which concentrated the bulk of the engine's mass around the centre of the bike, the Mk IV gave excellent handling.

Eric got straight down to the job of improving the Mk IV into what was to become the renowned Mk V Victor - universally known as the JBR, or John Banks Replica.

Despite Banks being known in the Cheney team - with at least some small degree of affection - as "The Destroyer", Cheney built the GP bikes from thin wall 1¾" x 17 gauge Reynolds 531 tubing for the main spine and employed ⅞" x 18 gauge in the sub-frame. This was bronze welded - which made for an extremely light and yet strong construction.

I'd like to add a real pub quiz bit of history here because it illustrates how Eric did business.

Eric always argued that although everyone else in the British bike frame building business was using the legendary Reynolds 531 tubing, the company's T45 tube was better for motocross. T45 was, strictly speaking, a tube for the aircraft industry but Eric always argued that it was stronger than 531 under shock loading – as in launching off a huge jump with the limited rear suspension of the day.

He may well have been right, because I saw many of the frames made by other small manufacturers break but never a Cheney – not once, ever.

However, the JBRs, and Heanes' Thumpers were all constructed from 531 – and I have written confirmation of this fact from Eric. I wonder if Eric switched to 531 because Heanes had purchased a huge quantity of this tube for the Thumper project - Eric always had an eye to saving a copper or three.

Eric's eccentric chain adjusters, whose angle is altered by a vernier cam, kept the rear wheel accurately aligned and flex free in the swinging-arm - and provided an instant trade-mark for the JBR.

An alloy 6" Rickman hub was used at the front, whilst a 7" magnesium Rickman hub provided the rear stopping power. The rear brake plate was reworked to take a fully floating torque arm with cable operation. Fully floating rear brakes were another one of Eric's passionate beliefs.

The suspension was state-of-the-art with Eric's own front forks and Koni rear dampers. The Cheney forks were manufactured from billets of solid dural which were machined by the old London gun firm of Mollants, using an Eldorado gun drill which Eric imported from America. This meant that the forks could be finished to an extremely tight tolerance - there are no bushes in the design - in one pass and the end result was a front fork about as good as one could get at the time.

Eric was equally busy with the engine. First, it was lightened by machining away alternate fins on the head and the barrels - worth 1½ valuable pounds (0.7kg) because the weight was so high up on the engine - then a hand-made alloy clutch was fitted, along with slimmed down primary chain case and timing covers which carried the footrests

The traditional Gold Star steering head angle of 62 degrees was used for straight line stability whilst a wheel base of about 54½" made for nimble turning on corners.

Because Banks liked to rev the engine, a ¼" (6mm) was machined from the flywheel which had the extra benefit of reducing oil drag. The downside was that the flywheel became ridiculously light for an off-road bike.

Shortened Gold Star valves were used for both inlet and exhaust, and a 34mm Mikuni, from a Suzuki TM400 motocrosser, fed the mammoth inlet port whilst the gas exited through a drain sized, and totally unsilenced, exhaust pipe which wound its way underneath the engine.

The end result of the 200-300 hours spent on each machine was a bike which weighed some 235lbs (106kgs) wet and produced around 40bhp. This was right up with the last works BSAs and the team was competitive.

Best of all, the JBR played right to Eric's strengths. Machining flywheels, fabricating special parts and working directly with one of the world's greatest motocross racers fed directly into Eric's heart and soul: making 500 identical Heanes Thumpers didn't!

This was a pity because the core of the bike – fuel tank, side panels, frame and swinging arm – became the Heanes Thumper so you can see the scope of that project, had it ever gone ahead to its full potential.

It was through this GP bike that I got to know Eric, and John Banks, on a personal level. The new JBR first appeared at the Cadwell Park TV scramble in February 1973 and immediately attracted attention with its nickel plated frame, blue anodised petrol tank and side-panels and, rather eccentrically, the latest Preston Petty plastic mudguards which were bright orange. Banks too proved to be on the pace and BSA fans all over the world looked forward to the new season.

As might be expected from a team operating from little more than a four car garage, there were ups and downs. John led the French Grand Prix by a handsome margin, but then had the nylon heel of the contact breaker seize on the cam. However, he did finish a joint second at the American GP at Carlsbad, beaten only by Gerrit Wolsink on the factory Suzuki. At the end of the year, Banks had also dominated the British 500 Championship and was the last rider to win this Blue Riband event on a British bike: strange things happen at the end of an era.

Banks' memories of the bike, 22 years on, are fascinating. "Of all the bikes

I ever rode, I like the Cheney the best. It was the most satisfying bike to ride and I still admire Eric's enthusiasm. He always wanted to win and that was just <u>so</u> important to me.

"The man was brilliant. If he had been working for Honda he'd have made a fortune. Anything we wanted he did straight away and nothing was too much trouble

"I went out to win the World Championship and I seriously thought I could. I didn't want to be second.

"Duckhams had put up a load of money and the 20-40 mineral oil they gave me was s**t and the cam kept wearing out. Then I found out that the rally boys were on Duckhams 'R' which they (Duckhams) told me they never had so I told them that I wanted the same as the rally boys, and the bikes ran good after then.

"Eric paid Roy Read to come to the later meetings and look after the bikes and this let me get on with racing.

"My best ride was at Carlsbad (the then home of the US 500 Grand Prix). Alan Greenwood (the US Cheney importer) gave us a lot of help and the two bikes he prepared in America were faster than my European bikes. They had special cams and were really quick starters. Not like my works BSAs which crawled off the line.

"Carlsbad was really hot but I could stand the heat, and I got a really good start and split the works Suzukis of De Coster and Wolsink. These were the best riders in the world, on the best bikes, so I was really pleased.

"We could have done more with more money, but I have nothing but good memories about that season".

There is a final, somewhat ironic, twist to this story. In the 1990s, I heard about a "funny motocross bike" that was in Oxfordshire. It wasn't for sale but the farmer who owned it had lost interest and so it was sat there in the back of one of his barns.

On the way back from the Banbury Vintage Grass Track, where I had ridden my "standard" JBR motocrosser against the methanol burning Jawas and JAPs with reasonable success, we decided to track the rumour down.

There, buried deep within a storeroom, inside a palatial farm complex stood what was, without doubt, a very special JBR. After two hours of intense negotiation, we headed home much, much poorer - and with a JBR on the trailer.

I was beside myself with excitement and the same night, I 'phoned Eric and he confirmed that it was indeed one of the batch of bikes which had been built for Banks but, in this case, it was the spare machine which had never been delivered to Banks and, when finances got tight at the end of the season, had been sold to raise money.

The bike had clearly been little used from new but had not benefited from being stood idly for so many years. The restoration job was not difficult when compared with those heroes who re-cast crankcases on 1899 Whizz-bang specials but it did take a lot of time - and in the middle of the racing season too.

In fact, the job was more of a time-consuming nuisance than technically difficult. For example, all the tiny, button head Allen screws which Eric was so fond of using had grown to like their home and the only way of removing them without damaging the frame's nickel or the threads, was very slowly and extremely carefully.

We fitted new bearings on all the cycle parts, re-chromed the Cheney forks which, as luck would have it, were totally unmarked except where the dust shrouds had retained a thin, damp line of moisture and pitted the fork leg.

With time tight for the big classic meeting at Farleigh Castle, we took a chance on the motor which had plenty of compression and seemed to be running free. I am fortunate in having a mini-test track in our sheep's paddock at the back of our cottage so it was with some degree of excitement that we dragged the JBR to the top of the test hill in order to launch it down the slope and fire it up. For those not familiar with racing B50s, crisp ones are impossible to start on the kick-start; not even fourteen stones of muscle-rippling John Banks could manage it - so I have no chance.

With a skilled assistant - usually Carol my wife, head mechanic, team-manager and financier - we can start our B50 in a couple of paces but after three fruitless attempts with the JBR, Carol was beginning to think that I had lost my touch! The problem was that the flywheels were so light, and the compression ratio so high, that the engine would just not turn over on the wet grass, even with the benefit of a grippy, modern motocross tyre. Eventually, we got the thing spinning and half a thou' of throttle persuaded it into life. And what life too!

This was the most non-politically correct motorcycle in the galaxy, with a rasp and crackle emanating from its exhaust which would stun a bison at 100 yards. Yes, I was wrong; socially irresponsible; it's not sharing our paddock with the rest of Britain in a meaningful, bonding, neighbourly way but - ooohhh - you'd sell your first born son to hear that exhaust note! For an evocation of the heart of motorcycling, I would put it right up there alongside Hailwood's Honda 6.

Testing continued for only another ten minutes - even the good grace of our neighbours can be stretched too far - and then we were off to Farleigh Castle, never having ridden the beast in anger.

Now, at this point, the story should finish with boy-racer-journalist-makes-good-riding-the-bike-of-his-dreams. Except, well - there always has to be an exception doesn't there? In this case it was the simple fact that putting a good, clubman runner on a GP bike does not make the amateur into a world star.

We arrived at Farleigh Castle to find the circuit deluged with rain, and the track as greasy as a roadside burger. The JBR produced little worth-while power until about 3,500 rpm, at which point it came on the cam like a road-racer. Shut it off and the thing stalled. Ease round corners on a whiff of throttle, as I was so used to doing on my "normal" Cheney, and the works motor coughed and banged until it was back in the power-band once more. Once in the power-band, there is nothing, but nothing, which will touch this bike for speed - and up the long, straight climb at Farleigh, we passed everything in sight; truly, a memorable experience.

The handling too, was a revelation with a precision and accuracy which our standard Cheney could not match. Certainly, Eric's efforts in the weight saving department seemed to have brought about miraculous results since very few classic motocrossers get within a mile of this machine in terms of handling.

The problem was that the bike intimidated the rider. Despite the quality of the handling, and the superb brakes and the Warp Factor Five motor, I hated riding the thing. It is not a user friendly motorcycle in any sense of the word, and it needs the skill and fitness of a GP star to be of any practical value. You might think that you're good but this bike will let you know if you really are.

When I complained to Eric, he summed up the situation easily and as accurately as ever: "Your balls aren't big enough! It needs a real man to ride it." Which, sadly, is true.

I had another couple of plays on the bike but on each occasion I rode it matters got worse, until I eventually gave up, covered this rare example of exotica with a pristine cloth and put it reverently in the back of my workshop.

Eventually, the Cheney found a home in American enthusiast Jim Godo's private museum - a fitting resting place for a unique piece of history.

I need to add a concluding comment which illustrates a key difference between Clews and Cheney and it's one which is now being buried beneath the soft duvet of nostalgia. Generally speaking, you purchased a CCM and got what you paid for, to the specification ordered and – more or less – at the promised delivery date. Of course, there were aberrations and disappointed customers but, largely, purchasers got what they paid for and at the stated delivery time.

The same could not be said for Eric who was in almost constant financial problems. This meant that some of his business practices were very questionable. There were even tense "discussions" between him and me about delivery dates for my bikes: that's how bad things got on some occasions!

I love Eric too much to go into detail but it does need recording that for ordinary, retail customers Eric was often not a paragon of virtue.

But Cheney and CCM were a long time in the future. To get the story back on the correct timeline what I needed was a replacement for the awful Greeves.

Chapter Twenty

If Only . . .

I want to devote a whole section of the book to the Victor not because it was a great machine but rather because the motorcycle is an almost perfect icon for the utter mess which the country had got itself into and also the confusion this chaos caused.

I had been educated at an Army school. I had learned to stand up straight and sing the National Anthem lustfully at the end of every cinema performance either at RAF Idris or one of the Army bases around Tripoli – and you stood up smartly too or were taken on one side for a "word" by one of the many military personnel. "British is best" was in our very DNA.

On the one hand, there were an awful lot of young people and especially men, like me, whose blood was red, white and blue and who had a passionate pride in Britain. We wanted to buy British, support Britain and walk with our heads held high because we were proud. All this sounds very old-fashioned now, and maybe jingoistic too, but it wasn't in the 1960s.

Everyone, quite literally every person, knew someone who had fought in the war and the overwhelming view was that the huge sacrifices which had been made had brought about world peace. As I have noted from my own family's experience, there was an immense cost to these efforts which often resulted in personal and family tragedy. Regardless, there was a feeling that what Britain had done in going to war on the 1 September, 1939 was right and an act which was worthy of great national pride.

Now, we wanted to continue to be proud but we felt that British industry was letting us down. Before getting on to BSA, let me give you another example both of my patriotism and what the results of being loyal to Britain meant in practice. Once more, the story is slightly out of chronological order but it does illustrate how bad was the mess with anything made in Britain.

By the time 1972 had arrived, things were looking up for me in so many ways that I could afford my first new car. I was also getting to understand how to make the best of the hand of cards I had to play.

One of the salesmen from a local Ford dealer was something of a grass track fan and, like a number of grass enthusiasts, liked the quirky sight of a motocross bike mixing it with the real grassers.

He would come across and chat in the paddock and there was always some spare coffee in my flask for him: a plastic mug of coffee being the 1972 equivalent of a MotoGP hospitality centre!

I was chatting to him about getting my first ever new car, and how excited I was, but also that I didn't know where to spend my hard earned, precious cash. He was maybe ten years older than me but still as enthusiastic about cars as when he had first started selling them, straight from school. He was one of the senior salesmen, and so carried some clout in the company, and he said that he would talk to his Sales Manager, and the Dealer Principal too.

The next week, he had got a really good deal worked out for me on the basis that I was a "Sports Personality". It was interesting that the idea of sportsmen starting to have some marketing value was just beginning to become widespread. I was given the brief to ham it up when I met his bosses, gloss over the actual race results a bit, and everything would be good.

The following week, I rocked up at the dealership – smart, presentable and articulate as normal – did a bit of fine tuning to my actual race results, without actually telling overt lies, and everyone was happy. The dealership had been in contact with the Ford factory in Dagenham - and between the factory and the shop, I was made a happy bunny with the promise of a bright red, Mk II Escort in GT trim.

At the time, almost everything was an extra cost on a Ford and so the dealer gave me a nice radio, better carpets and a tow bar. For the first time in my life, I was also going to drive a car with electric screen washers, instead of having to pump the fluid on to the screen with a big black button.

I was particularly pleased to have an Escort because they were built in the nearby Halewood plant, on the south eastern side of Liverpool, so it was doubly patriotic – British and made by Scousers, who I had come to like rather a lot during my time at college.

The Escort looked really nice and I couldn't wait to pick it up. There was a bit of a handover, with hands duly shaken, but no pictures or a press release. This was good because I was still learning the PR / Celebrity game, and how it was played.

I was given a thorough pre-flight briefing, with special emphasis on the running-in procedure and the need to bring the car back promptly for its first service at 1500 miles. The first service with the cars of the day was really important because there was, invariably, a list of problems to be fixed – most minor but others more significant. The first oil change was critically important because this took with it the debris from the original build and the running in process.

I couldn't wait to go to Chester and show it to my long term girlfriend and take her for a drive into Wales.

First impressions were good. The 1300cc engine was really peppy for the day, the four speed gearbox slick, and handling firm but sound. The all new disc brakes worked a treat, and I was looking forward to a wonderful life ahead as a member of the motoring elite.

This feeling lasted until about 600 miles, when the electric screen washer packed in. Hey, what's the problem? All new cars have a few snags. Then the windscreen wiper motor gave up the ghost and I was back to the bad old days of peering through the rain streaming across the windscreen. Still, it's only a few minor bits...

Then the posh carpets split – quite literally fell apart - and were replaced at the first service. The clutch refusing to disengage came a bit later – about 3,000 miles – but that's what you get if you're rough with a car. Me? Rough? You must be joking.

And what's a bit of odd front tyre wear? What do you expect, a lorry?

Then there was the door retaining strap which let go. It was blowing a gale, the wind got behind the door, snatched it out of my hand the retaining strap came right out of the door. Maybe this was my fault for not holding on to the door more carefully and they did do a good price for repairing the crease on the right-hand side front wing. I suppose that was kind.

The apogee of the Ford experience was reached at under 6,000 miles. I drove up the hill from the ferry port at Uig, on the Isle of Skye, and there was a tremendous bang. The alternator belt had snapped and one bit had given the inside of the bonnet a real whack. Now, I had to coax the Escort to Portree on Skye, before the battery ran flat.

And there was worse to come. In pre-internet days, getting hold of spare parts was a complex job and, being a new car, no-one had an alternator belt for the Mk II Escort. This had to come from Inverness to Portree 120 miles away on the other side of Scotland – and by "special delivery". It actually arrived along with a pile of other bits but I was charged as if the whole journey had just been for me. After all, what use are tourists if they can't be screwed?

Another two nights of dinner bed and breakfast, some nice walks around Portree, a walloping bill, and we were on our way south again.

This was the reality of supporting British industry.

By the time I got home I was heartily sick of the Escort and just wanted to get shut of it. Of course, my car wasn't the only one leaving Halewood in this state so no Ford dealer would have anything to do with the new cars, except in direct part exchange for another brand new one.

The saviour came from a rather unlikely source. Mazda were just building their nascent dealer network and had a tiny outlet in the back streets of Southport. I think Mazda had just told them to get cars out, regardless of the deal - so I part-exchanged the Escort for a 1200cc Mazda saloon and didn't lose too much money.

I want to be scrupulously honest in these stories, rather than pick and choose the facts to make a case. The truth is that the Mazda did not look nearly so sharp as the Escort, nor was it as nice to drive as the Ford. In fact it was a bit bland and, except for escaping from the build quality and reliability nightmare which was the Escort, I wouldn't have looked at the Japanese car.

But here was the sting in the tail. Dull as it was, the Mazda never missed a beat in 50,000 miles and I hammered it everywhere. Other than being heavy on tyres – that should be "other than me being heavy on tyres" – and normal servicing costs, I never spent a penny on the car.

The final conclusion was that I never bought another Ford but I did have a series of Mazdas which simply ran faultlessly – even when driven flat out all day, every day, which they always were.

I wasn't the only one to make this shift. There was a huge Datsun dealer near us – Datsun was the first trade name for Nissan vehicles – and they sold the Datsun 100A Cherry for under £1000. One of the lads I sort of knew, rocked up at a race with a brand-new Cherry which he had bought on some ridiculously good hire purchase deal.

At a time when the British manufacturers would have liked to charge extra for the air in the tyres, the Datsuns came with a really top notch, for the day, list of standard fittings. There was a radio, two speed windscreen wipers and electric screen washers which actually worked. All this was wrapped in a three door, hatchback body with a decent amount of boot space.

Compare this to the similar sized Hillman Avenger made by the London based Rootes Group. In base form, an Avenger was £10 cheaper than the Cherry but came with only one sun visor, no fresh air vents and the passenger seat was fixed. What was worse was that Fords were considered to be paragons of reliability compared with Rootes' cars!

All Datsuns were known to be the gold standard for rusting and of course they were the butt of jokes for this reason. I had a good sneer, along with the rest of the British patriots in the paddock, but we said less about the fact that the Cherry never once went back to the dealer for rectification. This might sound unexceptional now but it was remarkable, and comment worthy, in the late 1960s.

Truly, the Japanese were changing the way we thought about all vehicles – car and bike – and sadly, British industry was forcing us into the arms of foreign companies.

*****

The real reason that I didn't want a Victor was that it was a truly awful motorcycle in every way whilst being a wonderfully clear window on all that was wrong with the British motorcycle industry.

The Victor should have been a world beater but wasn't, because of a mixture of appalling management, at every level, and a BSA Competition Department which was completely out of control. At the risk of having a contract taken out on my life by BSA fans, it has to be said again that the Victor was utter rubbish – and in so many ways – and is one of the best examples of a missed golden opportunity which exists in the motorcycle world.

First, let's put the bike into a historical context.

The Victor was based on the bike which Jeff Smith used to win the 1964 and 1965 World Championships, and these successes led BSA down a blind alley. A key part of the two World Championship wins was Jeff Smith. I am not a fan of his but there is no arguing that he was a ruthlessly fine rider and a master tactician. He was also arguably the first rider to take motocross racing professionally.

I once saw an old 8mm film of World Champion Torsten Hallman collapsing in a heap at the end of the first leg of a GP, because he was so unfit. By contrast Smith actually trained with Maurice Herriott, an ex-Olympic silver medal steeple chaser, running up the 1:4 test hill at the back of the BSA factory and along the banks of the Grand Union Canal. Okay, this was a galaxy away from how athletes train now but it was a start - and a window on Smith's dedication and mental attitude.

He also had genuine, lavish works support and could afford to race a fragile bike knowing that it would be rebuilt, or even replaced, at the end of every GP. This was vastly different from the way CZ went racing.

Finally, Smith was in the right place at the right time winning his two World Championships before two-strokes came to the fore. When they did, East German policeman Paul Friedrichs beat Smith three times in 1966, 1967 and 1968.

Regardless, on the back of the Victor's success in GPs, BSA sold a production bike and it was full of fundamental flaws. For a start, it had a very short, 52" wheelbase, which Smith loved but lesser mortals – like me – found it nervous and unsettling. The BSA forks were rubbish compared with the suspension on CZs and Huskies and, interestingly, was soon replaced by Italian Ceriani suspension even in the BSA competition shop.

The BSA chassis also contained a real threat to riders. There was a large gap between the fuel tank and the saddle on a Victor. Hit this space with legs splayed and the consequences were dramatically painful. This was such a well-known design feature on the Victor that Moto Cross Motors, in Oldham, offered a foam filled leather pad to bridge the gap. With no fear of being challenged under the Trade Descriptions Act, it was called "MX Motors Knacker Pad."

The motor should have been good because, although it made less power than the big, single cylinder, 500cc machines which were still being used in motocross at the time, the 441cc unit construction engine was vastly lighter than older designs.

The snag with the Victor was that the engine was not a clean sheet of paper design. Its antecedents went all the way back to the 150cc Triumph Terrier engine introduced in 1953. This motor became the 250cc BSA C15 which was then stretched and bored until it morphed into the Victor.

BSA claimed that the engine produced 32hp. The best works motors might have made this power but no production engine ever did. I actually raced the last works BSA ever to leave the factory and this was the 499cc B50. My bike was built by the best fitters at BSA and it gave only 32.4hp on BSA's dyno, so there was no way that a 441cc Victor rattling down the production line was ever going to make the same power.

Not only was the engine down on power but it was also fragile, with a very weak gearbox and clutch – both grossly under-engineered for racing. This was fine for Smith, and the other works supported riders, but not for the under-class like me, who actually bought the bikes.

No CZ rider ever used the clutch after the start because the gearbox was unbreakable. By contrast, stamping gears in on a B44 was a sure way to break it.

Finally, the Victor was cursed with Lucas Energy Transfer ignition. In theory, this got rid of the need for a battery and coil, or a magneto, and should have been a real technological leap forward. It wasn't because of poor quality control, and matters were not helped by the high compression Victor being notoriously difficult to start even when it was at its best.

*****

Compared with the distribution network of CZ or Husqvarna, BSA were light years ahead. The factory was also in the right place at the right time and had the finances and production capacity to totally dominate the world motocross market.

Here are a few things to consider. In 1962, the BSA Group was the tenth biggest company in Britain. Not only did they own the BSA, Triumph and Ariel motorcycle brands but their portfolio contained almost every aspect of engineering it is possible to imagine, from guns to car bodies, exotic steels, machine tool manufacturing, rare earths and specialist steels. There was nothing which could not be made within the group.

In terms of distribution, BSA products had the world by the throat. There was still an immense pool of goodwill from the benign dissolution of the British Empire and in the major Commonwealth countries of South Africa, Australia and New Zealand, BSA virtually held a monopoly.

If things were good worldwide, then this was nothing when compared with what was happening in the US.

The BSA Group was the first non-American motorcycle company to establish a nationwide presence in the States and their dealers were fanatically loyal.

It's worth remembering just how far Honda was behind BSA, to make sense of what BSA threw away. Honda came to America with one small warehouse, based in Los Angeles, which opened on June 11, 1959. There were just three employees and to save costs they all shared a one bedroom apartment. During the day, they unpacked the Hondas arriving from Japan and built them up on the warehouse shop floor, by hand. In 1960, the first full year of operations, American Honda sold fewer than 2,000 motorcycles.

The truly amazing thing was how Honda overcame the inherent hostility to Japanese products following WWII. The War in the Pacific had primarily been an American and Japanese conflict yet, only fifteen years after the ceasefire, here were Honda ready to sell to what had been their country's arch enemy.

By contrast, BSA Group products – primarily Triumph it has to be said – enjoyed an incredibly positive profile with a loyal customer base. When the Victor GP came to the market in the Autumn of 1965, the off-road market in the US was, quite literally, on the point of exploding. If, and that is always the most deadly of all prepositions, if BSA had manufactured a strong, reliable, easy to ride dirt bike which could have been used as an enduro, desert racer and motocross machine it would have sold in many tens of thousands.

This is not me looking back at history through rose tinted goggles. Remember the Dot deal which fell through because I couldn't get my £5 commission, and Nick Nicholl's willingness to fund a brand new bike? In the late 1960s, dirt racers were the absolute hot sales ticket.

Instead, the factory produced the dreadful B44 GP and, in some ways even more unforgiveable, Triumph didn't offer any dirt bike to their dealers. This is an important factor because although belonging to the same group, BSA and Triumph dealers were sworn enemies. In fact, it was often joked that a Triumph dealer would rather sell Hondas than help a BSA man!

There was a fix for the whole mess which was both affordable and achievable – and without a huge investment. I am aware of the solution because I sat with Reg Dancer, BSA's PR chief, and gave him my ideas. The way forward was for BSA to concentrate on dirt bikes, and for Triumph to lead the road machine sales.

BSA could have produced Victors for racing and then taken the superlative Triumph Daytona engine to use as the basis for a dual sport bike. Additionally, a strongly engineered, single cylinder four-stroke would have also been perfect for a military motorcycle which could have world-wide sales.

In fact, this is sort of what happened – but vastly too late – with the Triumph Adventurer. This was effectively a BSA B50MX chassis, housing the very fine Triumph Tiger 100 engine. If this had been launched alongside the B50MX in 1971, it could have provided extra income for virtually no additional tooling or development costs.

The story is actually even more tragic than this. What the Adventurer lacked was a five speed gearbox - but this was available straight off the shelf and, again with virtually no tooling or development investment, from the British Quaife Engineering company based in Kent. It was merely a question of striking a deal with Quaife and then taking delivery of the five speed clusters.

Incredibly, the tragedy got worse. Triumph had a genius development engineer called Doug Hele. Doug was not a great designer but he had magical talents for making cheap fixes work – and work well. Down in his little development shop at the back of the Triumph works at Meriden, all sorts of wonderful things were created. One of these "black" projects was a 560cc Triumph Adventurer, the additional capacity being achieved simply by over boring the standard 490cc engine. The result was an utter peach of an engine with a smooth, torquey power delivery which was years ahead of its time.

Could the story get worse? Yes, actually, it could – and did. Hele always described the 500cc Triumph engine as the best motor the factory ever made – and with justification. In a Metisse frame, the engine took Don Rickman to victory in the British Motocross Grand Prix, and Triumph development rider Percy Tait rode to an incredible second place at the Belgian road race Grand Prix in 1969, beaten only by fifteen times World Champion Giacomo Agostini. It was also a world class enduro engine, used extensively in international competitions.

Finally, the Tiger 100 was one of the few British motors with Japanese standards of reliability - and it was even easy to start.

So, the BSA Group have a superb motor, five speed gearbox apart, housed in a very competent chassis and all that is required now is to promote it. Of course, no-one would have thought of Bud Ekins in North Hollywood, who was not only the finest desert racer of his generation but also owned one of the largest Triumph dealerships in the world. This was the same Bud Ekins whose best mate was an arch Triumph fan. His name? Steve McQueen – at the time the most bankable movie star in the world and owner of multiple Triumphs.

What if games are always fun. What if Triumph/BSA had supplied Bud with a 560cc, five speed Adventurer in 1970? Would history have been re-written and would the income from the world's first true dual-sport motorcycle have bailed out the British bike industry? I still lose sleep wondering...

The situation was all the more tragic because the Japanese weren't even in the game. Suzuki, soon to be the dominant force in world motocross, didn't even have a production dirt bike in 1970. They had made only 200 of the dreadful TM250 racers before abandoning the bike as worthless.

Honda didn't launch their XL250 – the first genuine dual sport bike – until 1972 and, worthy though this bike was, a 560 Adventurer would have eaten a garage full of XLs before going out and winning every dirt bike race in America. That's how easy the target was.

*****

It would be convenient to say that my ideas were just the patriotic dreaming of a very young and inexperienced journalist: convenient, but inaccurate.

BSA's total production in 1963/64 was only 18,000 motorcycles – a drop in the ocean compared with Honda.

Far worse was that the 18,000 units were spread over 42 different models, or variants of models. Some of the production figures are utterly ludicrous. For example, only 31 examples of BSA's C15 motocross machine were made. A mere 31 bikes was a production level smaller than even the tiny British manufacturers like DMW or Cotton. Remember that Dalesman, working from an old chapel in Otley, made 30 bikes a week.

I've not just chosen one particularly extreme example to illustrate a point. The SS90 was BSA's top sports 350 and yet the factory made only 160 of these bikes.

The reasons that common sense did not prevail were predominately political, rather than engineering issues.

The Triumph Trident/BSA Rocket 3, which was the Group's flagship motorcycle, is the best example of the poisonous atmosphere within BSA/Triumph.

The Triumph Trident was drawn by Doug Hele after work, in his front room. This is what Bert Hopwood, BSA Group Engineering Director, thought of the model in 1981.

"The Triple machine which found its way to market in 1968 was a flop and it was not until we reverted to the original prototype style that it started to sell and earn revenue. It *(the BSA/Triumph Triple)* should have been in production in 1963, thus five years of production were lost, the Japanese became ever more firmly entrenched and our reputation suffered yet another severe setback."

So what went wrong? As ever, the core issue was a weak senior management and political in-fighting which made the Roman court of Caligula look like a play school Christmas party.

Let's start at the very beginning. The often quoted myth is that Bert Hopwood and Doug Hele, Triumph's Chief Development Engineer, were like father and son. This is wrong in fact. I came to know Doug reasonably well, and I was the last person to interview him just a few days before his death. Hele's view of Hopwood was unambivalent: he neither liked nor respected him.

In 1962, Hele had been headhunted from Norton by Hopwood. Doug jumped at the opportunity because Norton had been taken over by AMC and was becoming very much the junior partner in the enlarged company.

Hopwood, to his credit, saw the end of the road for the 650cc twins. In particular, he disliked the harshness of the larger Triumph twins as ever more power was squeezed out of them. The problem was that the twins were the children of the autocratic Edward Turner, whose word was law at Triumph – and within the wider BSA Group too. Senior management's adoration of Turner was to be a major issue in the Triple tragedy.

Hele, an enthusiastic advocate for three cylinder engines, felt that the only solution was to add another cylinder to the 500cc Triumph Twin and so provide a stop gap Triple until the planned ohc engines came on stream.

Turner famously thought the idea "potty" – not for any engineering reasons but simply because the new engine was not a Twin but a Triple.

Regardless, Hopwood recalls the moment that he claimed the Triple egg was actually fertilised.

"One evening, late in 1963, after everyone had gone home, we sat in his (Hele's) office and to amuse ourselves we laid out the basic outline of what later became the 750cc, three cylinder Trident.

"We thought that the result was very encouraging indeed, but in view of the rather abortive conversation which I had already had with the Managing Director (*Edward Turner*), this drawing was filed away as a memento."

In fact, this is not what happened. Doug had a drawing board in his front room at home and there, in his own time, he drew the Triple engine – and, in view of the constraints he was working under, he was very proud of the design.

This is Hele again. "He *(Hopwood)* was keen to claim credit wherever possible. The Triumph T150 Triple was entirely my design regardless of what Hopwood, or anyone else, said later. I drew the Triumph Triple completely unaided and on my own."

Doug had the complete engine drawings finished by early 1963. It's worth remembering that this is a full five years before Honda's 750 four cylinder machine and even a year before the Japanese factory's launch of the CB450 twin.

This point needs stressing. Triumph could have been selling their 750cc Triple when the biggest, and fastest, Japanese opposition came from the 450cc Honda.

The BSA Group stood in front of an open goal, with the ball ready to kick and the opposition team not even in the stadium – but only by concentrating a lot of effort on the bike.

Much as I admire Hele, and my admiration - and affection - for this wonderful engineer is truly unbounded, Doug was not a great designer. A more apposite description would be to say that he was the world's best garden shed designer and the Triple reflects this. As a piece of practical, cost saving engineering, using the minimum of new tooling, the engine is the work of genius. Critically, it could have been garden shed cheap, as well as garden shed simple, to put into production.

Not that the first version of the Triple engine was fit for purpose, because it wasn't. Norman Hyde was an apprentice in the Triumph experimental department and remembers that Hele's first version of the Triple was full of faults.

"There were problems with the oil pump which was of shaft drive design. The iron barrels were also a real issue and caused the cylinder head to leak. But the biggest issue was with the gear primary drive. The co-efficient of expansion of aluminium, and the distance between the crankshaft and the clutch, meant that the gear drive was never going to be successful – and it wasn't!

"The bore and stroke of the engine was altered from the original 63mm x 80mm, which was the configuration of the pre-unit Speed Twin, to 67mm x 70mm used on the unit construction singles."

Despite the engine not being ready for production, Hele took the finished design into Meriden and there were two reactions. First, Hopwood took over the project and claimed credit for it. Secondly, it immediately became mired in BSA Group politics.

With the nominal retirement of Edward Turner, although he did remain as a Non-Executive Director of the BSA Group and his looming spectre still walked the corridors of power both at Small Heath and Meriden, McKinseys - a US company of management consultants - were brought in to completely re-vamp the company.

Harry Sturgeon was appointed Group Managing Director. He came from the Churchill Grinding Machine Company, another BSA company, but knew nothing about motorcycles.

The politics are important to the practical story of the Triple because all the BSA Group senior management had bigger fish to fry than Doug's garden shed special. Harry Sturgeon was obsessive about increasing production and, from an outsider's point of view, Triumph were selling everything they could make so what could possibly be wrong?

As McKinseys tried to build a single, highly centralised motorcycle manufacturing entity within the BSA Group so the infighting and desire to protect individual empires became ever more frenetic.

One Triple prototype, the P1, was made and, in a wonderfully ironic reprise of Turner's shoe horning of his Speed Twin engine into the chassis of Triumph's single cylinder Tiger 90 in 1937, Hele squeezed the new three cylinder engine into a Bonneville frame. And what a lovely thing it was too – very Bonnevilleish and yet clearly different.

There were initial problems with the width of the engine and cylinder head gasket sealing but these were quickly resolved, and the bike was ready for production in the Autumn of 1965 – ready for the critical, spring selling season in the USA.

Norman Hyde again. "The bike had flaws but we had skilled fitters who were capable of looking at fits, and suggesting solutions to management. I was an apprentice but even I was involved in the discussions. Bert Hopwood would come down and say to me, "Well young Hyde, what do you think of this?"

So what stopped the Triple going into production? First, and most importantly, the re-organisation of the BSA Group motorcycle manufacturing in an attempt to unify it and the demotion, or early retirement, of key managers.

Ariel was closed and the already tense relations between BSA and Triumph reached new heights. It was said, with a degree of justification, that Triumph would rather share their research with Honda than BSA – and, to be fair, vice versa was equally true!

Then there was a chaotic dilution of effort. Hopwood wanted a modular family of singles, twins and triples and these were to be based around an 83cc single which would morph into a 249cc triple. There was to be an eight speed, dohc, GP racer and a six speed sohc road bike. All this was wonderful – but nothing happened and meanwhile, the eminently production ready Triple prototype remained at the back of the queue.

Turner also had his hand in the pie and, in semi-retirement, had designed the disastrous BSA Bandit/Triumph Fury twin which suffered from a multitude of engineering problems.

It's worth recording just how bad this engine was. Here is an extract from Hopwood's report on the bike to the BSA Main Board.

"The complete motorcycle *(BSA Fury/Triumph Bandit)* we have on test now has 5,400 miles registered and in this mileage 3,000 have been completed by a tester who rode most of the time at very low speeds because of the severe problems.

"The machine used four pints of oil every 100 miles and the tests are worthless because of a lack of power. The other 2,400 miles by various riders embraced four complete rebuilds of the engine unit due to failures of the crankshaft, gudgeon pins and main bearings.

"The frame of the machine has already been redesigned due to excess flexibility in the main, which constituted a hazard and the front forks are also considered to be fundamentally unsafe."

*****

Another shambles was taking place at Small Heath and this was a very different elephant squeezing into the Group's already overcrowded R&D bathroom.

Jeff Smith had won the 1964 and 1965 World 500cc Motocross Championship and the BSAists were determined to get a third world title – if only to put their sworn enemies at Meriden in their place!

BSA Competition Manager Brian Martin's idea was to build the lightest 500cc motocross bike in the world. It was to have an all titanium frame, and the engine was largely magnesium and titanium. In terms of engineering, this was at the far end of cutting edge – and it was a disaster.

On paper, the bike was a world beater. Four-stroke pulling power and traction with the weight of a two-stroke should have swept all before it - but things went incurably wrong, right from the start, and the Ti bike was soon scrapped.

Not only did the Ti BSA consume a huge amount of money and engineering time but there was another, unreported, problem. Before his untimely death I was very close friends with Fred Barlow who, as an apprentice, worked on the Ti project. Fred and I spent many happy hours discussing the tales of the numerous "foreigners" which were done by BSA tool room staff to help the race team. These unofficial jobs caused BSA Works Manager, Al Cave, to call Fred, and his race shop colleagues, "The worst of professional thieves…" because they not only stole materials but vital, and irreplaceable, tool room time and staff, from production R&D effort.

In addition to the fundamental mistake of trying to race an unproven design in a ridiculously short space of time, the BSA Competition Department itself was unfit for purpose from top to bottom. Too much effort was focussed on Jeff Smith and other riders resented this. The feeling amongst those I spoke to was that they were always going to be second in the queue behind Smith, because of the closeness of the relationship that Brian Martin and Smith enjoyed, and also because they were full time BSA employees, who worked together at factory, whilst other riders just paid visits there.

The BSA team was huge too. I have a copy of Jeff Smith's 1966 book "The Art of Motocross" because, at the time, I was a real Jeff Smith groupie. The fly leaf is signed by the whole BSA team and it really is a who's who of British motocross. Clearly, as always, Smith is at the top but beneath him are Dave Nichol, Vic Eastwood, John Banks, Alan Lampkin and Arthur Lampkin: a fabulous line up!

Running a team this big, plus trials and road racing, was very expensive and of course there was the constant haemorrhage of parts, and even complete bikes, through theft which took place on an industrial scale. This was not a case of the odd "foreigner" being done on works time, or a few spare parts going missing, but the organised, determined and extended stealing of many tens of thousands of pounds worth of parts, engines and even complete bikes.

*****

Could things get worse? Well, yes they could – and considerably so too. At the time, distribution for the BSA Group products in America was a shambles. Triumph Baltimore and Triumph Los Angeles handled Meriden products whilst East Coast BSA sales were in the hands of BSA New Jersey and, in the west, by the privately owned Hap Alzina Company based in Oakland, California.

Johnson Motors had been bought out by the BSA Group but the old rivalry between TriCor, on the East Coast, and JoMo on the West still remained. In short, the situation was a total and utter chaotic mess with rivalry not only between East and West Coast BSA Group organisations but a BSA versus Triumph pistols-at-dawn shootout too.

If the rivalry between Meriden and Small Heath was fierce in England, it was near psychopathic in the US with each organisation running their own race teams and often battling it out for publicity with their sister company. It would have never happened in Japan.

The realpolitik of the situation was that any new BSA Group product which looked like a money spinner had to be given, in fair shares, to both BSA and Triumph dealers. This, I feel, more than any other factor, was the reason for the two different versions of the Triple.

Meanwhile, in this maelstrom of political infighting and management ineptitude, Hele's garden shed special took a back seat which was a real shame, because the bike worked a treat. Now acceptably slim after some more Hele tweaking, the engine produced a reliable and consistent 58hp at 7,250rpm – against 45ish hp from a Bonneville – and was smooth and torquey. Almost as important, just like Turner's Speed Twin, the emotional gap from the old bike to the new one was narrow because the new Triple felt very Triumphy.

Again like a Speed Twin, the weight was perfect being only 40lbs (18kgs) heavier than a Bonnie. Now, Triumph owners could have a much faster, smoother and sexier bike but one which didn't alienate them: perfect in every way for the 1965 season.

But no. That would have been too sensible. Two completely different Triples were produced – one a BSA version and the other Triumph. Each bike had so many differences that they were effectively two different motorcycles, ramping up the cost of the tooling, and production, hugely.

The crunch came when Harry Sturgeon, who had been very ill with a brain tumour, announced the news that Honda were about to release a 750cc four cylinder bike. Now this really was a gigantic tank parked on the BSA Group's lawn, and the Board went into full panic mode in an attempt to give their dealers, both Triumph and BSA, something with which they could compete.

The big issue was that, at launch, the Triples were hugely out of date. Let me illustrate this point by going through the starting procedures for a Triple and a 750 Honda four.

First the Honda. Switch on petrol. Close the carburettor chokes. Press starter button and the engine will start – every time, without fail. Wait for 15 seconds until the bike has warmed up. Open chokes. Ride off. Continue riding until fuel is needed.

Now a Triple. Switch on petrol. "Tickle" the outside of the two Amal carburettors – a wonderfully sanitised verb which means that you hold the float chamber down until petrol slobbers all over your gloves and on to the engine.

Then, set the cable operated choke at ¼, ½ or ¾ position according to the ambient temperature and swing the long kick starter until the engine coughs into life.

If you "wet" the plugs – easy to do in the cold – remove the spark plugs. Kick vigorously about 30 times to clear the excess fuel from the cylinders. Replace plugs, with the spare ones you keep in your jacket pocket, and kick again. Ideally, ride until you can stop somewhere near the crest of a hill so you can bump start it easily in case of sulks.

In 1958, this was acceptable. Ten years later it wasn't.

As well as a lack of electric starter, the Triples had four speed gearboxes and drum brakes. The Honda had a five speed 'box and a disc brake.

The really, but really, frustrating thing is that BSA knew all about five speed gearboxes, again through Quaife, and they had been using Airheart disc brakes on their American road race bikes for years.

At this point in the story, it would be easy to criticise Ogle Design and the mess they made of the Triples' styling. Certainly, at the time I was right at the front of the loathing queue. As a sixteen year old, I knew what a British sports bike should look like and it was predicated on being sleek and feline - with an undisguised eagerness to go fast.

Now, with the benefit of long sight, and maybe even a tiny smidgen of wisdom, I can see what happened. In 1967, anything was possible – as long as it was "modern" – and with a capital M. You could walk past a tip and see Victorian mahogany sideboards piled up for firewood, simply for being old-fashioned. I had, very briefly before she dumped me for being far beneath her social standing, a girlfriend whose proudest possession was a piece of plastic on a pink, Terylene cord which her brother had brought back from Carnaby Street, London's hippest address. Modern was good – and every-thing else was bad.

Ogle Design had already styled the Raleigh Chopper bicycle – a truly awful thing – and were now given the task of making the Triples properly space age. The problem was that the brief from BSA was vague and confusing. Jim English, from Ogle, remembers the shambles. "We were told they *(BSA)* wanted a flashy American look, like a Cadillac. We really let our hair down doing futuristic stuff. I never thought that BSA would go for my flared silencer with three tail pipes. To be honest, as a motorcyclist, I thought that the Triumph they brought in *(the P2 prototype)* looked fine just as it was.

So instead of the lithe, slim, sporty and eager 120mph sports bike we all wanted, Ogle gave us a dumpy, square machine borrowed from a Flash Gordon comic strip – and we enthusiastically reviled it.

Most of all, we hated the "ray gun" silencers which gave the bike a big fat bum - and, in the interests of political correctness, I'll not explore this area further!

Despite anything Ogle tried do with the Flash Gordon styling, kick-starting a four speed gearbox and drum brakes made the Triple old-fashioned at launch.

And so it went on - appalling management with a total lack of vision; corrosive political infighting; corruption and theft; and militant trades' unions.

So no, the Japanese did not steal the British motorcycle industry but were given it on a plate, gift wrapped and hand delivered. Truthfully, I used to cry at the tragedy.

If the big issues were the ones which made the headlines for me, there was an even worse humiliation. Lost in the maelstrom of corruption and dishonesty was a wonderful, truly magnificent layer of great engineers – ones like Warrington Tech was producing in the thousands. Alongside the engineers were superb tradesmen – men who could make anything for you and to the highest standards in the world. These wonderful people were dragged into the abyss along with those who instigated the fall.

This is not me simply looking back and longing for a golden time in my life. Once again, the facts support what I say.

Look what our engineers and tradesmen – and tradeswomen too now – can do when they are well led. Six out of the ten Formula One car teams are based in Britain and those that aren't use British parts. I know one small, and very discreet, company in the Midlands whose main customer is Ferrari.

The UK has more than 30 vehicle manufacturers and in excess of 2,350 component firms supplying parts. It employs upwards of 770,000 workers and the industry generates an annual turnover in excess of £64 billion, making it the largest sector for UK exports and earning £27 billion a year in revenue.

An incredible 44% of the world's smallest satellites are British made. Now we are building a cheap, efficient way of launching these from Boeing 747s which will be based at a new space centre in Cornwall.

Perhaps the most poignant example of all is Triumph Motorcycles – a privately owned company which is now a world leader in the bike industry, producing superb machines to the highest standards. Entrepreneur John Bloor took Triumph from oblivion in 1983.

I could go on because the success stories are endless. Well led, we have the best engineers and workers in the world.

But, as my first year at Balfour Road Boys' Secondary Modern School came to an end, I was very tightly focussed on the immediate future when Mr Parsonage summoned me to his study on the first floor of the school.

Chapter Twenty-One

Good Try - But No Goldfish

I sat on the edge of my chair facing Mr Parsonage. I always got the feeling that he would have felt more comfortable, and relaxed, if staff had been marched into his office by the school's Regimental Sergeant Major, brought to a halt before his desk and then have us salute before we were told to stand at ease.

As a poor second best, I called him "Sir" – and meant it – and sat bolt upright. It was one of those good news/bad news meetings. He was pleased with me on many fronts – my enthusiasm, how quickly I had learned and my dedication to the kids I was teaching. So, top marks all round.

The bad news was that I was in a professional cul-de-sac and had to get out. I was to apply for teaching training and become a qualified teacher. This would be essential for me and good for education.

Further, I was to do this immediately. Right. Dismissed. About face. Quuuickkkkkkk march. Left, right, left right, left, right…

I was always quiet in the staffroom but on this occasion I buried myself on the back wall, almost hidden by one of the big, cast iron radiators. I was truly frightened of what I was facing. I could pitch the Tribsa into a corner at 60mph, a gnat's eyelash away from half a dozen roaring JAPs, or leap downhill surrounded by riders who would have me off in a flash and be ice cool and clear headed.

I had ducked and dived and dealt in all sorts of dodgy situations and never blinked. Yet now, I was hunched in a corner - silent and afraid. I was frightened of leaving the protective womb which Balfour Road had become; of being without the safety and protection of kids who said, "Hiya Sir" and smiled at me in the morning, and the gentle ribbing the older, wiser teachers gave me. Losing all this I feared.

Even more, I dreaded being exposed as a cheat – someone who couldn't really teach but was a fake. I doubted, deep within my soul, my intellectual ability – whether I had the brain power to succeed in an academic career.

These demons gnawed at my mind as I drove home in my Morris Oxford van.

****

Ironically, what saved me were the years of getting sacked: I already had a lot of experience of rejection before I even applied for teacher training!

That night I sat on the edge of my bed, not brooding but laying out a plan in my mind. Fact one: I had to leave Balfour Road. Fact two: I had been told to apply for teaching training and Mr Parsonage would demand to know why if I didn't. Fact three: the odds were that I would never be accepted for a teacher training course. Fact four: if I did get in, and they sacked me – which was an absolute certainty – I needed to be on home territory so that I could get a job as a labourer, gofor or whatever: for sure, there would be something I could do to earn some money.

I chose to apply to S. Katherine's College of Education in Childwall - a very upmarket suburb of Liverpool. I never visited the college before I applied and nor did I have the slightest clue whether it was good, bad or indifferent. My main thought was that if I was thrown out after a few weeks, something which I thought was very likely, then there was nothing much lost and I would be near enough to Warrington to find work again in an area I knew well.

As well as being conveniently near to a known escape route, S. Kath's also had another strong attraction. At a time of rapid change in the criteria for teacher training admission, it still accepted students with five good "O" Levels when many other colleges were beginning to demand two "A" Levels as a minimum.

The urban myth, or it may have even been true, was that if you put S. Kath's down as your first choice of college, and were suitably enthusiastic, then you would be accepted on the grounds that the regime was so tough that you would either succeed or die trying!

I knew that my letter of application was going to be a deal maker, or breaker, and so I toiled at it for days. Before the advent of electronic word processing, redrafts were time consuming and tiresome but I didn't care. I somehow had to explain away the time between leaving school and joining Balfour Road Boys' Secondary Modern School. This task demanded some real creative writing, involving a lot of rearranging the facts - and the occasional manufacturing of new evidence.

I was helped hugely by what I was told was a very strong reference written by Mr Parsonage. I think he must have told S. Kath's that he approved of me - and so should they.

A letter eventually arrived asking me to attend the college for interview. I was overawed by S. Katherine's and fell instantly in love with the place. The college had been built in 1844 and, except for the new teaching block, which was an ugly and graceless building, it oozed history and tradition.

Instead of the urban Liverpool which I had imagined, S. Kath's was set in huge grounds with formal gardens and enormous sports fields: it was so gracious that it could have been one of the Oxbridge colleges. The intention was to provide the best possible education in Britain for female teachers. The college scarf – all very Oxbridge – was purple and white and gave the college alumni their title, "The Purple Virgins." The purple part of the soubriquet was still intact when I sent in my letter.

I wasn't given a tour of the college or even a hint of welcome or hospitality.

Instead, I was shown immediately into a large, wood panelled room lit by a lovely, dappled light streaming in through the mullioned windows.

The centre piece of the room was an immense wooden table which seemed to stretch out forever, like an airport runway. There was a chair at one end and I was directed to it. On the table was a stack of lined paper. I was told to write why I wanted to be a teacher and why S. Katherine's College of Education should accept me for teacher training. With that, the clerk left the room and the heavy, wooden door clicked purposefully closed behind him.

Outside, I heard a BSA twin being kicked into life. It coughed at first and then caught and ran sweetly on two cylinders. After a few moments, I heard the harsh click of first gear going into place and then the bike pulling away. Then there was silence - and I was left to my own fate.

It was another case of: "When the flag drops – the bull**** stops."

It's absolutely true - and very apposite for many situations I have faced.

Now, the flag had dropped and I was writing for my life.

On one side of the chasm was an endless succession of worthless jobs which I hated. I knew about this existence all too well.

On the other side was a real profession which I loved.

All that I had to do was walk across the tightrope from my past to my future life.

Strangely, I had no doubts or concerns. I wrote furiously, for fear of running out of time, but with skill, accuracy and passion. Expressing ideas in good, clear, standard English held no fears for me.

After a long time, the clerk returned and asked me if I was finished. The timing was good because I had just concluded the final redraft of the essay. The pages were covered in corrections and addenda but they did show that the writer understood how to improve his work.

He took the application and told me to report back at 2pm.

I didn't know where to get any food but eating wasn't much of a concern so I drank some water out of my hands from the men's toilets, and then went back to my car and read *Motorcycle News*.

In the afternoon, I met three tutors who had all read my application. They were pleasant enough and chatted about the points I had raised in the essay and, surprisingly, only very little about what I had done at Balfour Road. I think their view was that I hadn't been much more than a child minder, and that I had everything still to learn about the teaching profession.

I answered their questions with confidence and enthusiasm and, when I left, even a sliver of hope that perhaps I had not made a complete mess of things.

Three weeks later a stiff, formal letter arrived, informing me when and where I was to report for Teacher Training – along with a terrifyingly long list of books I was expected to have read before October. Three years at S. Kaths was not going to be a paid holiday!

*****

But beneath the surface of the maelstrom I was trying to swim through, I had a secret guilt: I desperately wanted to be a motorcycling journalist – more even than a teacher. From my side of the fence, there wasn't a problem. I liked bikes, knew a fair bit about them and I thought that I could write.

This was not how it looked from a potential employer's point of view however. First, I didn't know anyone with influence in either the magazine or motorcycling worlds: absolutely no-one. This meant there would be no back doors opened with nudges and winks and no-one waiting to welcome me because they had been in the Navy with my dad.

So, it had to be the mainstream way into journalism which was through a National Union of Journalists' course. At the end of the training, you got a NUJ union card and could apply for a job on any newspaper or magazine in Britain - and the rest of the world too, for that matter.

Every arm of the media was totally controlled by the NUJ and this was definitely restrictive. Against this was that the NUJ course was excellent and produced fine, professional journalists with a high level of competence.

The snag was that in order to get on the course you needed two "A" Levels – one of which had to be English. Compare this to the standards of material you see on-line from the current crop of journalists!

But I didn't have any "A" Levels, and so was banned from applying - and that was that.

The lack of NUJ card didn't stop me from trying. I got a really snotty rejection from *The Motorcycle* which was the combination of the two long standing, and rather august, magazines *The Motorcycle* and *Motorcycling*.

I never even got a reply from *Motorcycle Mechanics* or *Motorcycle Sport* which was somewhat ironic because I later became a major contributor to both publications.

Only Robin Miller, the then editor of *Motorcycle News*, was enthusiastic. He was prepared to take a bit of a chance on me, possibly, if I could touch type and do short-hand. I wasn't able to do either so again it was, "Good try – but no goldfish."

Having been so happy at Balfour Road, the secret quest had been put on hold but, for better or for worse, some deity in a little used part of the Multiverse was about to have some fun with me.

My Auntie Edie was about to go to America on holiday. This was a big deal within our community because no-one had ever been to the USA – and I saw a golden opportunity coming out of her trip.

Strictly speaking, Auntie Edie wasn't my Auntie but my mum's cousin. She was loud, smiling and very, very fond of me. I asked her whether she could bring back an American bike magazine for me to look at and got a big, wet, soppy kiss and a promise that she would. And I had more than just reading the mag in mind...

But the American magazines had to wait because the cliff face I had to climb now was S. Kath's.

*****

I arrived at S. Kath's on a lovely Autumn day, keen, eager and desperate to see what this brave new world had to offer me.

By 4pm I wanted to give up, go home and die.

Everywhere there were posh kids, with bags full of good "A" Levels. My fellow students were relaxed and confident. They smiled and tripped off their successes and backgrounds. Yes, "A" Levels – some of them even three! Grammar school, minor public schools, Dad owns his own company, Mum's a headmistress at a girls' grammar...

And now Frank, tell us about how you won 10 shillings at a grass track – we'll all be fascinated to hear about that – NOT!

I went into full blushing mode and stammered and tripped over my own tongue and generally sounded like some medieval village idiot who had just been dragged before the Manor Court.

My first day finished on a really spectacular high. I went into the toilets, gave the roller towel machine a sharp tug to dry my hands and it crashed down on my ankles, leaving me in a heap on the floor.

The only question was whether I was going to get thrown out of college for being stupid in a public place, wrecking their towel machine – or both.

The following day, I went in to see Mr Leyland, my English tutor, in his small office in the English Block overlooking the Junior Common Room. I told him that I was too thick to be at college and I was going to leave.

At this point, I learned another invaluable lesson. Geoff Leyland didn't like me much personally. I never did discover why this was but it didn't matter in practical terms because he offered me something far more important than kindness. Geoff was the consummate, dedicated educationist and his behaviour had a huge influence on me as my career progressed.

Despite a lack of affinity with me, he behaved as the complete caring professional and for this I admire him tremendously. He listened, carefully and patiently, to all I had to say and then explained that every first year student in every college in the world was finding it tough, in some way or another, in these first few days.

He didn't make any silly or patronising statements about me being as bright as the other students, or even being able to manage the rigours of tertiary education but, in his strong Liverpool accent, he said that it was too early to say what was going to happen and that I should forget about what the other students could, or could not, do and stick it out for a couple of weeks.

After two weeks, I could come back and see him and then we would decide, together, what to do next. In the interim, he would be my only contact within the English Department and, for two weeks at least, he wasn't going to throw me out.

Mr Leyland lifted an immense load from my shoulders by giving me a tiny breathing space and fourteen days to find a solution. If I was running dead last, at least I was still in the race!

*****

The following week, Geoff's Tutor Group crammed into his small study and we were given our first assignment. The brief was simple: "Write a critique of a play, book, poem or even a film. Write as much, or little, as you want. Don't worry about anything. Just write what you feel comfortable with."

It was a subtle test which was going to tell Geoff a lot about us. Did we have the basic trade skills of essay writing, without which a student cannot successfully manage an English course, and could we organise a task ourselves, as independent students in tertiary education rather than school pupils?

With that, there were smiles all round and we filed out. I really was between a very big sledge hammer and an extremely large anvil with this one. I was far too shy and embarrassed to ask any of the other students for help and equally reluctant to say to Geoff that I really didn't have the vaguest clue what to do next – not one molecule of an idea.

Clearly, I had read thousands of books but what sort of literature was acceptable for the assignment? Did it have to be very high brow, serious material or could it be science fiction? Were fun poems good or did they have to be the metaphysical stuff I never liked and couldn't much understand? The alarm bells rang loud and clear.

More out of desperation, and a complete lack of alternative ideas, I decided to take myself off to the cinema in the Old Swan district of Liverpool, and review a film that was currently making national news and receiving rave critical reviews. It was The Graduate – the story of young man a little older than me, who is first seduced by an older woman and then falls in love with her daughter.

The film received a ton of Academy Award nominations for Best Picture, Best Actor and many more, and Mike Nichols won the Academy Award for Best Director. With this sort of success, I thought that the film might pass the worthiness benchmark.

I sat in the semi-darkness of the cinema and wrote like a fiend from hell. It was a surreal experience. Around me, popcorn was being munched, Kia-Ora orange was slurped through straws and contented sighs came from happy couples.

Meanwhile, I sat on the edge of my seat and wrote for my life. If the roof had fallen in or tigers had appeared in the aisles and eaten viewers, I wouldn't have noticed. The flag had dropped and I was on a mission.

Essays at S. Kath's were graded in five levels. At the top was an A grade. No-one ever thought about A grades in English because they were impossible to obtain. Not only would the grammar, spelling, syntax and vocabulary have to be perfect but the arguments presented in the essay would have to be subtle, accurate and convincing. A grades were pure fantasy and didn't exist in the real world.

Good students got Bs. Anyone with a B+ was celebrating. A good, sound essay was a C. On a bad day, and they had better not be too often, a D+

would just about do. Don't even think about an E because this was hyper-dangerous territory. A metaphorical yellow card was shown and a rewrite was needed.

I handed in my Graduate essay and retired to a safe place to await the incoming fire. With luck, I would get a straight D grade or even perhaps a D+ if things went astonishingly well.

Somewhat surprisingly I hadn't found either the research for the critique very hard or the writing of the essay itself. The characters in the film were clearly drawn and unambiguous, and the plot was straightforward and episodic. Even the music, by Simon and Garfunkel, was strong and easy to analyse.

A week later, Geoff always marked quickly out of courtesy to students, I was sent a note asking me to see him. Maybe out of kindness for my state of extreme angst, he immediately slid the essay across his desk to me. There, in the top right hand corner was a C+. I gulped. The expression, "I couldn't believe my eyes..." is much misused but in this case, I couldn't. I was utterly speechless. I had written a film critique and achieved a C+. This was the equivalent of a podium finish at an international motocross meeting.

Geoff paused to let me savour the moment – another thoughtful act - and then said: "It's a good attempt - but it's not right. Let me show you."

And then, with a smile and infinite care, he unpicked my essay word by word by word. He showed me where I had misused a semi-colon because a colon was more accurate punctuation. Then he demonstrated how to add weight to an argument by putting an additional idea in parenthesis, and when to avoid using the vernacular when Standard English was essential. He was teaching me to write Standard English accurately and succinctly - and it was a truly wonderful experience.

I listened in near silence. Geoff explained. A light came on in my brain and we moved on.

Another explanation and another light. Yes, that's obvious.

More explanation. Now I see!

It was like opening up a mothballed factory. All the information was there in my head, it just needed Geoff to show me where it was stored and what to do with it.

After the tutorial, I skipped down the slatted wooden steps with a smile which nearly split my face. I had been wrong. I could do this college thing!

Chapter Twenty-Two

Brave New World?

My lovely Auntie Edie did not bring back one magazine, as I had asked, but fourteen. Goodness only knows where she got this number from but I went down to her house and collected them – along with a tsunami of wet, sloppy kisses and long hugs.

The mags were the most eclectic mix of motorcycle literature I had ever seen. At one end of the market were very serious, main stream magazines like *Cycle World* and *Motorcyclist* and, at the other, some seriously hard core *Chopper* publications featuring riders you wouldn't want to meet even at mid-day in bright sunlight!

The Greeves had gone – what a delight that was - and, for the first time in three years, I was without a race bike. This was no hardship because my mind was focussed 100% on making my new career work in education. Well, perhaps not actually a whole 100%...

Every time I read a motorcycling magazine, I did so with a lust and aching which matched any biological urge. I really thought that I could write about bikes but there was no way this was going to happen in Britain – so what about America? After all, the Americans spoke English, sort of, and they rode bikes so the big bits of the project were already in place. All that was needed was for me to get hired.

It was time for another creative writing session. Taking the core facts that I knew about bikes and could write, I then gave the truth a little bit of a massage in terms of my experience and work which had already been published.

Finally, I bet the kitchen sink - £5 actually - on buying some really nice notepaper. That weekend, I toiled over fourteen individual letters. My two-fingered typing wasn't bad but each letter had to be perfect so I pecked away, letter by letter, like a cypher clerk operating one of those Second World War code machines – terrified of making a mistake and having the message misread.

The next problem was posting them to America. Air mail letters were expensive and normally sent on tissue thin, blue paper. My missives were big, heavy, clonky things and weren't cheap. The saviour appeared in the form of another clubman racer who knew that I was in a state of semi-retirement and came sniffing around for a bargain, like a hyena circling a wounded wildebeest.

He went away with a gallon of Castrol "R", some Greeves' sprockets and my lightly used motocross boots – and I headed to the Post Office with the capital for an international sales pitch.

As the Postmistress took the letters, I felt like kissing bon voyage to each one individually but, instead, maintained a stoic face. Now came the waiting.

About three weeks later, two air mail letters arrived almost simultaneously. The first, from *Cycle World*, was meticulously polite in a very "Dear Sir or Madam" way. It thanked me for my letter and said that they had no requirement for my work.

The second came on notepaper much worse than mine. It was from *Motorcycle World* in New York and, in a couple of sentences, asked me to send them a story and some photographs and they would consider the piece.

I must have re-read the letter a thousand times expecting the text to change to, "No, we don't want you and don't bother us ever again."

But the words wouldn't change, nor did they try to escape from the notepaper. They did say send us a story and they did say we will consider it.

I was rolling down the runway for take-off.

I should add that *Motorcycle World* was not only the big bet to launch my journalistic career – but that there was no "Plan B" since the other twelve magazines never even bothered to reply!

I couldn't wait to tell my mum the good news but the reaction wasn't what I expected. Two big, fat tears quite literally rolled slowly down her cheeks. She held both my hands and said, in a very soft, quavering voice: "Please don't let bikes ruin your life, love. You've done so well getting into college and you'll be a teacher and have a good job and not be like me and your dad.

"Don't waste all this just for bikes."

It was the best of advice, given with all a mother's love. Both my mum and dad had left school at fourteen years of age and no-one in our wider family had even stayed on at school to do "A" Levels. Now, here I was at college and succeeding - with an incredibly high status job waiting for me.

Motorcycles were working class. They were dirty, dangerous and noisy, and belonged to my old life - which I should leave behind. By every measure of common sense and logic, she was right and her advice could not have been more accurate and kind.

The problem was that I was in love again and when I thought of *Motorcycle World* I could see my name there. If I had to swim the Atlantic to deliver the story to New York by hand, I was going to write it.

The big question was what to write about. The motorcycling season was coming to a close and although I had made some rather optimistic promises about my contacts, the truth is that I knew no-one of even minor importance in the bike world.

I was involved in a high stakes game of poker with Fate and Destiny, and I had just been asked to show my hand of cards.

At the time, the Wirral 100 Club ran sand races on an oval track laid out between the high and low waterline on the beach at the end of New Brighton Promenade. I had been to the races with Sammy Green and found them interesting because of the eclectic range of bikes competing. There was everything from small capacity 250s all the way through to the biggest, 650cc British machines. Road racing, motocross and even trials bikes raced against each other.

I thought that maybe this odd mix of machines just might make an interesting feature – but for a rather strange reason: I wanted to write a story that I would like.

This idea needs a little explanation because it ran against all received wisdom – and common sense too. The sensible thing would have been to go down to New Brighton Prom and write a feature in the same vein as those which I had read so many times before. It would say that the conditions were like this or that and Joe "X" won the 250cc race on a Yamaha, and Brian "Y" battled from a poor start to take the 350 class on his BSA and so on. This was motorcycle magazine reporting and it was clearly the right thing to do.

The problem was that I didn't much enjoy this sort of writing. I wanted to know how it felt to be there - to see the races and hear the bikes. Also, I wanted to know what it was like for me, the clubman racer with no contacts, to be at the event.

This was a very naïve view of life because ordinary riders didn't, and don't, influence affairs. Teenagers with rubbish bikes were spectators in the world of motorcycling – not players. Regardless, I decided that I would go down to New Brighton and write what I saw, heard and smelled.

In taking this approach, I had one enormous advantage. Because of my lack of "A" Levels, I hadn't followed an NUJ course and therefore I had never been taught to write "properly". Further, I had never worked for a newspaper or magazine and therefore had never been influenced by established writers around me. Because I didn't know what was right or wrong I simply wrote what, and how, I felt was right: it really was no more complex than that.

Without knowing it at the time, I had just exposed the mother lode in what was to be a very rich goldmine for the rest of my life.

I was my readers in that first article, and I remain my readers today.

I might have had dinner with some senior executive from a bike company, or be sat in the motorhome of a World Champion who rides at one of the events Carol and I used to organise, but I always did so as an outsider.

First by accident, and now by design and intent, I am the eyes and ears of the ordinary motorcyclist – and I am incredibly proud to be so!

Down at New Brighton Prom I sat on the sea-wall and wrote what I saw and heard. I didn't deliberately choose to write in a very literary style, but I simply used the language which I felt best described what was happening. It was as simple as a decent tradesman using the correct tool for the job. At the time, I saw myself as a literary tradesman – and still do for that matter.

If I needed a verb, I chose the verb which best explained the action. When the verb needed qualifying, I used an adverb – and that was that. It wasn't a case of being clever or pretentious but just getting the correct spanner for the right literary nut and then using it properly.

Today, much is made of the need to avoid "difficult" language in a story, for fear of alienating the reader. I think that this is a most pernicious form of political correctness, which is patronising in the extreme to readers who have not had the same range of literary experience as the writer.

What gives the author of a piece of writing the right to say whether it will be too challenging for the reader? To do so is an act of supreme intellectual arrogance and I will have nothing to do with the idea.

So, in a manner which came naturally to me, I chose to treat my readers as my equals. I wrote about the piercing screams of the unsilenced two-strokes battling with the angry calls of the gulls which had been driven away from their beach. I told the reader about the rich, near narcotic smell of the sea water, burnt on to hot exhausts and mixed with the soft aroma of racing "R".

I took them down onto the beach and, through my words, let them feel the wet sand clinging to my boots and, most of all, I said what a great time I was having and how much I loved being there.

It wasn't a difficult job. I saw, and heard, and smelled everything easily, made a few, a very few, notes - and then had an ice-cream. I really liked this journalism business!

Before I had even left the beach, there was a fuzzy outline of the article's structure in my mind and, back in my room, I tapped away at the Adler and things came fairly easily.

I still work in exactly the same way today. First, there appears a mist – never a fog – from which people, structures and smells poke out so that I can see the first hint of what they look like. As the concept progresses, the mist clears away and there is a story plan in front of me. After this, it's just a matter of filling in the spaces – rather like a literary "painting by numbers."

I was digging around in the back of our office last year and came across an ancient box with copies of my early stories. They should have been thrown out decades ago but I am both congenitally untidy and always nostalgic about my early writing.

Here's the first paragraph of the story I sent to *Motorcycle World*.

SANDRACING IN BRITAIN

The harsh bark of a big AJS single is drowned by the scream of a racing Yamaha howling through the gears, and both of them give way to the thunder of a mighty Vincent twin. Everywhere are machines to make the motorcyclist's mouth water, road racers, scramblers, road machines and grass irons. Exotic Japanese two-strokes, pre-war British singles, every type and breed of bike ever thought of, racing together.

It's not the greatest example of writing in the world nor is it anywhere near as good as my later work but, nonetheless, it is a remarkable effort because it shows the potential that lay within me. Without any training, experience, guidelines or any other support I was able to sit down and, typing away on my knee, produce a very respectable and competent piece of writing.

I finished the article in one long afternoon and a bit of an evening, and then made an appointment to see Geoff Leyland. Again, I must praise his professionalism towards a student for whom he had no real fondness.

I explained that I had a commission, here was the story I had written and would he please have a look at it for me?

A couple of days later, Geoff was always prompt with work, there was a note in my pigeon hole to go up to his study.

I had barely eaten or slept for fear of the results and, as each hour passed, it was becoming ever clearer just how much this story meant to me. There was literally nothing – physically, mentally or intellectually – that I wouldn't do to see my story in print. Truthfully, if *Motorcycle World* had said that I had to eat a bowl of broken glass, washed down with a glass of concentrated acid, my only question would have been: "What do you want me to drink – nitric or sulphuric?"

I had to see that story in print.

Geoff was all smiles. "It's not bad, not bad at all."

I nearly fainted with joy.

"Let's have a look at it."

And so we did.

"This was a bit pretentious – just ease it back a little.

"Here, you have over written it slightly – give the reader space to join in the story without choking them with detail.

"Look, if you use a dash you can join those two sentences into one and make the story tighter. See what I mean?"

And I could see what he meant – and instantly too. Everything made sense and I couldn't wait to do another draft.

What was also exciting was that Mr Leyland spoke to me in a manner which said that I was a writer and that he was completely confident I would understand the points he was making. This made me very proud.

And then came some truly memorable words – and these are verbatim, because they have been burned into my brain for five decades.

"You know, that article is okay. You might even get some sort of fame writing about motorbikes with a story like this."

At the time, I thought that it was a very odd thing to say.

I carefully put the precious manuscript into an envelope with a batch of 10" x 8" photographs. The pics were okay, because I had taught myself photography as a young teenager, but they were not brilliant. Today, they would be rejected out of hand but, because the print quality of *Motorcycle World* was so bad back then, you could get away with a lot more.

If there had been a God of Aspiring Journalists, her shrine would have been in my bedroom and covered in votive offerings. I was desperate.

I took the package to the Post Office near our house but was reluctant to hand it over when my turn came at the counter. It reminded me of how I used to be with our daughter Elizabeth when she was a baby going to toddler group. "No, that's my baby – be careful with her!"

Eventually, mainly because a very big bloke was behind me waiting to post his "Pools" entry, I gave in and passed the envelope over. More prayers:

Please God, don't let there be a fire in the Post Office.

Please God, don't let the plane crash going to America.

Please God, don't let the Viet Cong invade New York and machine gun everyone at *Motorcycle World*.

The following morning, I was waiting for a reply – whilst the letter probably still hadn't left Warrington!

Three weeks passed. I had failed. The River Mersey was helpfully close, just a couple of miles from college. All that I had to do was find a suitable block of concrete and a piece of rope, wait until high tide and then chuck myself off the "Iron Promenade" and drown.

The only thing which kept me from ending it all was the frantic pace of work at S. Kaths. The college viewed the first year as a weeding-out process and the workload was absolutely non-stop. We literally jogged from one seminar, tutorial or lecture to the next and in between we barely stopped for breath. It was truly a case of what doesn't kill you will cure you and the college was determined to find out how much we really wanted to be teachers.

Eventually, a white envelope bearing an American stamp and an air mail sticker arrived. Yes, the piece was very good and they wanted to publish it. Would I accept $50?

I couldn't believe my good fortune. I was going to be published! I sat and re-read the letter over and over again, letting the words wash over me like a warm shower after a winter ride. I had done it. No more notice board adverts and club magazine rejections: I was a professional writer.

The time flew by until a large, mid-brown envelope arrived from America. In it were two copies of *Motorcycle World*. One magazine I kept for many years until, very sadly, it got lost when we moved house.

I cut my article out of the other and kept the pages with me all day and every day. As we were waiting for a lecture or tutorial to start, I would melt into a corner and look at the byline: "By Frank Melling" it said. Frank Melling's name was written under a piece of real journalism, in a real magazine. Nothing in the world could make me this happy.

Chapter Twenty-Three

Goodbye to the 1960s and All That

The first seminar I attended at college was a discussion of Shakespeare's sonnets. At the end, we were given an assignment to produce an appreciation of one of the poems. I had never written a poetry appreciation before and was too embarrassed to ask Miss Iredale, who led the seminar, for help.

I had become loose friends with a super bright and very confident lad and, as everyone filed out, I pulled him to one side and confessed the mess I was in. He was dismissive of my concerns – as he would be, having done "A" Level English. He had probably been doing poetry appreciations since he could speak and so they were just a normal day's work for him. Outside the seminar room, he leaned on the wall and gave me a brief and somewhat brusque explanation of the task. He said that I should write about the narrative of the poem, how the characters were drawn, the language and metre.

Despite the darkness of the winter night outside, my head almost exploded with lights coming on inside my head. The golden key was that I already knew about literary criticism because, without ever consciously knowing it, I had subconsciously done hundreds of poetry appreciations over many years. Now, I was like one of those bear cubs who fish for the first time and find out that they understand exactly what to do because nature has already put the skills inside their heads.

I worked really hard at the assignment but it wasn't like the drudgery of painting shelves; the near catatonic stress of struggling with mechanical engineering at Warrington Tech or, worst of all, drowning in the bottomless pit of administrative paperwork which was the Post Office. No, this work was nothing like any of those experiences.

In fact, it was more play than work. Yes, I had to check my ideas thoroughly and take meticulous care with my writing but it was a joyous experience to do so. Joyous? You might think that this is an odd word to use about sitting in silence, concentrating intensely, but I used to enjoy myself so much that I'm surprised I wasn't arrested for having too much fun.

I used to find an empty lecture room and sit, alone and in total silence, only occasionally thinking about what incredible good fortune I was experiencing – being paid, through my student grant, to do something which was so intensely satisfying.

There was another wonderful experience about to arrive. I collected my assignment from Miss Iredale and it was graded B-. This was really good –

absolutely a step on the podium. Miss Iredale was much quieter than Geoff Leyland so I didn't get much feedback regarding how my work could have been improved but, as I sat in silence in another empty room, I could see how to do better. B- was okay but...

And of course the "but" was the same face that you see at the end of a GP when the rider who has finished second, or even worse third, looks as if he has just had his arm amputated – and without anaesthetic.

B- was on the podium but a straight B or even a B+ would be better – so, so, so much better.

Mid-way through the following year, I would have been suicidal to receive a mark as low as B- but at this stage, just before Christmas, I hadn't quite learned to have dreams so ambitious.

The dynamic of tutorials also shifted – and the situation was just like racing. At first, I expected to come last in everything and in every way. I was too frightened to say anything for fear of looking stupid or, worse still, intellectually shallow and incapable of managing the ideas which were being discussed. Now, my assignment marks had a huge effect on my self-confidence. Little by little, I began to understand that I was at least as bright as any of the other students: this was even better than racing!

I had found my place in the world and I liked it very much.

*****

I was so ecstatic with how my life was changing that I actually forgot about the cheque from *Motorcycle World*. The by-line on the story was of far more importance. Eventually, I took the cheque into Thomas Cook, the travel agent. The clerk asked me to sign on the rear and then counted out five £5 notes, a couple of £1 notes and some change.

In those happy days, there were no passports to present or ID checks. Instead, trust was everywhere. I had presented a cheque, Thomas Cook believed it to be honest and so bought it from me.

I walked out with my wallet fatter than it had been for many months. It was a wonderful feeling.

*****

I can't remember much about Christmas that year so I guess that it must have passed without any major trauma. On Boxing Day, I drove out to the other side of town and walked along the Bridgewater Canal at Stockton Heath. Even after all these decades, I can still remember the railings where I sat, watching the neon tinted, yellow mist as it hung limply over the perfectly still waters. Across the canal, a group of mallards dug around in the weeds for food, oblivious of the fact that it was Christmas. Through the dense, enveloping blanket of the winter's evening I heard a car pull away from one of the houses adjacent to the canal and then accelerate through the gears and away into the blackness.

I sat alone, and lonely, longing for companionship. I should have been much sadder than I actually was but the choice to sit on the cast iron railings in the cold, watching ducks and listening to the sounds of the night, was entirely mine: it was this freedom which protected me.

I could have been with my dad, down the pub – laughing and singing and getting hammered with the lads. My dad would have loved that. He would have shown off his son to his drunken mates – a proper man at last.

Then there was the option of being with my mum and visiting her friends, or maybe my cousins and Auntie Inez – that should have been pleasant.

The problem was that now I knew why I was different. A magazine had paid to print my work and my assignments were well received at college. It wasn't that I rejected my intensely working class background out of snobbery or a feeling of superiority. On the contrary, I admired the skill of the tradesmen and the gallows' humour which sent me out on an RSJ with a burning torch. No, it wasn't any new found sense of superiority – not at all. The problem was that I didn't fit in – nor did my enthusiasms and aspirations. No-one understood them – and sharing them was impossible. This is why I called my autobiography "A Penguin in a Sparrow's Nest" – I was an alien forced to live in a foreign world.

*****

For dramatic effect, I ought to write that I woke up on 1 January, 1970 and had some intense, revelatory moment which said the 1960s were over. The truth is, I didn't: there was not even one molecule of awareness or interest.

For a start, no-one knew that we had just experienced "The '60s" – or had any concept of what they were. We knew the Beatles, the war in Vietnam, the Cuban crisis which had nearly led to World War III, the price of petrol and a bag of chips. But this was all. As for a bigger picture, we had none – and not just at my end of the social spectrum either.

However, what I did know was important to me. Now, I knew how to hold a girl's hand and kiss her gently. I knew how to make great starts at a grass track, win ten shillings and where to stand to get my prize money. Thanks to Sammy Green's wash house I understood how to make money from Villiers spares.

I also was certain that I didn't want to be an engineer, work at the Post Office or become a petty thief: all this I knew.

So, I had scrambled enthusiastically through the 1960s and survived it with a smile. Now, I had the 1970s before me, and what a roller coaster ride this was going to be.

Wyrd bið ful aræd

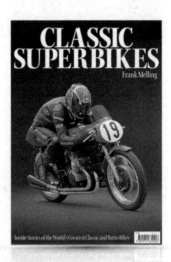

CLASSIC SUPERBIKES

There are many great books about classic motorcycling which are packed with fascinating technical information and critical dates in a bike's production life. Classic Superbikes isn't one of them!

Instead, these are the stories of bikes which keep you awake at night just thinking about them. There are no sensible machines which you buy just because they are good value and spares are easy to find. These are motorcycles which you dream about riding, the best of the best of the best.

You're never going to find a grown up reason for owning a 1957 Gilera Four but there are plenty of bikes you could have, like Melling's favourite MkI Norton Commando or the fabulous Triumph Street Twin – the bike which always brings a smile to the faces of the Triumph staff who designed it.

Each story is told in Melling's quirky, original style – peppered with unique anecdotes and oozing enthusiasm for the big, bold bikes he loves so much. You might agree, or disagree, with Melling's opinions but for sure you will want to read on.

A PENGUIN IN A SPARROW'S NEST

Amazon Top Seller

"A Penguin in a Sparrow's Nest" is far more than a story about motorcycling and journalism. Instead, it recounts the inspirational journey of a sixteen year old who left his Council House to become a shelf painter and went on to be one of the most prolific motorcycling journalists of his generation.

This true story could almost be a fictional novel because it is an epic tale of overcoming adversity, avoiding death on many occasions, huge efforts - and a lot of success.

On the way, Frank was fortunate to enjoy a good night's sleep in a brothel; witness the gates being closed at the BSA factory forever; discover the delights of skiing on a motorcycle and appreciate the benefits of not listening to paramedics discussing his imminent death.

Every page is filled with warmth, humour and highly original stories which are a wonderful window on growing up in the 1960s and 1970s. The voyage Frank takes you on during "A Penguin in a Sparrow's Nest" is unique but one always driven by passion, determination and boundless optimism.

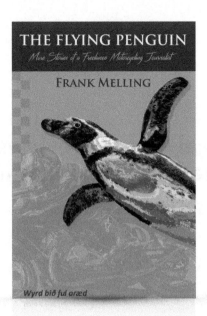

THE FLYING PENGUIN

This is the second part of Frank's autobiography.

There are plenty of near death stories, from almost drowning whilst trapped under a Honda enduro bike to looking down the business end of a Colt .45 in the backwoods of Missouri.

The humour Melling has become so well-known for is everywhere, including how to be an imitation World Champion - when there are free hotel rooms on offer!

On the way there are broken bones, broken bikes and broken relationships - all precariously balanced on the knife-edge of a freelance journalist's permanent state of insecurity.

Melling also tells the hidden stories behind his phenomenally successful Thundersprint - the biggest motorcycle event of its kind in Europe - and why he eventually brought it to an end.

But "The Flying Penguin" is far more than a book of motorcycling memories. Melling is as much a historian as a journalist and he provides a fascinating, and unique, insight to the last 30 turbulent years of British social history.

Real Amazon reviews of Frank Melling's writing:

A brilliant relaxed style of writing, like chatting to your mates in the pub

Absolutely superb

Frank writes beautifully. I cried with laughter and I cried

A superb writer with a sometimes hilarious use of metaphor

Frank's descriptive and witty style shines through in every story

Melling writes in an inviting style, quickly drawing the reader into wanting to hear more

I have just finished this book. I am normally a bedtime reader, but found myself reading this, morning, noon and night.

Intelligently written and highly recommended.

Another of Frank's books which is filled with his invisible glue that urges you not to stop reading until you reach the last page.

This book is pure entertainment and contains emotion and experiences which are credible and so real.

One of those rare books that hold you until you regretfully turn the last page.

A thoroughly enjoyable read. The best motorcycle writer there is.

A master story teller and hugely respected journalist, produced a book I found difficult to put down